It´s Broken, Let´s Fix It

Springer-Verlag Berlin Heidelberg GmbH

Gerard M. De Beuckelaer

It´s Broken, Let´s Fix It

The Zeitgeist and Modern Enterprise

With 81 Figures

Springer

Gerard M. De Beuckelaer

Kalmthoutsesteenweg 54/1
2950 Kapellen
Belgium

GerardDB@skynet.be

Library of Congress Cataloging-in-Publication Data

Beuckelaer, Gerard M. De, 1943–
It's broken, let's fix it: the Zeitgeist and modern enterprise/Gerard M. De Beuckelaer
p.cm.
Includes bibliographical references.
ISBN 3540673253 (alk. paper)
1. Corporate culture. 2. Organizational behavior. 3. Industrial management.
4. Capitalism. I. Title.
HD58.7.B484 2000
658.4'063 -dc21 00-033825

ISBN 978-3-642-08672-4 ISBN 978-3-662-04890-0 (eBook)
DOI 10.1007/978-3-662-04890-0

http://www.springer.de

Originally published by Springer-Verlag Berlin Heidelberg New York in 2002.
Softcover reprint of the hardcover 1st edition 2002

Cover design: KünkelLopka, Heidelberg
Data conversion: perform electronic publishing GmbH, Heidelberg
Printed on acid-free paper SPIN: 10761810 45/3142 GF- 5 4 3 2 1 0

To Helena Mueller and Dr. Hans Wössner
who made this a better book
than I could have written by myself

Preface

We used to have this saying: "If it ain't broken, don't fix it." That was a powerful piece of wisdom. It meant: "If something should, against all odds, function properly, then do not touch it, you might make things worse!" But then, the re-engineering fashion emerged, and somebody whom I used to deeply admire as one of the most brilliant teachers I ever saw at work, when he was still an Assistant Professor of Electrical Engineering at the Massachusetts Institute of Technology (MIT), coined the phrase: "If it is not broken: break it!" Now that is obvious non-sense on a logical level, but is it on a social level?

Society, and thus business, is driven by fashions. Some of us call it fads. There have been more of those than I care to list here. The more colorful, the more exuberant the statement, the more attention it gets. Attention translates into book sales and lecture fees. But it does not stop there. Very obviously, the more you pay for a speaker, the higher the distribution numbers for his book, the "truer" his message must be! We will revisit the "strange loops" caused by recursion often in this book. Let's start with one example. Did I pay a lot for this lecture because it is good, or is it good because it is expensive? One can very easily see a mechanism here that will make us gravitate towards ever louder and shallower truths.

As a matter of fact, I see the world as we have known it go down the drain rather rapidly. We all know that it was by no means the best of all thinkable worlds. It had terrible faults. The question is: are we deliberately replacing it with something better, or are we just shredding it, without having a real alternative? I believe the latter. We don't know what we want. We just know that we don't want what we have any longer. That is a fairly childish way to deal with reality.

Is there anything that can be done about all this? Probably not! Evolution is as slow, but also as unstoppable as a glacier flowing down the mountain. But as we will see further, through the curious miracles of recursion, we are not only the products and subjects of evolution, but also its accomplices! We do have a choice. Free will does exist and it does matter. The only way I have to exercise my free will is to write this book. I do it with hope and without illusions, as I did most things in my life.

Modern enterprises are the engines that drive society. Stop them, and nothing goes anymore. Prosperous nations would go to the pawnshop. The rich would suffer just as much as the poor – maybe a bit later, but for that they have so much more to lose. What is this elusive creature "enterprise" really like? What would we have to show if we wanted to treat it as a biological species? Could we place it properly into taxonomy? Would we be able to thoroughly understand its survival/reproduction mechanisms? The sad truth is that we know dearly little about it. But we totally depend on it. Doesn't that worry you? Don't you think that, for something of such a paramount importance, we ought to have a plan B? Unfortunately, the only "plan B" that has been experimentally tested so far – communism – resulted in the most cataclysmic bankruptcy in history, killing millions of people, and impoverishing even more. Let's face it: there is no plan B! Of course, we know that provided we are wise enough to keep our fingers from certain critical buttons, and assuming that we find no other even more sophisticated way to destroy life on earth, the capitalistic enterprise will not be the last and ultimate form of economical organization. Nothing is forever! Somewhere in the future, the values will change, the technology will change, and we will have another system. But these changes, especially the value changes, are so slow that if there were anything viable in the offing, we should already see it now quite clearly and we don't. In plain words: if we want to remain anything more than a society of hunters and collectors – and just figure how many, or rather how few living human beings such a system would allow; also consider the inconceivable atrocity it would take to get from here to there – we are stuck with the capitalistic enterprise, as we know it today. Until somebody finds the silver bullet that will ultimately replace and supersede the capitalistic enterprise, we have no other choice than to make the best of what we have got through continuous improvement. That's what this book is about. Let's try to understand things, and then find ways to improve them, without breaking more than we already have.

One more thing: my writing style is not exactly what you expect in this kind of book. Apart from the fact that I would have great difficulty expressing myself less directly, and that English is not my mother language, there is another reason. This is *our* world I am talking about, mine as well as yours. Together, we carry responsibility for it. And I am talking about it to *you*, a *person,* not an abstraction. So I try to write as if we were having a personal conversation, as potential partners in making this earth of ours a little bit better, a little bit safer. Of course, I feel passionate about this, and that will show in the language. If you feel disturbed or even offended, I apologize. I did not mean it that way. On the other hand, the situation is far too serious to allow for niceties.

Randolph, New Jersey, July 2001 Gerard De Beuckelaer

Table of Contents

1 The Merits of Capitalism

We, humanity, have a very real interest in prolonging the life of capitalism to the maximum possible extent. System changes always go hand in hand with indescribable suffering. In many cases, that suffering is far greater than the evil the system change tries to eliminate. To give an example: not even the worst czar did anything comparable to driving 6 million farmers into starvation. So the introduction of communism in Russia was, from a human standpoint, rather counter-productive: it increased suffering. It never liberated the working classes, as it advertised it would, but quite contrary killed a considerable portion of them. Frequent system changes are, given the statistical risk that they will make things worse, rather inefficient. So, if we are ever going to replace capitalism by anything else, we better make very sure that this is a genuine improvement. One way to achieve this is to refine capitalism to the point that only a truly formidable, visibly superior competitor could have a chance to pick up the gauntlet. Many people will reject this approach. It simply is not heroic enough, not strongly enough anchored in irrefutable moral ground. It carries the putrefying smell of resignation. People always had a tendency to prefer "heroic" to "smart". That cannot be helped, and in a way humanity's willingness to follow the new and colorful ideas, without involving our brains too much in the decision, provided for the necessary abundance of experiments that make evolution work. But times have changed, and so has technology. In a day and age where a massive world scale conflict is likely to involve thermonuclear devices, it seems advisable to use somewhat more brains, and somewhat less guts to plan and shape our future.

So let's all work together to improve our capitalistic enterprise. It sounds very logical, doesn't it? But how are we going to do this? First of all, let's try to get a somewhat better understanding of capitalism.

2 Why Was the Winner Victorious?

To call capitalism a winner is an understatement. After it's crushing victories over fascism and communism, and after the slow, but seemingly inevitable decay of democratic socialism, it is today the only serious contender in the field! This total defeat happened to competitors that had such grand ideologies (= value systems) that they were able to inspire masses. Some of them were intrinsically so much more noble, so much more in line with our ethical understanding of society. I never saw the popular masses stage a demonstration to support capitalism. One would be ashamed being seen marching in such a rally. Who wants to openly support something as shabby as greed, except for some rare lunatics in the higher income bracket? How could a system that is so blatantly and obviously at odds with our ethical and religious values become so victorious?

The answer is simple. Capitalism relates to much deeper, to much more fundamental layers of our existence than the thin and fragile – but readily visible – outer layer that encompasses such things as ethics and religion. The problem is that we *want* to be seen as if this topcoat, although it is thinner than the edge of a razor blade, extended into the inner core of our being. This is not just hypocrisy. We really *want* it to be true, for ourselves as much as for our fellow humans. Wishful thinking, although completely remote from reality, is one of the most powerful forces in our world.

But all the wishful thinking and all the hypocrisy in the world, which are such powerful forces that they are able to disturb financial markets and to destroy the careers of American politicians, could never stop the victorious march of capitalism to the summit. How could that happen? It is almost frightening: capitalism is, if not completely, then at least to a large extent, aligned with evolution.

3 Introducing Evolution

I do not believe that I have to explain to a person who read this far that we, as individuals, as a species and as a society, are the result of evolution. I say this as a convinced Christian, without the slightest feeling of contradiction. Evolution, the instrument that God created and then used to let us emerge, is not a bit less impressive and awesome than the biblical story. Genesis after all describes the same phenomena, only using the extremely simplified language that was necessary to be understood by the audience at that time. Has anybody noticed that even the sequence of creation, as mentioned in the bible corresponds quite precisely with the sequence we now know, through overwhelming evidence, as the one followed by evolution? I do not want to enter into a debate with the Christian fundamentalists. I despise fundamentalists in general, irrespective their color or conviction. I believe that they should be locked up, if possible in mixed teams, so that they could punish themselves by making each other's lives miserable. I have however a very special problem with the Christian fundamentalists, because they try to sail under a Christian flag. As paradox as this may look: they do not just insult my intelligence, they also hurt my religious feelings with their pharisaic self-righteousness and intolerance.

But how does evolution work? Its beauty is in its simplicity. Please put your imagination into overdrive and picture the following scene.

Just let's assume for a minute that God had contracted an architect to build the universe.

The Lord had, of course, to make his intentions clear to the architect. After explaining the more intricate details of space, time, energy and matter and their delicate relationships, the real brute force part of the job was done. The architect had understood the principles, went to work and soon we had a universe. The Lord took a little break, overwhelmed by the beauty of his creation, became very pensive, and said:

"I want this beautiful universe to be inhabited by an abundance of diverse living creatures, in ever and ever varying compositions, spanning the inconceivable distance between the primitive matter you made to build this universe, and some quite sophisticated facets of my own being."

The architect answered: "Well, teach me the design principles, then I will build those creatures for you."

But the Lord said: "It would take you 3 million years to build even the minimum diversity that I have in mind, and I am not going to pay your appalling rates for that long. Further, you would probably build me a static set of creatures, and I am not so sure that such a thing would be wise. I have thought of something much better. I am going to give you the principles and grand design for a biology system that basically takes care of itself. Better still, it will be totally based on the science I thought you so that you could construct the material universe. It will be a universe in eternal motion, in eternal progression. Not even the closest two snapshots will be identical. It will be a universe where no part is eternal, and yet the whole is. It will appear as if inanimate matter could learn. And the sheer perception of life will fulfill the products of life itself with awe. That will teach them a lesson about recursion. It will put a veil of mystery over my works, so that my creatures can love and admire me even deeper."

The architect cleared his throat and observed dryly: "Boss, with all due respect for your infinite wisdom, this does not sound like a cheap solution to me. In fact, I have a gut feeling that it is going to be a lot more elaborate than all the quantum mechanics and high energy physics mumbo jumbo you made me do to create the material universe and you surely remember what that cost."

The Lord smiled his infinitely benevolent and compassionate smile, so that it filled the whole newly formed sky, and sighed: "You see, my son, that's the difference between us: I have *real* imagination."

Then he began to explain:

"What we really will create is not some bunch of creatures, but a process that will inevitably lead to them. We need a huge amount of experiments spread out over an unimaginable amount of time, always different, but somehow remembering past experiments. We also need an arbitration mechanism to decide which experiments are successful, lead into the generally right direction so to say, and which ones should be aborted right away. Then the 'great experiment', being the sum of them all will lead to awesome creatures."

The architect did grasp the grand design: "Sir, I am much impressed by these thoughts, but I see no way to do it. The arbitration mechanism for instance: I believe you will want it at the same time tangible and unobtrusive. That will be awfully hard to do. And how can I make future experiments remember the outcome of previous ones?"

The Lord looked a little bit disappointed, but only on the far side of the horizon, and spoke: "Oh, you faithful but weak servant. Had you just remembered the algebra course I taught you as the very first thing, you would understand that the answer is recursion! But I will get into some more detail. You need a blueprint of a creature, and then you need the creature itself. But the blueprint needs to be made by the creature as much as the creature by the blueprint. Tell me honestly: did you really totally *forget* about recursion? The elements you constructed according to the principles I gave you have an infinite potential for forming the strangest combinations. Later, intelligent creatures will discover this, and call the science that governs these combinations chemistry. They can also form very large chains, once in the future to be called polymers. Of course, we will be limited to such polymers that can be constructed under the given conditions at any place where we want to start our chain of experiments. Watch this little pebble: they once will call it Earth. There the conditions are such that the elements already started to combine into molecules like ammonia, water, carbon dioxide and methane. Others, more complex of course, are to follow soon when the temperature drops a little further. I can see the conditions that we will have there in a couple million years quite clearly. Remember: I am the one who taught you physics! Now let me teach you some chemistry: pretty soon, one of these horrible thunderstorms that devastate the planet as the result of your lacking understanding of the electrodynamics I tried to teach you, will generate some amino acids. And more, and more. Amino acids are very useful building blocks when you want to create something that *lives* in symbiosis with the environment down there. You can polymerize them under the present conditions to form parts of cells. This is a bit complicated, but given the almost infinite amount of time and experiments I can afford myself, it will somehow happen by sheer statistics. I hope you do at least remember that course! In that place, DNA seems to be the material of choice for the blueprint. It is composed of building blocks that are also needed for the creatures themselves. It can grow an immensely long molecule, so that its code of four base pairs can represent an unimaginable amount of information, able to describe the most complex creature you can think of, and still fit into the confines of a cell nucleus. Now building DNA can only be done effectively *within* a creature. It's not a simple thing. Enzymes are needed. But enzymes are again mainly built from amino acids. An energy transportation system is needed. But that can be made very efficiently using phosphoric acid plus the same sugar and one of the bases we needed to make DNA. On the positive side: DNA can be replicated by fairly simple mechanisms.

So, now creatures start to build DNA, but how does DNA start to build creatures, which is of course the gist of the whole 'recursion' idea? For that to happen we need replication or procreation as one will call it later. The idea is again simple. During its limited life span, the creature makes 'copies' of itself. It transfers its construction plan, in the form of DNA to them. Then it dies and returns to the inanimate world."

The architect was speechless for some time, and then ventured: "Lord, I can see the mechanism in all its grandeur, but how is this going to lead to a self-generating system? We will only generate those creatures that are the result of my shortcomings in electrodynamics, and some rules of chemistry that I assure you I understood and implemented correctly. And why, in your name, should they ever want to make copies of themselves anyway? Even worse, why should they ever want to die after enjoying the incredible feeling of life?"

God slightly shivered at so much lack of understanding, and a whole galaxy shook.

"They will not want to die. But it will be necessary. Remember that I mentioned an almost infinite number of experiments. How could we ever do that if we were not able to throw away the remainders of previous experiments, and turn them into ashes for future use? Even our vast universe would soon be overpopulated. So we will have to provide our creatures with a clock, and when their time is up, they will be discarded. None of the parts shall be eternal, only the whole of my creation will be, as I am. Now let's come to the copying business. Not all of them will show an urge to do that, but those who don't will be immediately extinct as a species, and therefore no longer of any consideration. They are just failed experiments. But trust me, some will have the urge, because it is the closest thing they can get to what I am: eternity. They will be striving towards me. In all their ignorance they will have understood that to be the right thing, and they will survive and thrive for many millennia."

"Dear Lord, I still fail to see the point of generation after generation of identical beings. Why do you not just let them live, they must be longing for eternal life!"

"First of all, they will have eternal life, not as individuals, but as parts of the whole. Then, I do not intend to have *identical* copies from generation to generation. Chemical influences and cosmic radiation will make sure that there are subtle changes. Not too big, because that would cause a too high number of failed experiments, and thus exterminate the species. Not too small either because that would lead to a static genome, and you already pointed out that such a thing would not make much sense. We will have just enough variance to provide for the necessary experiments. If you want to get more insight in this, I strongly recommend Stuart Kauffman's 'The Origins of Order' [7]. The math is not too difficult after all the stuff you had to learn for the creation of matter, and the consequences are fascinating."

"But, Lord, how can that be? Stuart Kauffman is not going to be around for quite a few billion years."

"Fascinating, isn't it? For you, things like past and future exist. But I invented the concept of time, as you should very well recall, and I am not subject to it. For me, there is only present, encompassing the whole future and the whole past."

"I follow You so far, my Lord, but now tell me: how do we construct the arbitration mechanism that decides which experiment is successful and which one should be abandoned?"

"Recursion again, my son! Creatures will over time become very fond of procreation – reproduction. Otherwise, they go extinct, you know! They will get so fond of it that they will in the end start to fight each other over the opportunity to reproduce. Only the fittest will obtain that opportunity. So, the species will become fitter and fitter. Until there will be a – statistically rare – considerable but still viable genetic deviation. Then a new species will emerge. And also the species will compete with each other, mainly for food. The considerably weaker ones will end up extinct. So there will be an eternal upward spiral, leading to fitter and fitter creatures, distancing themselves more and more from the crude matter that was their origin, and approaching me more and more. Oh, there will be dead ends and aberrations, and I will mourn over them as they happen, but in the large scheme of things, they do not matter."

"My Lord, I start to understand, but the consequences are terrible, and hard to accept from a loving benevolent God. For instance, the meaning and sense of death is now so much clearer than the meaning and sense of life. Are you really sure you want this?"

"I will love all my creatures, and embrace them in the larger scheme of things. They all contribute and belong to my creation that is, quite opposed to its components, eternal, like I am. Even those that have no biological descendants, but exercise influence on the future by shaping the phylogenesis of their species will in a certain sense immortalize themselves. As long as they understand that and know me, death will not be a catastrophe for them. But let's understand each other: eternal life does not come as an automatic bonus of being born. One has to do something for it. That something can be good or bad, and that is what it will be for eternity."

"Lord, You are greater than great. I comprehend now. I also believe that I am out of my job."

"Indeed, my son, because you already did it."

The architect fell on his knees in awe. He suddenly understood that he had eaten from the fruit of good and bad, as creatures after him would, and that he had forever lost his innocence. But he also knew that God loved him nevertheless, and always would.

The world as we know it emerged. And God saw that it was good.

Please, take your imagination out of overdrive before you hurt yourself!

For me, evolution is the most amazing thing I ever saw. It is full of mystery and contradiction. The basic principles are fairly easy to understand and paleontology can trace back the "big picture" that we see today in its development with amazing scientific accuracy so that the results of evolution acquire a kind of plausibility. But still the true inner workings of this phenomenal creation machine totally elude our imagination and our comprehension. If we cut small fractions out of the whole stream of events, we are able to understand them to a quite impressive degree. But with larger portions of even past reality, we are at a total loss. No wonder that we are for instance completely unable to predict with any degree of accuracy what evolution is going to do next. Not that we would worry too much! Many of us never look beyond the next quarter, and only very few ever worry about anything beyond their own life span.

But this property too must have been shaped by evolution, and it is totally oblivious whether this shortsighted perspective was once a contributor to our amazing past success, or will be the main attribute of a failed experiment, the instrument of our future demise. Our perception of and our thinking about evolution are of course as well shaped by – evolution.

While the machine forms creatures, the creatures also shape the machine. As the creatures become more diverse and complex, the machine becomes more and more powerful and mysterious in its capabilities and products. I do not believe that we will ever be able to comprehend the full power and beauty of the course creation takes. Indeed, if one looks at the world the way I do, there is no way to talk about creation in the past tense. It is still going on. We are in the sixth day of the biblical story, and it is not even noon.

If we have no chance what so ever to understand the big picture, we might as well try to work with the couple of details we can understand. The governing principle of evolution is obviously competition. Individuals within a species compete for procreation. They do so mostly very effectively without spending a single thought on the *meaning, the purpose* of what they do. There is no need, they follow their instincts. Species, too, compete with each other for resources. Both "competitions" take place simultaneously and intertwined. But evolution, given the almost infinite time and the almost unlimited number of experiments, arranged things so that they do not significantly interfere. That is the recursion thing again. Most aspects of evolution, as we observe it today, are shaped by evolution itself. If there is not sufficient competition for procreation, the species will evolve too slowly to survive the competition from other, faster evolving ones. If the competition for procreation is so fierce that it severs the cohesion within families, tribes and ultimately the species itself, the competitors eliminate each other, and thereby weaken the position of the "race" to such an extent that it can no longer survive external pressures. This poses an interesting question for environmentalists. Sure, humanity has created an immense amount of pressure on the environment. But if we look at the species that are threatened by this pressure, like for instance the big cats, should we not also consider that extreme competitive behavior of the males, of course as such a result of evolution, with consequences that only allow for families with a few males only tolerating their own offspring, weakened the species to such an extent, that relatively little would have been sufficient to drive them over the edge? When you look at the nature films that are abundantly available to us these days, you can observe how hard lions (in this case meaning the lioness) have to work for their daily meal. Would they not be more successful if they could hunt in bigger groups? If you look at the tiger, that is threatened worse, you see an even more extreme case. No cooperation at all except for procreation. On the other end, species that have developed a strong cohesion and cooperation within families or even tribes seem to do a lot better, although they are subjected to even greater stress.

This is absolutely no argument to absolve humanity from its responsibility and guilt towards nature. It is also not a cheap way of saying: "The big cats did it to themselves." I do however offer this as a thought, because it will find an application when we discuss the evolution of the species enterprise.

As creatures became more adapted, and thus more powerful, social organization became more complex. Many entities started to play a part in the "game of life": individuals, families, tribes, races developed within one species. And guess what: according to the rules of evolution, they all started to, *had to* compete with each other. The covert, and at the same time paradoxically very clear goal of competition was always to increase one's representation in the future gene pool. The more complex the creature, the less direct competition takes place between single individuals. More often its goals are achieved by making considerable "detours", securing resources, a reliable food supply being one of those. That of course can only be done effectively by the group.

Then emerged Homo Sapiens, not only the first creature able to have an inkling of understanding, but also the first genus capable of denying the truth, however overwhelming the evidence (see Christian fundamentalists), or simply ignoring it (see most of us).

With humanity, the number of entities interlocked in competition with each other rose drastically:

- villages
- nations
- religions
- political parties

and many more.

Put that on top of the individuals, families, tribes, races and species that already existed. This has complicated the situation immensely. Individuals often belong to many of those entities. All too often, the different entities one individual belongs to get at terrible odds with each other even in deadly competition. The conflicts and tensions that arise from this can tear a human being apart and often provided the themes for great literature.

The complexity of the thing defies any representation, but let's give one simple, rather old example, represented in Fig. 3.1.

Romeo and Juliet [17] belonged to deeply stacked different entities, that were locked into deadly competition. The poles of the conflict, the pope and the emperor, were so far remote from them that one can assume those played no role in their lives and their decisions. They created their own entity and a very strong one on top of that: they became lovers. That entity was totally at odds with the larger scheme of things. To say that they did this deliberately and consciously would be exaggerated, but it happened. From now on, something had to break.

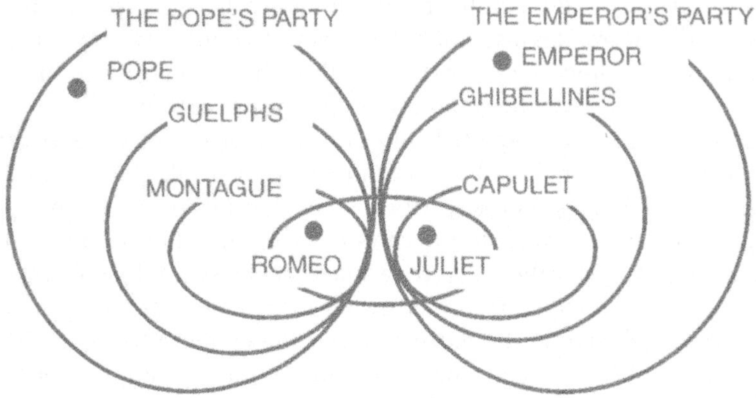

Figure 3.1

For some time, they still had the possibility to choose what would fall into shambles.

They could have severed the ties between them. That would have generated the situation represented in Fig. 3.2.

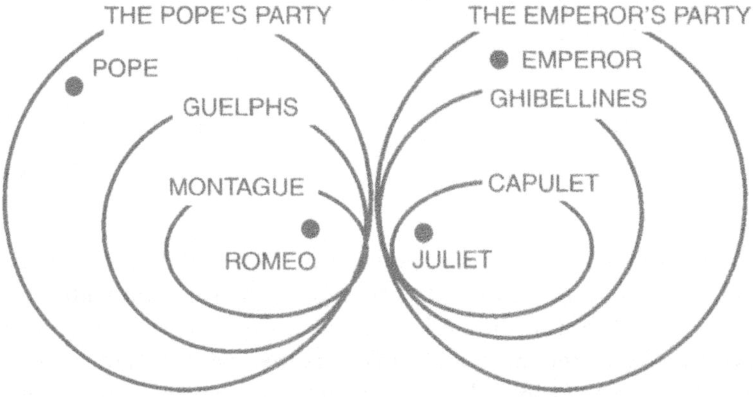

Figure 3.2

This would have been a perfectly acceptable situation: the status quo ante. They could also have disengaged themselves from their families and clans by fleeing, which would have lead to Fig. 3.3.

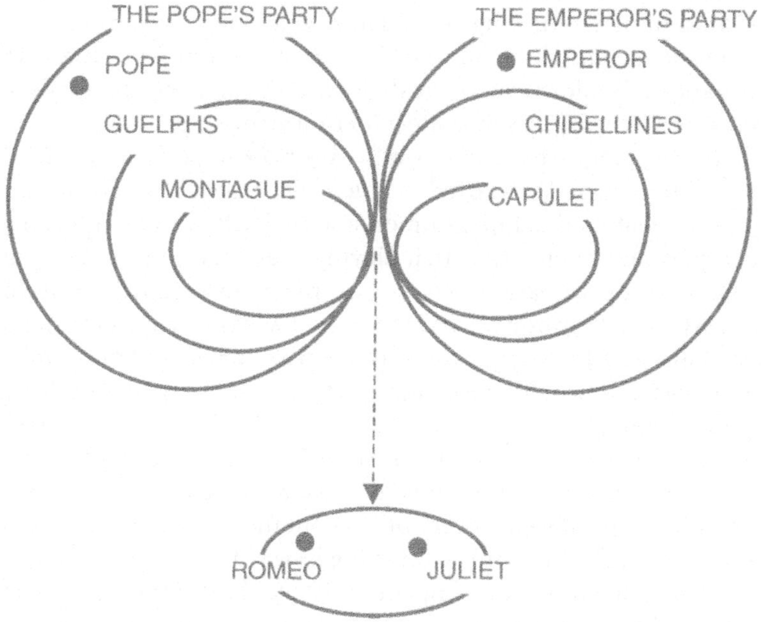

Figure 3.3

That would have removed the offending set, containing elements belonging to the opposite clans, and thus would have greatly reduced the stress in the system. But of course, they did not do any of those things. After some time, even that choice did not exist any longer, and the anomaly was destroyed. That leads to Fig. 3.4.

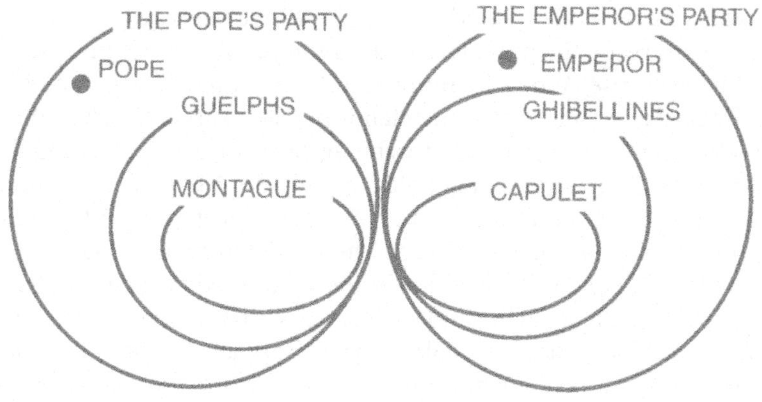

Figure 3.4

Interestingly, from the standpoint of the clans, this situation is identical with the one the alternative "fleeing" would have generated. Even from an evolutionary standpoint, the whole thing makes sense. Genes that lead to such disruptive situations should not be replicated: experiment failed, materials recycled. The rest is maybe history, but great literature for sure.

But it did not always have to be that deadly. We became so fond of competition that we sublimated it. We started to invent activities and to create entities with no other goal than competition on and by itself. Games and sports clubs are examples. One could argue that playing chess does very little to improve your chances for procreation. But on the other hand: competition seems to be able to creep into every human activity, even it was not originally intended. Take a game like golf. In essence, you play against yourself, but the number of twists that we came up with to make a competitive affair out of this after all would easily fill a book.

And then suddenly the situation reverts to square one. Soccer fans start to kill each other in the European stadiums, turning a sublimated competition into a very real one again. We know very little about these mechanisms; we already elaborated on that. The more astonishing how readily we are willing to interfere with them. One factor in competition is health. It certainly contributes to the probability of procreation on several levels. Health problems are clear signs of failed experiments. The art and science of medicine has the highest prestige of all arts and sciences among the popular masses and, no miracle, look what it tries to achieve: to reduce the suffering of mankind. But then look at what it does. In the past, health problems like diabetes or poor eyesight would have drastically reduced ones chances to reproduce, either by getting killed in young age or being less eligible as a mate for procreation. Medicine can now deal with these problems to the point where they are no longer in the way of a quasi-normal life. Even children that are born with severe, sometimes genetically caused defects are treated to the point where they can live and procreate. Great, I am ready to applaud. The question is: Where will this lead to in an evolutionary sense? Won't be more and more people diabetic? Will we all have to wear glasses, or have some elaborate laser surgery? What about some even more radical and rare diseases, being cured by genetic techniques? Will we be faced with an increasingly older population? Is medicine in fact fighting evolution? Would that not be a totally losing proposition? Question over question, and no reasonable answers. There *seem* to be easy and reasonable answers like: If a child is born with considerable hereditary birth defects, fix it so that it can live a normal life, but sterilize it, so that it can not procreate. But this only *seems* easy and reasonable. Apart from all the difficult moral questions, there is also a very practical one. How can *we humans* with our terribly limited understanding of evolution decide that this is a *failed* experiment, that has to be terminated here and now? Couldn't it be that we are looking at the next phenomenal jump in evolution, but we just don't recognize it?

Wouldn't it be much wiser to let evolution make that complicated decision? There is this piece of advice I always give to business people who believe that they should have their say in technical matters: If you do not understand it, don't touch it! Of course, nobody follows that advice and I saw so many fingers burnt, with a totally unchristian amount of deep satisfaction. But in the case of interference with the fundamental base of evolution, and procreation is such a thing, extreme caution is the right prescription.

But it's not just medicine. We are well on the way to "defeat" evolution by other cultural changes. Today it is not the most successful ones, the fittest that have the largest offspring. Quite to the contrary, many of them elect not to have children at all. That is of course, in an evolutionary sense, totally absurd. Why succeed in competition, and then not replicate? But who are we to understand the abysmal depth of creation? Maybe this is just another correction, another set of failed experiments. I can almost hear God say to his architect: "Do you see now how beautifully this works? My children erred in their objectives and are clearly lacking understanding of and respect for my creation. They tried to forget me, to live as if I would not exist. Do you see how they reign themselves in? I do not even have to move a finger!"

In the meantime, it is quite fascinating to see how competition thrives totally out of context, as if it were hard-wired into our behavior, and more likely than not it is. People that cannot reproduce any more, or that have elected by their own volition not to do so, go at it with an – evolutionary – totally senseless vengeance. The "DINK = double income no kids" movement *must* be a dead end – anything with "no kids" in it is by definition.

But it also is not only just cultural. The moment Stanley Cohen and Herbert W. Boyer[1] discovered recombinant DNA technology in 1972/73, they changed the world much more drastically than any inventor did before them. Indeed, I am willing to also include fundamental developments like the invention of the wheel and the control of fire in the previous statement. Curiously enough, hardly anybody outside of a narrow circle of scientists noticed. I am convinced that even today very few people recognize the names! When you look in the encyclopedia for "Boyer", you find an actor, a Canadian folk singer, a politician from the past, and a couple more quite uninteresting people, but not one of the inventors of recombinant DNA technology.

Why didn't anybody notice? The answer may be that this is optically totally unspectacular. You need a quite powerful microscope to see anything. And most people would not understand what they saw if they even had an opportunity to look through it. But even if you understand what you see, you also

[1] Strange enough, these brilliant scientists did not – yet – get the Nobel Prize. But they got the very prestigious MIT Lemelson Prize. I am still proud to have been the jury member that forwarded them for the nomination.

understand that you see very little. The true seeing happens indirectly, through a set of very sophisticated analytical methods.

When the world saw "Dolly", the first cloned sheep, they got a bit more excited, but only a bit. After all, Dolly looked so much like a normal sheep. There are a number of activists cautioning against genetic engineering. They want their governments to impose controls that span a spectrum ranging from strictly enforced laboratory conditions up to a total ban. They organize rallies against genetically altered food. They managed to create sufficient fear among the Europeans to let them strictly curb the latter.

The debate about genetic engineering fatally resembles the one we once had over Nuclear Power. In those days, we were living in Germany, and we saw the struggle happen on television. There was a recurring pattern. One side would say: "This is all the devil's work, and it will exterminate whole cities, if not humanity, and besides, this is all just about acquiring a Nuclear Weapons capability." The other side would proclaim: "This is totally under control and completely safe, and besides, we have signed all the relevant international treaties to have perfect control over the plutonium." Nobody said things like yes but..., or no but... They all possessed the eternal unlimited truth. There were no buts.

The outcome was very interesting. The environmentalists have found something else that will destroy the world: CO_2. Obviously, nuclear power plants do not generate that, but most of the alternatives do. The Swedish environmentalists are already making shy overtures to the nuclear industry. But the previous proponents discovered in the meantime that, in order to do this right, it becomes much more expensive than burning fossil fuel. This is of course a complete snapshot situation. It all depends on the availability of fossil fuel. It also depends on a conclusive clarification of this global warming thing, and that is by far not there yet. At the time of the debate, the former was badly underestimated, and the latter was not even a discussion topic. Even at that time, the debate seemed extremely strange to me. This was obviously not at all about discovering the truth. It was all about defending a predefined position, and *getting* right, without a trace of healthy systematic doubt. In those days I was employed by a large German chemical company, and earmarked to rise in the ranks. Accordingly, they trained me in the fine art of debate. That was where I understood where this ridiculously naïve discussion style came from. We do not just *know* the truth, we practically *own* it. There is no reason for a real debate: this is just battle. You do not have to convince your opponent; he cannot be convinced. The only problem is to sway the audience. You do not weaken your position by showing insecurity. I found this primitive. We were dealing with a lot of issues that were profoundly important for generations to come, and we did it on the level of Roman Gladiators! I got a distinctively Orwellian taste in my mouth.

The other side must have had similar schools.

Of course, I can see the logic behind all this. The popular masses want simple explanations, so that they can put their own judgment to work within the democratic process. But as technology and society evolve, there are less and less simple explanations. The decisive things in fact become more and more complex, loaded with more and more question marks. They could never digest this! So let's cheat a bit, and sell them the complicated issues as if they were simple ones that they can readily understand.

This was the moment where I decided that I did not *want* to rise to the top of either side. I would not have a piece of a world where everything was about power and nothing about understanding. I realize the moral inferiority of that decision. Just imagine Gorbachev [4] had made the same one...

Now I see the debate about genetic engineering evolving into the same direction.

So let's put a couple of things in perspective here:

1. We have always tampered with evolution by breeding animals and by cultivating plants.
2. The overall result of this was quite successful. It probably added, in a very quiet way, as much to our food supply as the more recent technology that allows the chemical production of fertilizers.
3. Even this, at first glance so innocent, so natural technology had a strong military significance. Horse breeding was, for many centuries, an affair of strategic national importance. The Mongolian tribes that we often call "Huns" could only accomplish the quite astonishing things they did by the grace of their horses. Well into the 20th century, horses played a crucial role in warfare. Let's just look at one somewhat colorful example from the early 19th century. During the Napoleonic wars in Spain, the British had a number of officers operating solitarily behind enemy lines in order to gather information. They did so in full uniform! The reason was that, if they were caught, they would not be shot as spies. How did they pull this off? They simply counted on their superior horses to get away. If they encountered opposition, those would highly likely have "standard" horses provided by the French army. British officers bought their horses themselves. You can very easily imagine a bunch of VW beetles chasing a Ferrari! It worked in most cases.
4. Even the "natural way" of animal breeding created monstrosities. We now have pigs with an extra pair of ribs that can hardly walk. We have pure bread race dogs that suffer under life long back pains and have a very limited life expectancy. We have thoroughbred horses that could never survive in a natural environment, with a so fragile skeleton that they have a high risk of breaking bones whenever they fall.
5. All this was basically done by "selection" that is by weeding out undesirable characteristics and promoting desirable ones. This was achieved by killing

one specimen, and breeding the other. Of course, there were confines. When a newly bred animal or a plant was not really viable, nature – thus evolution – would kill it and cut off the branch. We were quite powerless against that. All this seemed innocent enough, until somebody got the idea to breed a human super race. We all know to what misery that led!

But the gist of all this is: also in the so-called natural way, we produced species that evolution, if not tampered with, would probably not have generated. It was not evolution making the selection, we were doing it. Why do we call this natural?

What is so different about genetic engineering?

1. The most obvious difference is speed. It would certainly have been possible to produce a soy bean variety that is resistant to certain herbicides in a "natural" way, but it would have taken time, a lot of time, many generations of soy bean plants. Genetic engineering achieves the same result much faster. This is not only the most obvious difference, it is also the least dramatic one.
2. The fact that genes can be transported between species as different as a human being and a bacterium is much more spectacular. This is a frightening perspective. On the other hand, just think of insulin. Diabetics were traditionally treated with insulin that was extracted from pigs. Pig insulin and human insulin are very similar. I believe that there are only four amino acids different in a quite large peptide. Nevertheless, some people are allergic against it! Their fate was not rosy. Transferring human genetic material into a bacterium resulted in the production of *human* insulin. I would not call that a small achievement. My daughter biochemist is skeptical, but I would venture to say that something like this, introducing genetic material of a more evolved into a much less evolved species is something that nature would never do on it's own. But for the same token, who am I to claim that *we* are the more evolved species? A thorough look at DNA might lead to a different conclusion! The same technology is now used to develop medication against a number of vicious diseases that plagued humanity since its existence, rheumatoid arthritis being only one of those. The possibilities seem unlimited.
3. It is now possible to clone mammals. It is still not easy, but the experiment that led to Dolly has been repeated with other mammals and other people have developed methods to clone mice in a quite reproducible way.

Now look at the combination of 1, 2 and 3. This immediately creates horror visions of Adolph II, commanding 100 million cloned Rambos.

There is a lot of debate about the moral implications of cloning humans. At this point in time, there is no immediate danger. Doing such a thing would still be awfully difficult. But how to curb something that is basically possible, amidst a mind-boggling development of the supporting techniques? It is quite possible that human cloning gets within our reach in 10 years from now, but it is certain that it could be done in a routine way in 50 years.

But after all, genetic engineering is just another tool, albeit an extremely powerful one. Let's think about how we humans deal with tools:

- We hardly made any tool that, however useful and apparently innocent, could not be abused.
- If there was a potential for abuse, somebody did it. Even if the knife in your kitchen has the obviously wholesome purpose to cut bread, which happens to be an activity with a very ancient ritual component symbolizing the unity and sharing within the family, only your conscience prevents you from using that same thing to slice your neighbor's throat. The latter remains – luckily – the exception, but it has been done thousands of times.

Further:

- Genetic engineering is an inherently cheap technology. It may not quite look like that today. Fact is, one does not need gigantic particle accelerators or nuclear reactors. The necessary sophisticated laboratory equipment becomes cheaper and more powerful by the day.
- Genetic engineering facilities are easy to conceal. You do not need enormous equipment that could be easily spotted from air or space. It is already difficult enough to distinguish between a bona fide pharmaceutical plant and a nerve gas factory. Genetic engineering is so much more universal in its applications and it will be so much more ubiquitous, that such a distinction here will become orders of magnitude more complicated.
- Armies of human clones and the industrial production of engineered individuals have been a constant topic in all kinds of science fiction, including "Brave New World"[6]. Please do not take science fiction lightly! It stimulates fantasy, and that is as important an ingredient as technical skill when it comes to dramatic new developments. It all too often provided the vision for somebody else that suddenly realized: "This is after all technically possible," including such incredible things as diving to the bottom of the ocean or flying to the moon.

If you look at the combination of all this you see an activity of choice for rogue nations or even individuals.

How could we ever control this? Can we revoke our knowledge? Can we stop discovery? Can we forego the obvious promises? Can we police this, without the cure becoming worse than the disease? Should we attempt to proactively engineer morality into the human species, as the only possible defense? But even if we could do that, who would determine what morality is? Would that not be the true culmination of the original sin as narrated in Genesis? How is this going to play within the framework of evolution? Is this the ultimate method to prune the Homo Sapiens branch, in order to change direction? Is this the way to elevate Homo Sapiens to the next level? As far as I understand it, genetic engineering is just one more tool created by evolution that will forthwith play a role in evolution, and please do not believe that I find any comfort in this apparently simple explanation!

I have no advice, except "FASTEN YOUR SEAT BELT". After all the disruptions and dislocations created by the fact that our scientific technical surroundings developed much faster than the age old inner core of our self could ever absorb or adapt to, now the pace of evolution itself is going to accelerate. This may look quite poor as a prognosis, and it certainly is. But that's the nature of evolution. As poorly as we understand how we got here, the direction we are taking now is even more obscure.

Maybe the most promising approach to all this is plain naïve hope, unproven optimism as radiated by Pierre Teilhard de Chardin, the French Jesuit who probably understood more about the nature of evolution than anybody else. In his "Phenomenon of Man" of 1955 [18], he develops the grand vision of evolution ultimately culminating into point Omega, a state of unification with God.

- The communists loved him, because they smelled dialectic materialism.
- The pope and especially Cardinal Ottaviani hated him, probably for no good reason.
- A lot of the positivists and existentialists ridiculed him, because they believed to have better answers.

But looking at all the above, I can only be even more astonished by the assertiveness of our increasingly materialistic mind. We ridicule altruism, we don't even truly believe that it exists. We chuckle about the obvious futility of prayer. But ask yourself honestly: what is so much more effective about our "normal" ways to deal with creation?

4 What Is Capitalism?

Please remember that we started the whole previous excursion only because of the statement that capitalism is extremely well aligned with evolution.

But what is capitalism?

- an economic theory?
- an organizational principle?
- a value system?
- a philosophy?
- a political doctrine?
- a religion?

Or:

- just another rather insignificant tool that evolution developed to refine itself in a certain very short phase of its own evolution?

Or:

- the symptom and the source of a failed experiment?

Especially the idea that capitalism may have religious aspects will astonish, even shock you. By now, you should have discovered that I have a whole lot of appreciation and respect for the scripture. And does it not say: "You cannot serve two masters, you will have to decide between God and the Mammon"? Of course, there is a lot of religious tradition that claims that God will give you the Mammon, as a reward for a just life. If asked, most people would point here to the Jewish tradition. It always has been very convenient to blame everything, including the plague, on the Jews. May I just mention the story of Job, which we find in the so-called *old,* read *Jewish* testament. You may not quite remember Job's story anymore, so I feel compelled to tell it in a nutshell. Job was an upright man, a faithful servant of his Lord. He was also a wealthy, happy man. Then, apparently without any reason, God robbed him of all his earthly wealth and happiness. Not only his money and his family, but in the end also his health went down the drain. As I understood it, the purpose of the whole exercise was to teach Job the relative unimportance of earthly possessions. And of course, there is a happy end! That seems to be the Jewish position, unless the orthodox rabbis in Jerusalem have lately found a new twist I do not know about yet. They are after all fundamentalists, and you will know my opinion about those by now. In this case, however, I believe that we should acquit them. They value study, not exactly a moneymaking activity, so much above everything else, that they believe that it should take precedence over defense, not even to mention earthly wealth. That's a strong position to take in a state like Israel!

But surely, it was not the Jewish tradition that tried to tell us that money is the only value in life worth pursuing.

Let's rather look at Protestantism, especially Calvinism. That is where we find the doctrine that earthly wealth is the reward for the good, and poverty the punishment of the bad. We see this, as almost everything on earth, expressed in its purest crystalline form in the USA. That ground swell produced a lot of evil, particularly in the South, an especially hypocritical breed of racism being just only one aspect. In this day and age, Christian Fundamentalists exercise quite some influence in the Republican Party of the United States. Their fundamental belief is that poverty is self-inflicted. It is the punishment for a wrongful life. Therefore, taxpayer dollars should not go to social support programs.

So, surely the Catholic Church has clean hands. Well, I happen to be a catholic, and I know a thing or two about my church. For the largest part of history, the catholic hierarchy literally followed Christ in saying: "Let the little ones come to me." The problem is that they never meant children. What they had in mind was golden coins, or more recently, dollar bills. They did proclaim that avarice is one of the biggest sins, but what they had in mind were generous donations to the church. Saint Peter's dome in Rome is the epitaph of luxury. Even the paintings are no paintings, but incredibly detailed mosaics. In order to raise the enormous fortune that was needed for the construction, monks "sold" heaven. This must have been a more solid business practice than we have thought so far: none of the people that bought their salvation ever complained about not receiving it. The indignation of deeply religious people about these practices, among other things enabled the reformation. In the recent past there have been a number of financial scandals involving the Vatican and the "Banco del Santo Spirito", but believe me, comparing to the past, the contemporary Catholic Church is clean, and the Vatican is by far less wealthy than generally assumed. Some dioceses are filthy rich though, especially in Germany. The Catholics are much more Latin minded than their Protestant brethren. Accordingly, their standpoints towards wealth and poverty are much less clear. While some of the clergy in Latin America embraced doctrines close to communism, the general standpoint is still that worldly wealth is bestowed upon you as a blessing of the Lord and that the poor should endure their fate with dignity and patience, awaiting their reward in the life after death, respecting hierarchy, religious as well as worldly. Although these positions are much older than the subject we are trying to approach here, they did and do without any doubt contribute to the maintenance of social stability in the kind of class society that capitalism creates and needs.

There is another aspect to this. Although religions have done their bit to support it, I would not want to call capitalism a religion, but its competition – communism – certainly was one. I once believed that I had discovered this strange phenomenon. Unfortunately, later research revealed that Joseph A. Schumpeter published his observations about this in "Capitalism, Socialism and Democracy" in 1942 [16]. As this happened the year before my birth, I have some difficulty to uphold my claim to the discovery.

For one thing, like all religions, communism pretended to know the future. Their dialectical materialism philosophy did not only predict exactly where humanity was going, but also how we would get there: through a number of transitions that never could be reversed. There was not the slightest doubt that we would reach the blissful end point of the process, where we all would live happily. Obviously, they must have had long and intensive conversations with either God or at least his architect, so that they understood infinitely more about evolution than we do! They promised, in religious terms, nothing less than a world where the original sin would be wiped out. There would be no more greed, no more crime. Nobody would take advantage of another person. The bite that the biblical Adam took from the biblical apple would be reversed, and the snake would be vaporized by a laser canon. This is typically the kind of thing that religions promise. Like other religions, the communists deduced that there was no effort too great and no sacrifice too gruesome, if needed to progress on the road towards the goal. Communist soldiers, from Russia to Vietnam, often sacrificed themselves not a bit less fanatic, not better equipped and for no better cause than the children that Peter the Hermit rounded up for the first crusade during the 11th century. And then they said: "Religion is opium for the people!"

The dream had been dreamt before, over and over. Does not Schiller's "Ode an die Freude"[1], used for Beethoven's 9th symphony, proclaim: "Alle Menschen werden Brüder"[2]? It is a very powerful, extremely attractive dream. Especially young, idealistic people have a tendency to grab it. Confronted with the gloomy, utterly hopeless reality they reach out to it like a drowning person to a piece of wood. But it won't float – it contradicts evolution. I used to say: "Show me a decent person that never was a socialist, and show me an intelligent person who remained one." As far as I know the world, I probably did not invent this either. It is far too obvious for not having been observed and formulated by somebody prior to me. Just take it as a challenge, and let me know. In case you think that I am one of these brainless right-wingers, celebrating the demise of communism: I did not attend the banquet. I have known for all

[1] Ode to the joy

[2] All men become brothers.

my life that communism could never work, but I am still saddened by that. If it could work, we would not have to fear it. It only got into those monstrous aberrations because of the tension between its doctrine and the realities of life. That tension frustrated its leaders to the point where they lost their ideals, and just remained cool, selfish, almost inanimate power brokers. It took a man with the stature of a Gorbachev [4] to see the truth. His expression: "*Those who come too late are punished by life*" reveals a lot of insight in and respect for evolution.

Communism was not the only religion to commit collective denial of reality. My Catholic Church, too, when it ordered celibacy for its clergy did a very similar thing: ignore evolution. If anyone today is "totally appalled" by the cases of child molestation, that is a very puritan standpoint: holding very real people to impossible, very unreal standards. If you deny your priesthood a "normal" life what else than abnormal behavior can you expect? It can be classified:

- Many just cheat. They live guilt ridden, and are eternally subject to all kinds of blackmail and manipulation.
- Some develop sexual aberrations, or they had them to begin with. And for the record, on sound evolutionary ground, I believe homosexuality to be one very serious form of aberration. OK, I chalk down one more de-merit for political incorrectness.
- About 5% cope with the rules faithfully, while being absolutely "normal" people. Have you ever considered how much energy that must cost them, how it devastates their lives, their feelings? Are they ever able to do anything but staying chaste? Some are, and those become mystics. Maybe some people think that this small harvest is worth the whole misery. I don't.

So, maybe capitalism is a philosophy. Philosophy has a lot in common with religion: it attempts to explain the world. Capitalism does not try to explain anything to anybody. It gives simple, largely unproven recipes to optimize economic activity. So, it certainly is no philosophy. Communism was: it pretended to understand the world, its evolution, and the role of individuals in it. It didn't.

Maybe capitalism is a political doctrine? Well, I have severe doubts here. Liberalism, in the old European sense – laissez faire, laissez passer – is a political doctrine. This means that the government should not interfere in the economy, that it should in fact be as small and unobtrusive as possible. That obviously is a strong political statement. Capitalism never said anything like that. It simply calculates whether the conditions in a given place are conducive to its goal, and that is to make money, nothing more, nothing less, and then decides to stay or leave. Capitalism certainly had an influence on political doctrine, especially in the United States, but it never was one in its own right. When I hear people like for instance Jack Kemp speak, I do not see a capitalist in front of me. He may be quite wealthy, I hope he is, but surely, he is not as wealthy as he would be if he had devoted his life to shoveling dollars. I see a man who has discovered the promise of free trade and low tax rates. He wants our government, as a matter of fact *all governments* out of our hair. He is a pure liberal in the traditional European sense of the word. Before he sues me for calling him a liberal, we have to understand that the word underwent quite a change of meaning in the USA. While traditionally liberalism says that the government should not interfere (laissez faire, laissez passer), the term liberal in the contemporary USA means maximal involvement, and I can assure you: that is not what Jack Kemp is standing for!

Could it be that capitalism is a value system? Well, here we got something. What is a value system? It puts the priorities straight. What is more important? Being a good citizen, being a good parent, being a good person, being smart, being a respectable golfer, being a good Christian ... There is no end to the possibilities. What benchmark are we going to use to determine success or failure of our lives? What are we going to use as a reference point to take our bearings on as we grow up? Capitalism has the answer: money! Now what *is* money? In its most primitive form, it basically is a totally worthless piece of paper with strange things printed on it, so that it cannot even properly be used to write a note. It is created and maintained by aloof, secretive organizations called central banks. This is the kind of nonsense a scout from Alpha Centauri would report at home after his mission to earth. But humans know better. Money is what the inventors of money wanted it to be. It is the substitute for the ancient gold, the key to everything a human being may lust after: goods, power, services, sex and, most importantly, more money. Money makes the world go round! As so often, we sublimated the tool so that it became a goal in and by itself. People are obsessed with money as such, in the USA more than anywhere else. I often believe that they don't have eyes, just $ signs in their face. Europeans are of course not a trifle better; they are just more hypocritical about it. In Europe you will not see neighbors tell each other over the fence "how much they make", just so that the pecking order question is settled once and for all, but the power of money over social relationships, although less directly visible is just as strong. In Europe, the traditional teachings of the church, brandishing avarice and greed to cardinal sins are still too much alive to allow an open, almost intuitive worship of the Mammon as it occurs in the USA. But that does not really matter. Everywhere nowadays money is the generally accepted benchmark for success or failure. Thus, capitalism with its myopic focus on money alone is very well aligned with the main stream of our culture.

Maybe capitalism is an organizational principle. If it is, it is the simplest that was ever devised. "Maximize your profit" is a rather short statement. We should not frown at that. Something as wonderful and complex as evolution shows very simple primary principles, too. I could almost imagine the architect, during his vacation on earth, say to some people: "Cut the bull, go for the dough!"

Capitalism is certainly an economic theory. It simply states that, if everybody strives to maximize his benefits, in the end the whole economy will be in the best possible shape. There is of course no proof for the validity of such a statement, but the system seems to work more or less, in quite blatant contrast to everything else that has been tried up to now. This is what aligns capitalism with evolution. It follows the same pattern. No miracle that it works so well. Humans pursue money with the same thoughtless vengeance other animals reserve exclusively for sex. All those things that communism wanted to abolish: the original sin, greed, avarice, eternal battle between human and human, are the very basic drivers behind capitalism. Capitalism is about competition. The winner takes all. Capitalism puts the rights of the individual over and above the interests of society. Every individual does not only have the right, but the quasi duty to optimize his situation, no matter the cost to others. That is exactly the way evolution works, which brings us to the question whether capitalism actually plays a role in evolution. The answer is that it certainly does, like everything we observe about human life. The extent and direction of its influence elude our comprehension. Whether capitalism is an aberration leading to a dead end, or a core mainstream mechanism, leading to a subsequent higher level of existence, is something only our descendants in a distant future will know.

5 Contraction and Expansion

Enterprises do not exist in a vacuum. They exist within the confines of human society. Enterprises as we have known them in the past – and there is of course no guarantee that this will remain so – used to be about the cooperation of many towards a common goal.

Organization of labor and cooperation has clearly existed much longer in human society than what we call modern civilization. Given the observation that elements of cooperation and hierarchy also exist within primate groups, politics and all, especially among chimpanzees, it seems reasonable to assume that the underlying behavioral pattern is older than Homo sapiens. It certainly constituted an important advantage in the competition between species. Families and tribes that were good at it had a better chance of surviving and reproducing, and that is how any property of that kind in the end becomes a characteristic of the whole species. There is however nothing trivial about the spreading of such a behavior as cooperation. After all, the same males that hunt together, braving great dangers and sharing horrible hardships, still have to compete with each other for the opportunity to procreate. This requires a very delicate balance, but it was obviously found. I cannot imagine the length of time it must have taken, neither the drama it created in its wake.

Even today, things like cooperation and organization are not exactly reduced to behavioral trivia. Humans do neither like instinctively to share, nor do they cherish to be bossed around, but they will go along with it as long as there are substantial, immediate, visible and individual benefits to be gained. In an evolutionary sense, we see recursion striking again. Just contemplate this:

The fact that certain things needed to be done that an individual alone could not accomplish, forced society into more and more interlocked organization forms.

But also:

The complexity of social structure leads to an increased number of activities that require cooperation.

And thus:

We seem to be confronted with the eternal "chicken and egg" problem again, unable to clearly understand quantitatively what drives what.

We can only look at the facts. The degree of cooperation and organization increased with time. But the road was long and convoluted. It would also seem rather preposterous to adopt the viewpoint of dialectical materialism, and postulate that the movement never changes direction. History contradicts that. But it is still true that we never have seen a degree of organization and cooperation like the one we observe today. It is also true that the phenomenon has accelerated virtually exponentially during the last century. It is like a spiral, winding it's way up to ever more concentration, to always-larger organizations. We could now very easily fall in the "club of Rome" trap, and start to extrapolate, which would lead to all kinds of absurd predictions. In a way, that kind of approach is so much in line with dialectical materialism, that the realization would mightily embarrass many of the authors that take such positions. I can easily understand why economists can do such a thing. As opposed to chemical engineers, they were never exposed to the physical perils of exponential processes. Do you believe that to be irrelevant? A lot of dumb actions in this world have no other background than the absence of experience with physical exposure. The latter has a quite different learning effect from all purely intellectual exercises. Like it or not, we are not just cerebral creatures. If you once stood next to a run away polymerization reactor, your approach to exponential processes is, for ever after, a bit different. You *know* that the process will definitely not just go on. Of all the frightening possibilities, that is the one thing that will certainly *not* happen. Something will break. Hopefully the safety valve will open and be large enough. More desirably, one of your counter-measures might actually work, and rein the monster in before it eats you.

Further, there is clear historical evidence for alternating periods of concentration and dispersion, as if society were "breathing", inhaling concentration and exhaling dispersion almost continuously. Interestingly, a lot of these cycles can be traced back to technology. Just to set the stage, we might want to look at a couple of examples.

Some examples of innovations that drove concentration:

- Athens' superiority was the result of innovative naval technology.
- Alexander the Great's conquests became possible by innovations in infantry tactics.
- The Romans were able to control their vast empire by the grace of a road system that let them move troops with an unprecedented speed. They also had a better-organized army and improved infantry tactics, as compared to their competition.

When Vercingetorix managed to unite the Gauls against Rome, and that must have been about as easy as uniting all Irish behind the same idea, he managed to lay siege on Alesia. The extraordinary road system that the Romans had built allowed them to move in sufficient troops so that they in their turn could surround the Gauls. That was the end of the revolution. After parading the Via Sacra in Rome, as a part of Julius Ceasar's triumphal return, Vercingetorix was executed.

- The Arabs invented the stirrup, which enabled a more or less aimed shot with a bow from horseback. That was sufficient to provide them with a century of military supremacy, and contributed to the formation of their empire.
- Medieval Christianity invented the armored knight. This allowed the "Francs" to expand their territory into the Holy Land.
- The introduction of artillery, an expensive technology that only the king could afford to have, reduced the previous instrument of decentralization, the medieval castle to little more than uncomfortable housing, and enabled the unification of the great European nations.
- Napoleon, as one of the very few great leaders, personally created an innovation. He invented the mobile field artillery. It was enough to create a great empire, not to keep it.

But the examples of technological innovation driving decentralization and destruction of great organizations are just as numerous.

- All the Roman organization could not stand up against the fact that the Germanic tribes had steel weapons.
- Charles Martel stopped the Islamic armies with their superior light cavalry at Poitiers cold with the latest invention of the Franks: heavily armored infantry.
- During the whole medieval age, local potentates were able to defy the king, holing up in their castles that, if well designed, could only be taken at enormous, often prohibitive cost.
- The Dutch and the British were able to withstand the might of the 16th century European super power, the Spanish Austrian Habsburgs, by superior naval technology. Dutch and English ships could just turn a bit more into the wind than their heavier Spanish competition, and in naval battle, maneuverability and relative independence from the direction of the wind was everything.
- In the land battle between the Dutch and the Spanish that raged in the Netherlands, Dutch engineers cleverly exploited the region's abundant water. As described so brilliantly by Paul Kennedy in "The rise and fall of the great powers" [8] , the small Dutch nation literally bled the Spanish giant to dead.
- The emergence of hand held firearms, relatively cheap to come by, enabled local uprisings, like for instance the French revolution and certainly contributed to the disintegration of the Austrian Hungarian Empire.

There also are records of pathetically missed chances when leaders failed to recognize the importance of technological innovations. Napoleon was not known to be stupid or void of fantasy. His biggest problem on earth was a virtually invincible Royal Navy. Eliminate that and he could have conquered England. In 1807 Robert Fulton demonstrated his steamship to Napoleon and his staff, right at Napoleon's front door, on the Seine in Paris. Here was the solution to the Emperors worst problem. If you are no longer dependant on the wind, if you can even navigate against the wind, you have a very distinctive advantage. You can decide to fight or flee, and your – sailing – opponent is powerless against that decision. Napoleon did not see the promise and dismissed the idea.

If one of the parties in a conflict manages to implement a sizable improvement, and the other party ignores or underestimates it, that often leads to the great military victories that are remembered centuries after. There is absolutely no doubt about the fact that Nelson was a great military leader. But when he met the French-Spanish fleets at Trafalgar he had the benefit of a quite tragic misunderstanding. The French admiral, who absolutely had the opportunity to run, was under strict orders to engage any British force that had an equal or inferior number of canons. This order quite blatantly ignored the fact that the British had refined their artillery technique to the point where an English canon, compared to a French piece could shoot nearly double the number of rounds in the same time. The rest is history.

Today, we see a confused picture. While there are clear signs of a worldwide decentralization movement (contemplate how many "new" nations made our atlases obsolete, just during the last ten years), there is also a certain amount of concentration momentum visible. A true European union seems closer than it ever was since Charlemagne. NAFTA (North American Free Trade Agreement) is a reality waiting to expand. Mercosur is developing fast, binding the erstwhile bitter enemies in the Southern Cone of South America with economic ties that are soon to completely overshadow the animosities of the past.

One could argue that the concentration processes that are going on are all in the economic realm, while we see at the same time nations (or tribes) striving for political autonomy. But one does not even have to read Paul Kennedy to understand that economic, military and political power are inextricably intertwined. They feed and support each other, they are convertible into each other. It is in the end the sum of them that defines a great sustainable nation. Once we have a European currency, a European Army and a European foreign policy will follow, all of that controlled by a true European parliament. It is quite inevitable. Of course there will be a large local autonomy in cultural issues. That is neither new nor uncommon. All great multicultural empires of the past, beginning with the Romans, granted such freedom to the locals.

In the military sense, we are left with only one superpower: the United States. That is a quite desirable state of affairs for the world. In spite of all the justified criticism one might have towards American policy, especially concerning the third world, one cannot deny that the USA are not only the most formidable empire the world ever saw, but also the most morally inclined one.

They have the capability to strike just anywhere or anytime they want, but they use it with an unprecedented caution and restraint. Some people will dispute this. They will say that America interfered in Panama, Grenada and Vietnam, just like the Russians in Czechoslovakia, in Hungary and in Afghanistan. I will let you get away with this, as long as you are willing to put Alexander Dubcek on one level with Manuel Noriega. If you take that standpoint, we will have peace. All you will further hear from me is "Yeah, yeah".

I just wish the world a couple more centuries of "Pax Americana". That would probably be sufficient to solve most of our urgent problems. It is not likely. A number of elements are pointing to more and more resemblance with the Roman Empire. As in the latter case:

- No nation can truly defy the American might.
- But some lunatics try it from time to time nevertheless.
- And the USA cannot be everywhere at the same time, in spite of logistics capabilities that simply dwarf whatever the Romans had.
- They already lost a war against a third world country. To compare Westmoreland with the unfortunate Varus, who lost his legions in the Teutoburg forest, would of course be a stretch. Varus did not have to deal with a continuous stream of telexes and telephone calls from an ignorant Roman emperor or a bunch of equally unqualified agenda laden senators. Varus was no career soldier; he was a lawyer. It may look a bit strange to put a lawyer in charge of three legions invading Germany, but if you consider that nowadays we put lawyers in charge of big chemical companies, it probably wasn't all that awkward. I don't believe that Varus knew for a second what he was doing. I don't even think that Varus knew where the Yalu river or the Cambodian border were. I also believe that he never had heard of MacArthur. But Westmoreland knew, and beyond that, he knew very clearly how all these things related to each other. On the other hand, Varus did not have superior technology or firepower. Their opponents, Giap and Hermann the Cherusk, more frequently called Arminius, were probably equally formidable. But Hermann received his training in the Roman army. He knew them in and out. Giap's knowledge about his enemy must have been more theoretical. I do not recall that he visited West Point. Westmoreland did not feel compelled to fall on his sword, like Varus did. That has been out of fashion among the leading classes for quite a couple of centuries by now. In Varus's case, it seemed rather practical. The German tribes used to burn the leaders of their opponents alive. What a shocking brutality! Falling on your sword looks like a really attractive alternative in that context. It should also be remembered that 7 years after Varus's defeat Drusus, Tiberius's son, went back, recovered the standards of the defeated legions and took revenge with typical Roman thoroughness. That was a very wise move if you were a superpower, wanted to stay one, and could get away with it. I don't know

what restrained the United States, but it was probably more than just one of the above. But in spite of all that, the symbolic value will have been very much the same. The USA can be defeated, if... Of course, there still is a lot of "if", but the fact remains.

- The USA has started to build walls. This is going to astonish some people. How can I say such a thing, if we even can't build a decent fence along the Mexican border? But in the end SDI (Strategic Defense Initiative) and Star Wars are the modern equivalents of walls. In the old days, the most powerful nations had no walls around their capital. The enemy was simply not supposed to show up there. There were armies and navies that could make sure of that. As soon as Rome, under Hadrian, started to invest in walls instead of legions and fleets, its decline became inevitable. Walls do not project power: they literally are just delaying instruments.
- The American elite is losing its moral fiber. They are indulging more and more in hedonistic pleasures. The enemies of the United States heavily gamble on that: they believe that the American public could never support the view (on CNN of course) of body bags coming back en masse from some distant war. They may not be completely correct about that yet, but reality approaches their dreams a bit more every day. Rome was a great nation as long as the Roman matrons said to their sons departing for a military campaign: "Come back either with your shield or on it." Which meant: "I'd rather have you die than forsake your duty." I will not vouch for the Roman matrons or their sense of morality, but there was a stubborn kind of "right or wrong, my country" in this. In later days that changed, and then Germanic tribes, mostly lead by people with a Roman education and training, could ransack Rome, in spite of the walls. In the contemporary USA, one can deny the country one's leadership in times of need (or more clearly: dodge the draft), and then still become elected president. And have you even contemplated how many of America's enemies received their education in fine US academic institutions, military and civilian?
- The proliferation of weapons of mass destruction, and here is your technological innovation, is defining totally new rules. While nuclear technology is still difficult and expensive enough to deter most rogue nations, the same cannot be said about biological agents. That is a serious problem.
- In the East, a new giant is emerging. China has the oldest culture on earth today, and more experience with the tides of time, with the eternal sequence of contraction and expansion than any other nation.

All this does not yet mean that we have to fear the impending end of "Pax Americana". There are uncharted forces in the slumbering giant USA. Wake him up and suffer the consequences! Admiral Yamamoto, a great military leader, understood this very clearly. He knew that Pearl Harbor, as devastating as it looked at the time, did nothing to foster a final Japanese victory. Quite to the contrary: it woke the giant up, and by doing that it set Japan's demise in irreversible motion. The USA is still good for a couple formidable rebounds, if the American people can be mobilized behind a morally justifiable cause. But nothing is forever, also "Pax Americana" isn't.

Politically, the influence of the United States is enormous. It would be interesting to show how many of the political and military leaders in the world have been educated in the John F. Kennedy School of Government, West Point, or a dozen more absolutely fine American institutions. The increasing worldwide support for free trade may not be totally disconnected from that fact.

It is quite characteristic for the maze of evolution that, although we are perfectly able to rationalize how things could become the way they are today, and although we can clearly identify the basic driving forces behind future development, the outcome remains nevertheless totally unpredictable.

The drivers behind the contemporary changes are quite clear. They are information and communication, in the broadest sense of those words.

We are moving towards a world where almost all information will be almost immediately available to almost everybody. This means that information flow will stop to be a bottleneck for progress.

Today:

- Internet is a fact, and it is the fastest growing thing on earth.
- Even in huts with dirt floors you see TV sets.
- Americans could see the air raid on Baghdad during the Gulf War live on CNN.

What consequences will that have? Communication always played an important role in the dissemination of new ideas. Without the Roman road system, and the "Pax Romana" that allowed reasonably safe traveling, Christianity could never have spread like a wildfire, as it did.

Will Internet and "Pax Americana" achieve similar results in our time? Will they, as the Roman road system did, enable the proliferation of the new ideas that will lead to the demise of the superpower that made it all possible?

Will this ubiquitous and immediate availability of information drive further concentration, or rather enable fragmentation?

Will we see new "dark ages", as one normally does after the destruction of a great power?

But before it goes that far: what will this new, ubiquitous information availability do to the financial markets? Will it decrease time constants that once enabled relative stability for an intrinsically meta-stable system?

Very interesting questions indeed and no secure answer!

The prime question at hand here is whether we are, as a result of the current technology changes, looking forward to a period of further economic concentration, or rather fragmentation. Remarkably enough, one can make a case for both.

First of all the improvements in communications and the ready availability of information enables command and control of large and complex organizations to a degree that would have been impossible as little as 10 years ago.

In the classic pre-internet enterprise, we had this age-old notion of "control span". How many individuals can be managed, controlled, and lead by one person? Once you have resolved this, it is easy to calculate how many levels of hierarchy you are going to find in an organization of a given size. Hierarchical depth is a powerful bottleneck for the performance of organizations, and therefore a decisive limiting factor to their growth. We will come back to that. If utilized properly, the contemporary electronic tools, work flow tools like Lotus Notes deserve a special mention here, allow to vastly expand the control span, thereby reducing the hierarchical depth, and thus allowing larger organizations. That seems to indicate that technology will support further concentration.

On the other hand, modern technology allows you to run quite substantial businesses with just a handful of people. We see examples of that emerge in the telecommunications industry (there we have our old friend recursion again). Let's just suppose that the electronic market place will develop along the lines we believe to see today. Everybody will be a participant in that market, being supplier and consumer at the same time. A company will for instance be able to put intellectual work, like computer programming, up for bids on the net. Any individual can bid on it, eventually subcontracting parts to others. The purchaser can receive the "goods" via the net and pay via the net. This seems to indicate that there are opportunities for *smaller* companies, with fewer employees, using the services of a huge number of independent, one-person enterprises.

Which of the two scenarios will happen? Most likely: both of them at the same time. Which will be the dominant effect? There is no way to tell for sure from here and now. But let's look at a couple of examples.

6 An Example, a Scenario and Some Thoughts About Them

Yesterday I ordered a book from amazon.com. They provide a quite comprehensive search engine and also offer attractive prices. What happened?

- I entered Amazon's web site.
- I searched and found the book I wanted. In the meantime I was able to observe the enormous selection they offer about the topic I was interested in (history).
- Sometime in the past, I had to give them a whole bunch of data (address, credit card, etc.). At that occasion, I got a password.
- Now I just enter the password. I do not have to give them any more information.
- I selected the delivery option.

I promptly get an order confirmation by e-mail. Later I will get e-mail reporting the shipment of my book. And that was it! So far, no human intervention was required.

What will happen next? I have no inside knowledge, and this is pure speculation, but let's look at the alternatives:

- Amazon has this gigantic warehouse.
- The shipping order for my book appears on a screen.
- Better yet, shipping documents including a label with my address are printed.
- My credit card is debited for the appropriate amount.
- A clerk picks the book and puts it in the package.
- The package is shipped, according to my delivery instructions.
- The order is registered as "shipped" on the screen.
- The transaction automatically flows into Amazon's financial system.

But maybe Amazon does not want to have that gigantic warehouse. Maybe even after talking to their suppliers, the publishing houses and distributors, about putting books in it that still remained their property, thus eliminating the inventory carrying cost for Amazon, they still found maintaining and operating the facility too expensive.

So how about this one:

- Upon receiving my order, Amazon immediately orders the book from subject publishing house / distributor.
- All further steps as in the previous case.

But even now, having eliminated keeping an own inventory, Amazon still has the hassle of receiving and shipping the goods. Worse, there is a time delay that the customer will not like, so there is a better solution:

- My order is electronically forwarded to the publishing house / distributor in question.
- The shipping documentation is printed there. They have the Amazon packing material available.
- A clerk picks the book and puts it in the package.
- The package is shipped, according to my delivery instructions.
- The order is registered as "shipped" on the screen.
- My credit card is debited for the appropriate amount.
- The publishing house is electronically paid by Amazon.
- The transaction automatically flows into Amazon's financial system.

Still better:

- My order is electronically forwarded to the publishing house in question.
- It is forwarded to their production center, where they have a number of "book printing and binding robots". Those are basically a combination of:
  - fast (color) laser printer.
  - book cover embossing tool.
  - book binding tool.
- My book is produced there and the shipping documentation (labeled Amazon) is printed on the same equipment. The data for the book come from files where it resides in Microsoft Word format. Additional files define the cover and the binding.
- I am not certain that it pays to have the packaging done by the robot as well. It certainly seems possible enough.
- The package is shipped, according to my delivery instructions.
- The order is registered as "shipped" on the screen.
- My credit card is debited for the appropriate amount.
- The publishing house is electronically paid by Amazon.
- The transaction automatically flows into Amazon's financial system.

Or yet another one:

- My order is forwarded to Amazon's production plant.
- They have there a number of "book printing robots".

- My book is produced there and the shipping documentation is printed on the same equipment. The data for the book come from files where it resides in Microsoft Word format. Additional files define the cover and the binding. Agreements between Amazon and the publishing houses define things like paper quality and cover texture. Amazon gives the publishing houses the opportunity to supply their own materials.
- I am not certain that it pays to have the packaging done by the robot as well. It certainly seems possible.
- The package is shipped, according to my delivery instructions.
- The order is registered as "shipped" on the screen.
- My credit card is debited for the appropriate amount.
- The publishing house is electronically paid by Amazon, now just for copyright + eventually material provided by the publishing house.
- The transaction automatically flows into Amazon's financial system.
- Same in the publishing house.

Yet another variant:

- Amazon sends me the book in electronic form by e-mail. I get a stiff discount for not requiring paper. After all, if I want, I can print the book myself.
- All other relevant other steps are the same as in the previous case.

What happened during this sequence of scenarios?

- Inventory went down, ultimately to zero.
- Human labor went down, ultimately to almost zero.
- The use of raw materials went down, ultimately to zero.
- The contact between original supplier (the author), and ultimate consumer (the reader) becomes more and more direct.

A couple of questions and observations here: What happened to the classical production factors? What were those again?

- land
- labor
- raw materials
- capital
- knowledge?

I did not see so far knowledge explicitly mentioned as a production factor, but I believe that it is about time to change that. Without knowledge nothing goes. All one can do is pathetically waste the other four.

In his very intelligent book "The Future of Capitalism"[19], Lester Thurow points out that it is rather easy to move knowledge and capital freely around the world. Labor can also be transported to a lesser extent. So production can take place wherever land, raw materials and labor are cheaper. But what if you hardly need any of those, like in the case of my "last-stages" Amazon? In that case you go

- where your consumers are, to minimize logistics costs,
- where taxation is the most humane,
- where political stability does not let you have nightmares about the security of your investment.

And that is not necessarily in the third world!

Now you will say: "That's just books, big deal!"

Wait a second: there are other possibilities, they just have not yet been exploited. Please put your imagination in overdrive again, we are going to have one more of those stories.

It is August 2010. My wife Vita and I are invited to a wedding party, a big formal affair. Now Vita has a problem of existential nature: what shall she wear? If one is not independently wealthy – and we are not – one cannot just go to a tailor and have something custom designed. But if one buys "ready to wear", there always is this dreadful prospect of seeing two other women with the same dress at the party. Although I fail to understand what would be so life threatening about that, I yield to the obligations accrued by 43 years of marriage and I am going to help finding a solution. What shall we do? Suddenly I remember the "Cyber Tailors" that opened a couple of weeks ago unceremoniously next to the post office. "Cyber Tailors?" says Vita, "You know that I don't feel at ease with all that computer hocus pocus, only the *word* Cyber makes my flesh creep!" But we go anyway. The store looks like, well not like a store. It's like entering somebody's quite pleasant living room. I am amazed: there is no high tech equipment visible. A pretty young lady, who introduces herself as Cathy, welcomes us. "Can I offer you something to drink, coffee perhaps? I just brewed some fresh one." While we sit down and sip our definitely low tech but delicious coffee Cathy asks: "What can I do for you today, folks?" "Not too much for me," I answer. "Just don't think so, we also have a lot of gorgeous stuff for men, especially for distinguished middle aged gentlemen like yourself." Well, that's a salesperson, calling a 67-year-old "middle aged"! Vita takes the initiative: "I need a dress, something really nice, but unobtrusive." "I am sure we will find something you will just adore," says Cathy, "but first we need to know you better. Please go into that cabin, strip to your underwear, push the green button and do as I will say."

Vita does as she is told. She enters something that looks like a rather large deluxe fitting room. Once she pushes the green button, a voice from the loudspeaker, more precisely Cathy's voice tells her that her measurements will be taken, and for that to happen she please might stand very still in the middle of the green circle on the floor. In the meantime, a number of ultrasound sensors record a geometrically perfect image of Vita's body. After about one second, the voice tells her that we are now going to record video imagery, essential to support her choices. She is asked to face the #1 on a wall, then the #2 through 4. She is then asked to walk along the white line on the floor, to the rhythm of the music, and make an elegant turn on the white circle, as if she were a model in a fashion show. The voice leads her through the moves, and then tells her to dress and come out, not forgetting the obligatory "thank you so much, dear".

Cathy asks us to sit down on a couch, facing a piece of white wall. I suddenly notice that there are no pictures on it, and I start to suspect something. Cathy pulls a drawer from her little Louis XV desk. It houses a keyboard, a joystick and a bar code reader.

Cathy hits some keys and says: "Well, folks, let's get on with our fashion show, featuring one of our most prominent models." The room gets dark, and the wall lights up with a projected image. This is a real fashion show, music and all, but the model that walks down the stage is... Vita! She is wearing a red cocktail dress, makes an elegant turn and walks back. She is looking absolutely delightful! Cathy looks at Vita. "Do you want to see it again?" "Well, the dress is not bad, but that red is a bit... well I mean, for my age." "No problem," says Cathy, "we can do all kinds of colors". We see the same thing in white, green, orange... you name it. Then suddenly Vita says: "I think I like the black one, but I believe that it would be good if we could lower the hemline by let's say one inch." Cathy pushes a couple of keys again, and there is the new hemline. Vita is quite enthusiastic by now, but Cathy says that there is a lot more decisions to be made. First of all the fabric must be selected. She opens a drawer cabinet, and pulls out a black fabric sample book. Quite amazing how many different kinds of black cloth one can make. Vita feels them with her fingers, and decides for a particular one. Cathy reads the bar code, and we see the show again, with that fabric. With a lot of good will I can notice some difference in the light reflections. Cathy suggests that Vita can make her dress really unique by applying some gold embroidery. She draws it on the image, and we see the show again. Vita is ecstatic. "And now the lining," says Cathy. When we look at the ultimate review, Vita suddenly exclaims: "But I don't have that kind of shoes, and also the stockings..."

"Nothing to worry, dear. That can be helped." And there goes my credit card.

Cathy says that the data will be streamed to Charlotte, NC, by the way via the Internet. First of all my credit card will be checked. If it is good, the plant will manufacture the dress today. The material and machine capacity are available, otherwise the fashion show would not have been performed. Vita wants to know whether there will be any fitting sessions. Cathy says that they would be utterly superfluous, as the system knows Vita's measurements almost to the micron, much more precisely than any human tailor could ever work, and asks what kind of delivery we want. They can do overnight for a couple bucks more. She tells us that they originally wanted to build the plant in Thailand, but personnel costs are so insignificant that it really does not matter. The additional shipping costs alone would by far offset the cheaper Thai labor. Add security considerations, and Charlotte was a no-brainer.

Please take your imagination out of overdrive. We better handle it with care, we are still going to need it.

Let's not go overboard: we still are far from there. But this is only halfway science fiction. Strangely enough, the science is there. There is nothing in the previous story that I could not do today. I would not have to invent one single thing, just cleverly combine technologies that already exist. It is the fiction that is missing, not the science. Fiction comes from *fingere:* to shape. In today's lingo, we would probably rather call it vision. As so often, not science and technology, but a clear vision of what those can achieve is the limiting factor on development.

But let's suppose this really happened – and it ultimately will! – Then what? There are a number of possibilities. The one that seems the most threatening and likely is that the virtual elimination of human labor from the process will result in mass unemployment. Spending power and consumer confidence will evolve accordingly, and our awesome ingenious factory will have very little to do, because there are no customers that can pay for its products. This is the old communist credo. The capitalists will try to reduce the whole economy to only one significant production factor: capital. The consequences of this process will ruin the system. This would be a quite frightening perspective, if we had no historic examples of similar processes.

Let's look at agriculture, after all one of the historically fundamental pillars of the economy. In the Middle Ages, the vast majority of the population was totally absorbed with the production of an inadequate and unreliable food supply. But we have of course difficulties to find reliable statistics from that long ago. We don't need to go that far back. Even if we look at the evolution of farming in the USA since as recently as 1900, we are quite able to make our point. It is interesting, let's look at the evolution of the population first in Fig. 6.1.

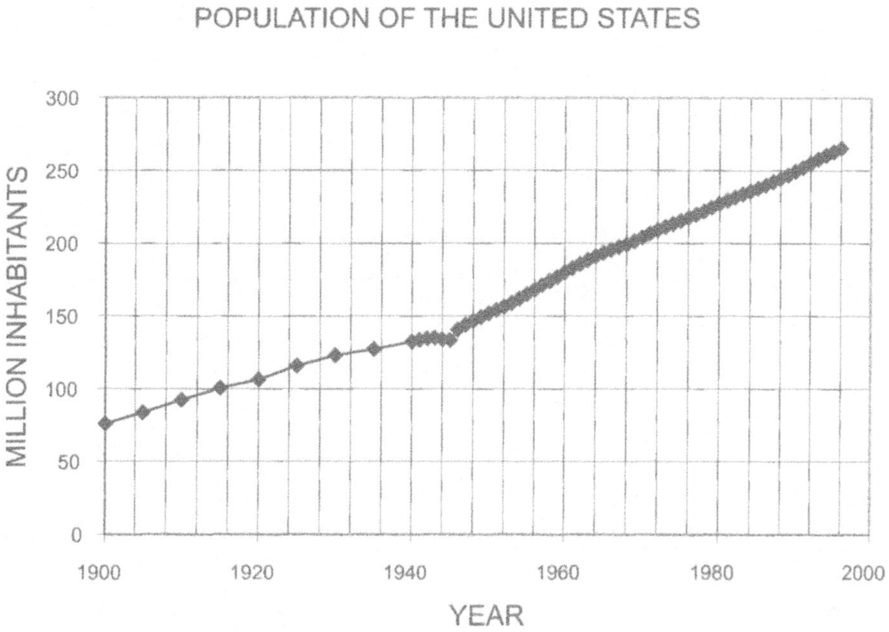

Figure 6.1

A quite impressive, continuous growth is obvious. It should not be a surprise that the total workforce evolved along the same lines.[1]

Now lets look what happened in farming over about the same period of time. This is represented in Fig. 6.2.

[1] All data material used in the remainder of this chapter has been extracted from the Internet and then compiled and processed. The main sources for your verification:
- Historical Statistics and Analysis on Unemployment, Poverty, Urbanization, etc., in the United States. Kelley L. Ross, Ph.D.
- http://www.census.gov
- http://stats.bks.gov
- http://www.usda.gov/nass/aggraphs/fl_frmwk.htm
- http://woodrow.mpls.frb.fed.us/economy/calc/hist1913.html

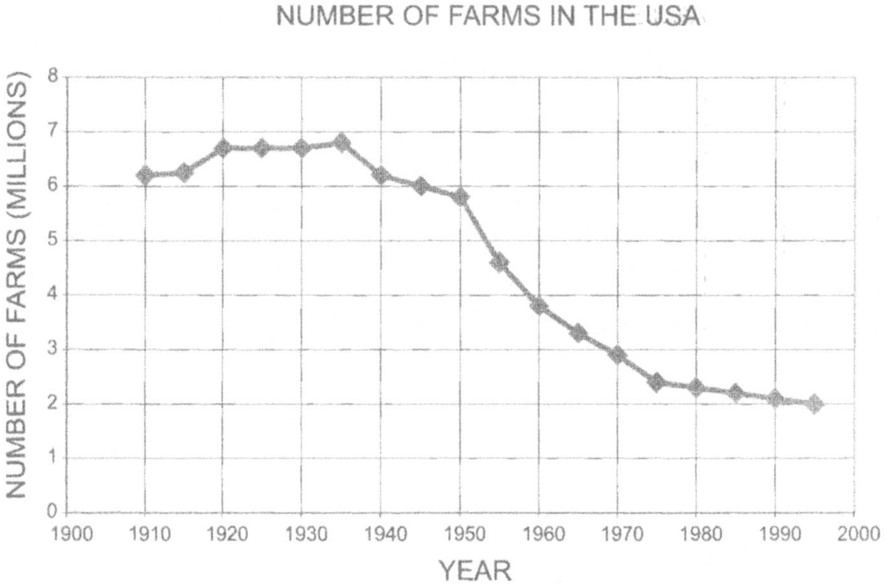

Figure 6.2

In the last 90 years, farm employment fell from 13.5 million to 2.5 million.

This becomes even more dramatic if you look at a drop from 15% to less than 1% of the population, as visible in Fig. 6.3.

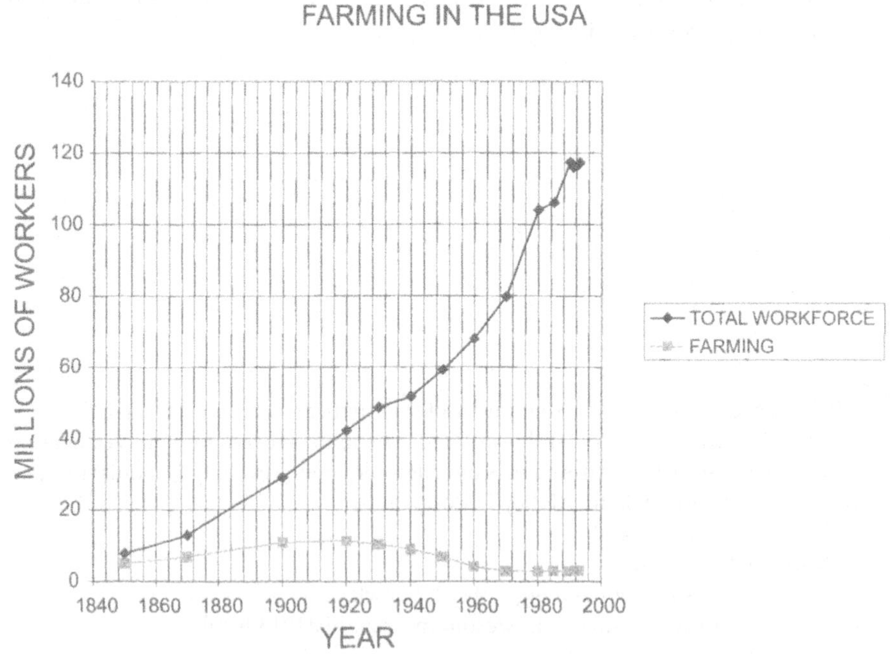

Figure 6.3

But only if we look at the proportion of farm workers in the total workforce does the earth shattering effect really unfold. That is what Fig. 6.4 shows.

Figure 6.4

So the main employment factor in the economy was literally wiped out! But what was the effect?

Mass unemployment? Very obviously not!

Let's look at the unemployment statistics in Fig 6.5.

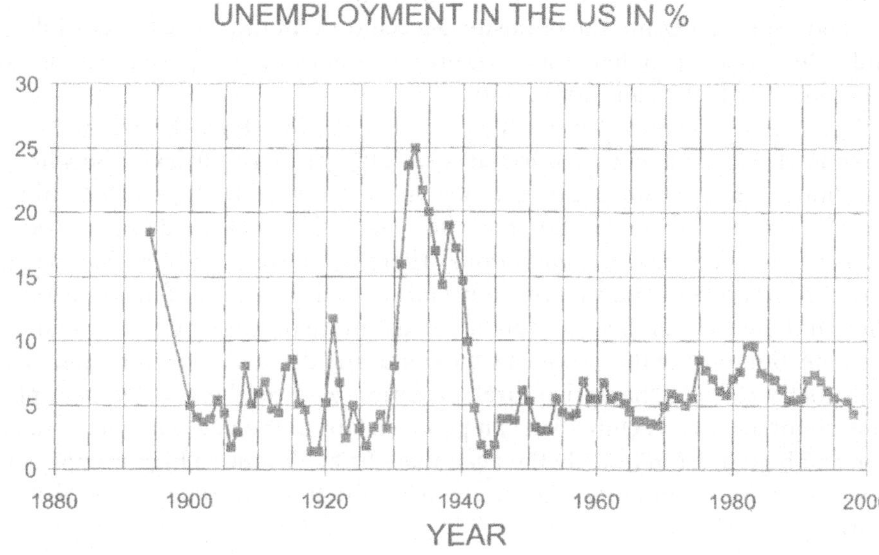

Figure 6.5

There is absolutely no correlation between the loss of farm jobs and unemployment. Some serious economists claim that unemployment has much more to do with the clumsy attempts of governments to manipulate national economies that with anything else.

Then, the general population must have become impoverished, sharing the burden of the lost jobs.

Let's look at poverty in Fig. 6.6:

Figure 6.6

If anything at all, we could prove a correlation between poverty and the *availability* of farm jobs, not their elimination.

Food shortage? Quite the opposite! Agricultural output rose by multiples, and if there is any problem, then overproduction, leading to permanent bickering with the European Community.

Improving efficiency never really caused any of the above detriments. Improving efficiency means that we, as a society, get more for less. The whole question is how the gains are distributed. As long as everybody gets something out of it, things are fine. The latter can however only be achieved by *slow* transitions. One needs several generations. There will have been men that never would be, never could be anything but a farmer. The slowness of the transition allowed them to hold their ground and to get more or less by until the end of their life. But most of their sons saw the trend, and decided to become dentists and stock brokers. The agricultural transition we used here as an example took about a century. Only then can people adapt to the newly created situation and benefit from it. Only then can there be at all times a high number of winners, and a low number of losers, which is the short formula for social stability.

The transitions that we can see coming in manufacturing today will not be that slow. They will not take a century. There are fundamental differences.

If I had lived in 1898, I could *not* have written the "agriculture story", the way I described "Cyber Tailors", not even in the wildest of hallucinations. A lot had still to happen to make the agriculture revolution even a remote possibility.

- Only mass-produced synthetic fertilizer would allow for the agricultural mass production that had to come. What we had in 1898 was Chili Guano.
- We had to find a way to chemically combine Nitrogen from air, and Hydrogen, essentially from water to yield Ammonia, Nitric Acid, and ultimately Ammonium Nitrate. After resolving all the difficult catalyst problems, we had to find ways to mass-produce Ammonium Nitrate in a reliable safe way. That was a daunting adventure that took a couple of decades to accomplish. What we had in 1898 were a couple of good ideas and tons of technological problems. Dozens of break-through inventions still had to be made.
- Farm equipment needed to be revolutionized. We had to switch horses for combustion engines. And if the ultimate outcome could have been clear for someone in 1898, even the fabrication techniques to mass-produce such equipment still needed to be invented.
- A massive re-distribution of land was necessary. Especially in a rural environment, this takes a lot of time, often generations.
- Crop protection agents and herbicides had to be discovered, and their production processes had to be developed.
- The logistics of modern agriculture, as such requiring a lot of quite sophisticated equipment, had to be developed.
- Millions of people needed to learn new techniques.

All this took time, lots of time. It did indeed *have* to last a century.

Not so in the case of "Cyber Taylors":

- Nothing fundamental needs to be invented: the technology is all there.
- The automatic, computer driven cutting and sewing machines are available today.
- Robots, that may be needed to transfer the work from one station to the next, are offered to the market place in increasing abundance and sophistication.
- The logistics are available: Federal Express, DHL, even the US Mail offer them right now, ready to go.
- The Internet is sitting there: a highway waiting for future commerce.
- People today are by and large computer literate. What Cathy has to do in our little story is not more difficult than your average computer game.
- The necessary graphics software is available.

Granted, some pretty advanced programming might still be necessary, but nothing more than a small clever team could accomplish in a couple of years.

None of the attenuators that slowed the agricultural revolution down to a humane pace is there. But the promise of profit lures. Tailor made, at ready to wear prices!

This will go fast!

But what if you increased efficiency too swiftly? What if you did this in a world of ubiquitous, immediate knowledge, also about price levels. The result would likely be deflation. There is nothing magic about deflation. Historically, there have been longer periods of deflation than inflation. It just never happened in our lifetime. We learned to fear inflation, which in short translates to "relentless scarceness of things". Why should that be so, now that we have a much better handle on natural phenomena that used to create such situations in the distant past? Does the natural course of evolution not rather point to an ever-increasing abundance? Would that not make deflation the more natural state of affairs? Such a thesis would by the way be supported by its more frequent occurrence in history.

When could we, in the modern industrialized world, ever link inflation to a natural disaster, like a totally failed harvest due to climatic conditions? Of course, even in contemporary Russia such a thing can still happen. But the farmers there never had an opportunity to see the link between their efforts and foresight and their gains.

Were our own inflationary periods in the West not mostly induced by shortsighted political action, nationally and internationally? Were they not more the result of clumsy attempts to tamper with national economies against the stream of evolution?

Would not a – totally illusionary – general acceptance of the fact that one has to *earn* a living mitigate most of the danger?

In spite of all the unanswered questions, there are many signs that we are in for a new era of deflation. It could be triggered by technology making stuff truly abundant. It could be induced by technology that lets us all instantly know "the right price", so that enterprises are forced to watch their efficiency even more fiercely than they ever have so far. And it could be accelerated by technology that helps companies to become more efficient at a high pace if they have the vision and courage to recognize the opportunity. All those components are present right now.

If you ever thought that inflation was bad, wait until you see deflation. I am almost certain that I will hate it. We are so accustomed to eternal inflation by now that it will be as if we suddenly had to drive on the left side of the road. There will be quite a bit of accidents!

Let's look at the Consumer Price Index (CPI) in the United States in Fig. 6.7.

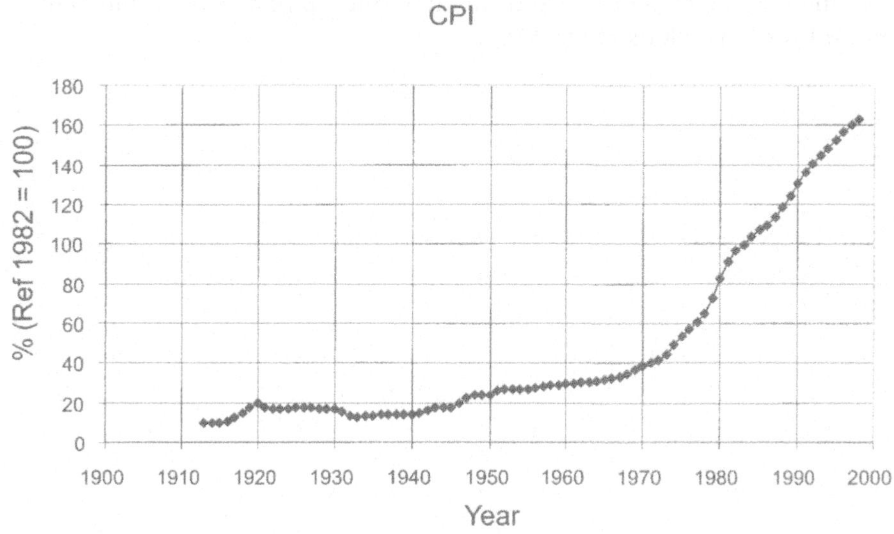

Figure 6.7

We see a period of relative stability between 1920 and 1945. From 1970 on, the curve takes off.

Now let's have a look at inflation in the United States. This is what Fig. 6.8 shows.

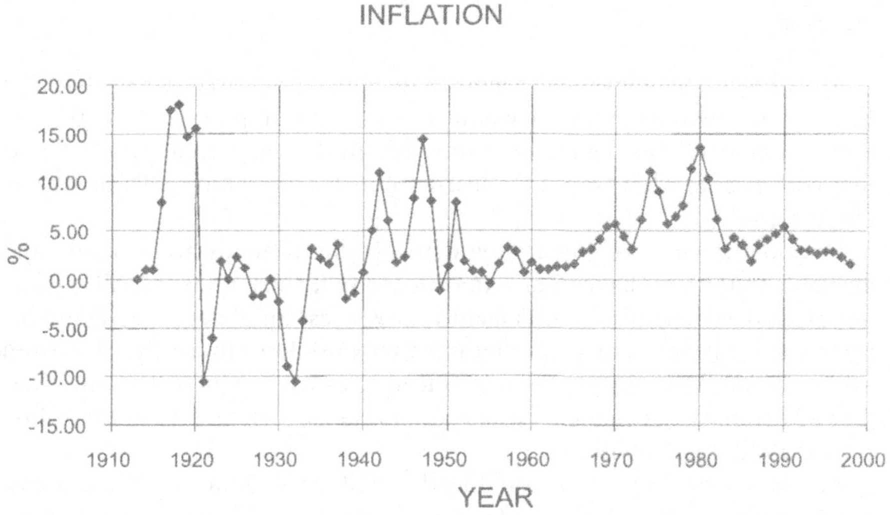

Figure 6.8

In the 20's and 30's we see periods of deflation. If you talk to people that have lived through those years, they will probably tell you that they have very few fond memories of them.

Is there a correlation between inflation and employment in the United States? Let's have a look at Fig. 6.9.

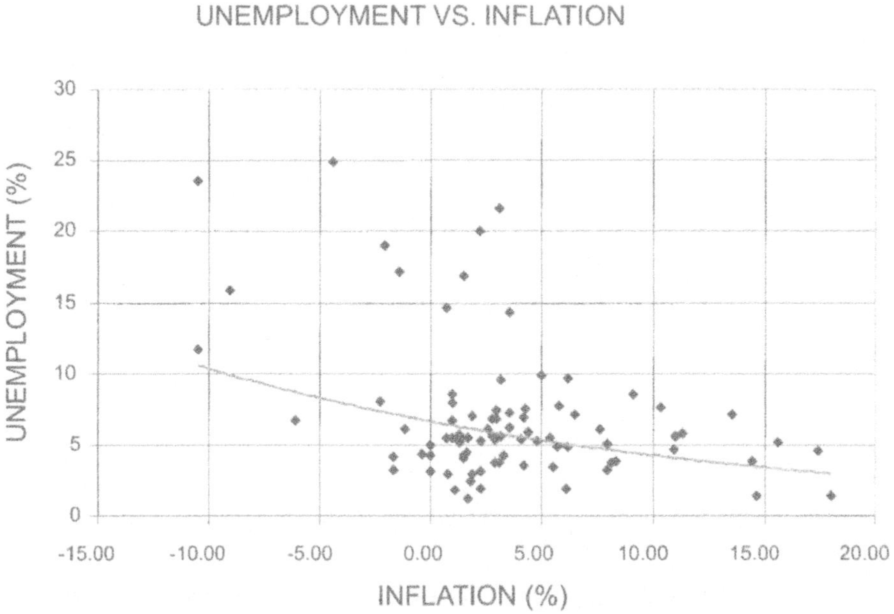

Figure 6.9

The exponential regression seems to indicate *some* correlation between inflation and unemployment. I would not call this impressive scientific evidence. First of all, the data strew quite a bit. And then, even if this were a perfect correlation, what would we learn from it? Correlation tells us nothing about causality.

Does deflation *cause* unemployment? Maybe! If goods are so abundantly available that prices have to give in order to sell, entrepreneurs will certainly not expand existing production facilities, even less build new ones. Quite contrary, they will close older installations that work less efficiently. That would lead to unemployment. It would also lead to efficiency increases, and therefore additional price maneuvering room to the downside, thus at least allowing for additional deflation.

But then: would unemployment lead to deflation? Quite likely! If a considerable portion of the labor force loses its revenue, spending power goes down, and so does demand. The existing production capacity shows a surplus. Prices will have to go down. We will sell less at lower prices and entrepreneurs will close inefficient installations, thereby creating more unemployment.

Probably both of the above assumptions and at the same time none of them are true. Likely, deflation and unemployment are both symptoms of a deeper, less visible, more elusive problem with the economy. I could imagine that they are interconnected by complex feedback mechanisms. They probably chase each other in the age-old "chicken and egg" fashion. I am no expert. This is something for the economists to lose their sleep over.

Nevertheless, historic data seem to indicate that at least moderate inflation and virtually full employment go hand in hand. Also, that seems to be a quite delicate equilibrium that can easily be destroyed from both sides.

It is conceivable that an "efficiency shock", exploding supply at much lower cost could start the spiral with the same deadly certainty as a sudden "unemployment shock".

There is another factor that we need to consider here. Innovation and modernization of the industry happens by the grace of economic cycles! I have worked all my life in the chemical industry. Our quest was to find ever more efficient processes, based on ever-cheaper raw materials to manufacture about 200 very basic chemicals. Many of those have been made for thousands of years! Take acetic acid – vinegar – as an example. First it was made by the enzymatic oxidation of alcohol, almost certainly invented due to mishaps in the wine making process. After that, the catalytic oxidation of ethanol was used. After that, the hydro-carbonylation of methanol, in different processes with ever decreasing pressure (and thus cost) were employed. Now, we make acetic acid from methane, which happens to be the simplest, cheapest, most abundantly available hydrocarbon one can find. But how did we *modernize* production technology? How did we come to the decision to close the plant that utilized the old technology, in order to replace it by a more modern one? The true and unglamorous answer is that we never made such a decision! I know not one single instance where we decided to shut down plant A, making product X, in order to replace it by the more modern plant B, also making product X, solely on economic merits. It is very hard to compete with old, totally depreciated installations. Innovation happens nevertheless. During an economic downturn, you have to curtail capacity. What installation will you close? Quite obviously it will be the one with the highest variable cost. So the old technology goes. Then the economy recovers, and you have to expand capacity. What do you build? The process with the highest return on investment of course, and that's the modern one. The net result is technology substitution, but with a time shift. That is how I saw innovation happen in the chemical industry's production equipment. In a totally stable economic climate, modernization would be a much slower process. Maybe we humans simply have to suffer for our progress.

The question is: what will all this mean for the future enterprise? If what I see coming materializes there will be:

- deflation
- revolutionary high tech available at short notice and affordable cost

- an aging population in the developed countries
- markets that shift accordingly
- difficulty to keep up with the necessity for education.

And worst:

- Because the capabilities of humanity are more or less normally distributed, there will be more and more people that cannot acquire the skills that are needed to be players in the new game. Thus there will be more and more "incurable" unemployment.

All this will put enormous demands on the future enterprise. It will sail through even more troubled waters than the contemporary one. It will need an agility that dwarfs what we have believed to be flexibility in the past.

There also will be enormous opportunities, waiting to be taken by the best. Will our enterprises be ready for the challenge? I am rather pessimistic.

7 The Enterprise

Of course, when we previously listed the kind of entities a human being can belong to, we omitted a very important one. We have many names for it: enterprise, company, firm, corporation, and if you would thoroughly research you certainly would find many more. We will try to deal with the enterprise as if it were a biological species, developing along the lines of evolution. I have no scientific evidence to support the validity of such a treatment. But it seems like nothing in this world is truly able to evade the systematic of evolution. It also seems that the enterprise was formed by a lot of trial and error from elements that could be found in the given environment, and subject to laws that pre-existed, much like the creatures we previously elaborated on. So, why not give it a try? It might be entertaining, provoke some thought and maybe, just maybe, somebody later comes up with scientific proof for the validity of the approach.

We will try to look at different aspects of this most visible and yet most elusive of all creatures. The longer I work on this subject, the more I despair of its complexity and size. We will only be able to brush rather superficially over the internal and external forces that influence the enterprise. But let's give that a serious attempt nevertheless.

7.1 Cooperation, Competition and Hierarchy

What is this illusive "enterprise"? What are its defining characteristics? First let's look in the dictionary. We find:

3 a: a unit of economic organization or activity, especially a business organization.

That's not a very precise definition. Enterprises come in an unimaginable multitude of shapes and sizes. If we want to find the main commonality that characterizes them all, we probably should look at the word "organization". Organization is of course nothing but a structured form of cooperation. Cooperation is probably the one common characteristic between all the diverse life forms that we call "enterprises". So let's have a closer look at cooperation.

7.2 The Roots of Cooperation

How did people, uncounted centuries ago, decide to start cooperating in enterprises? This seems innocent enough in terms of a question, doesn't it? Well, let's take a step back here. We, as a species are so terribly anthropocentric, so much convinced of ourselves! The question insinuates that cooperation is a human invention! That is probably not true. Cooperation is even today by no means a human monopoly. We know that animals cooperate, especially for hunting, have a social organization and leadership. Our cousins the chimpanzees, so touchingly described by the Dutch biologist Frans De Waal [5], do have a complex society, with pecking order, power struggles – including the "small favors" and back scratching we know so well from human politics –, political parties and intrigue. The diversity of cooperation in the animal world is stunning. Not only do wolves, lions, dingoes and hyenas hunt as groups. Also Orca's and Humpback whales show amazing collective hunting techniques. And cooperation is not restricted to hunting either. Meerkats cooperate in raising their offspring: they have "professional" babysitters. Should we now suspect that cooperation is so old that it was invented before the big mammals returned to the sea? Probably not! A more likely hypothesis might be that cooperation is such a powerful principle in general, that evolution re-discovered it wherever it was applicable.

But it still must have been hunting that gave the main trust towards cooperation. When you hunt, cooperation improves your odds dramatically. It is clearly an activity where the cooperation of n people yields a result far superior to just n times that what one individual could achieve. Tribes that practiced this invention obviously improved their food supply. That again enhanced their survival rate and strengthened their competitive position towards other tribes. It's really always the same and quite trivial: a property that however indirectly offers a competitive advantage towards procreation will in the end expand over the whole gene pool. We find group hunting and fishing everywhere with primitive human tribes that have survived up to now.

In order to hone the fine art of successfully hunting in teams, as we saw it happen almost everywhere, there are quite a couple of complex issues that need to be dealt with. It must have taken thousands upon thousands of years to achieve some of the things that are necessary to make a bunch of n people perform considerably better than n times the individual capability. To begin with: communication. Cooperation requires communication on many levels. First of all one needs to be able to share a plan. That sounds really simple, but one first needs to *have* a plan, and constructing such a thing requires a rather profound and socially shared understanding of the world, plus the necessary language to reason and communicate about it. Then, during the execution of the plan, unexpected things will happen. The group needs to react to those in a synchronized way. This can hardly be achieved by ad hoc discussion. There must be prepared - canned so to say - behavior modules available for those cases. There has to be a mechanism to "call" these modules into action. In this realm all kinds of communication, verbal and non-verbal, play a role. There is probably also heavy use of rituals, one of the most effective ways to manage recorded behavior. Further, n individuals can act a lot more effectively if they are practically controlled by *one* brain. That requires rudiments of social organization. There must have been powerful feedback systems at work as well. Hunting in those days could become a very dangerous, very strenuous undertaking. The glorious feeling of having accomplished something together, of having shared the danger and the excitement, of having visibly surmounted the capabilities of an individual person, must have done its part to reinforce group cohesion.

All these things had to evolve side by side, like in a skillfully choreographed ballet, an infinitely slow ballet for that matter. And as they proved to enhance success, they became part of the main stream of our culture.

Experience and behavioral patterns that people acquired while hunting as groups were later extrapolated into other activities. War was probably one of those, as it shares many characteristics with hunting. The study of the belligerent behavior of surviving primitive tribes has revealed an interesting paradox. Originally, warfare was much more like fighting between animals of the same species. The main goal was not the destruction of the opponent, but just the clear and permanent clarification of the pecking order. There were numerous rituals and symbolic gestures, aimed at keeping the killing to a minimum, involved in the course of a battle. There was an elaborate "code of honor". Only as society became "civilized", war deteriorated to the utterly uncivilized activity it is today. Even so, it is almost amusing to observe how much of the ancient symbolism is still preserved in modern armies.

But also in agriculture the merits of cooperation were soon discovered, especially in difficult environments where harvests depended on irrigation, or where marshes needed to be drained to provide arable land. Then suddenly "public projects" of gigantic proportions became necessary, requiring cooperation far beyond anything that was ever experienced in connection with hunting. The terraces built by the Incas, for instance in the Sacred Valley in Peru are impressive testimony of their engineering *and* organizational abilities at the same time. A similar level of achievements must have been reached millennia earlier in Mesopotamia. The "hanging gardens of Babylon" were reported as one of the marvels of the ancient world.

Another "marvel of the world", the pyramids, must have taken the cooperation of ten thousands of people. I don't believe that they were happy unionized employees. But who ever claimed that cooperation needs to be voluntary to happen?

Urban life required yet another level of cooperation. The supply of water and food, hygienic infrastructure (like sewers) even questions like the location of cemeteries needed to be resolved. It is interesting to see that the Romans had mastered all these problems to the point where we had to wait until the 19th century to see the standard of living in European cities climb to the same level again.

In all those millennia, ever more refined forms of cooperation established themselves as powerful and unequivocal tools of competitive advantage on the tribe level. The problem is that, for cooperation to work on the tribal level, it needs certain prerequisites on the individual level. First of all, when our hunting party came home, exhilarated with the experience of common victory, the companions still had to compete with each other for a lot of important things:

- procreation
- food
- power
- influence.

Cooperation thus always boils down to collaboration with direct competitors. That has to be difficult!

But there probably is still another level of competition below the individual one. Competition may also take place *within* one person. In his brilliant book "The Society of the Mind"[11], Marvin Minsky, without any doubt one of the great thinkers of our time, describes the mind as a society of competing agents. A simple example Minsky gives in his book is a child playing with building blocks. The "building agent" wants to build an ever-higher tower, the "wrecking agent" wants to topple it. In the beginning the wrecking agent has very little incentive. There is almost nothing to destroy. The building agent has the floor. As the tower grows higher, both agents come closer to an equilibrium, and in the end the "wrecker" will prevail, unless... another agent, like for instance "hunger" will guide the child's attention into a completely different direction. I find this representation quite fascinating. It rationalizes not only a lot of the behavior we observe around us, but also what we witness happening within ourselves. It makes the torn, tormented personalities, that populate great literature so densely, much more understandable. So let's just for argument's sake assume that two agents called "the cooperator" and "the competitor" regulate the balance between competitive and cooperative behavior.

The competitor is a formidable, fundamental agent. It is the engine of evolution itself. But the competitor operates on a number of levels. Very certainly fundamentally on a personal level, but also, more through reasoning, experience and inference, on a group/tribe level. The cooperator is also active on essentially the same levels:

- the family
- the close workgroup

- the enterprise
- the political party
- the church

...

As long as the competitor operates one level above the cooperator, they will amplify each other. Competition between groups will go very well with cooperation within the own group. But what if they address the same level: cooperation with the group, and competition within the group for the leadership? Then they will struggle, very much like the "builder" and "wrecker" in the building block example. Who will win under what circumstances?

It is a fairly safe assumption that the competitor and the cooperator will have a base intensity that differs considerably from individual to individual. Whatever measurable property of human beings you investigate, you always find something close to a normal distribution. I have tested this for shoe sizes, body length and weight. Whenever you try this with a random group of more than 30 people, you do not only find a pretty neat normal distribution, but also rock hard statistical evidence for differences between the male and female population. Believe me, it's a great game to play with an Excel spreadsheet and a video projector, especially in front of a crowd that does not believe in statistics.

Insurance firms and credit card companies have found very much the same in their own studies about spending patterns and the tendency to save. IF you assume that our more elusive and less measurable properties are subject to a similar distribution (and there is no proof for this, but it seems not unreasonable), you can start reasoning about this. Why should they be different after all? They are the products of the same evolution that grew our feet and our ears! Of course, as opposed to shoe size, education and life experience as well influence the intensities of our cooperator and competitor. But those are fairly random sets too!

On top of all that, there is of course the influence of the circumstances.

IF the leadership is accepted as competent,

- the closer the individual's fate is intertwined with the group's wellbeing,
- the more immediate a threat to the group's prosperity is perceived.

The more dominant the cooperator will be.

But, just to show through what a devilish maze we are moving:

IF the leadership is NOT accepted as competent,

- the closer the individual's fate is intertwined with the group's wellbeing,
- the more immediate a threat to the group's prosperity is perceived.

The more dominant the competitor will be.

We should understand that the competitor and cooperator are two quite different animals. The competitor has its roots in the R-complex, the oldest and deepest part of the brain. It is closely related to the most fundamental layers of our existence, to those faculties that support survival and procreation. The cooperator feeds on reasoning, which takes place in the Neo-Cortex, the relatively young outer part of the brain. But it's not all that simple; certainly the competitor *uses* the faculties of the Limbic Complex (seat of emotions) and the Neo-Cortex. The cooperator inevitably finds support in the group behavior function that is clearly located in the R-Complex. It also will be able to feed on noble feelings as they are represented (together with less noble ones of course) in the L-Complex.

A lot of what is happening in the struggle between competitor and cooperator is governed by mythical components. In the animal world, it happens very often that the challenger waits much longer than necessary to announce his claim to the leadership position. The mythos surrounding the leader is just too strong. That may be a clever mechanism devised by evolution to prevent too frequent leadership changes that would be damaging.

It is quite conceivable that, if we could accurately map our competitor and our cooperator, they would differ between individuals as much as fingerprints. So the outcome, the equilibrium that will finally be found, is never truly predictable. It can be unreasonable, unlikely and still successful as easily as the other way around. It is all part of the great game of evolution, part of Creation as it happens today, totally evading our cognitive powers, towering over the pettiness of our individual existence and understanding.

Cooperation is always an n to n relationship. It always is a bi-directional relationship as represented in Fig. 7.1.

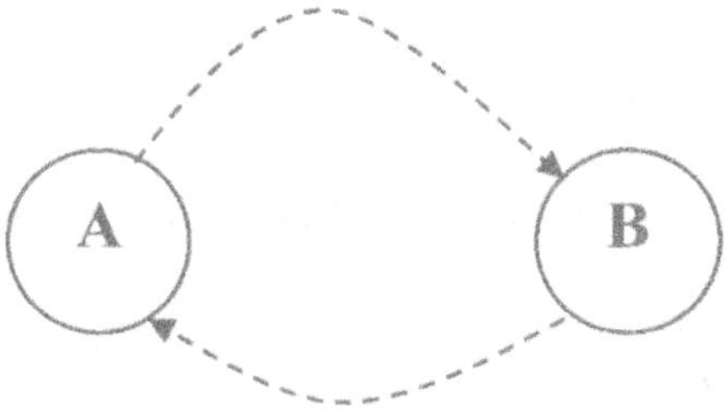

Figure 7.1

Even when A is the master, and B the slave, B will still expect and get something in return for his contribution to the relationship, if it were just food and shelter.

Even a one to one relationship is very rarely balanced. There is almost always one partner giving more, and the other one getting more. It will very seldom happen that A and B show a similar configuration of competitor and cooperator. Experience shows that such teams do not come together frequently. One of them will, all exterior circumstances equal, have a more pronounced competitor, the other a more dominant cooperator. That creates a quite broad spectrum, ranging from almost total dependency to almost total equality. The extremes will not occur too frequently. You don't have to believe me. The most common occurrence of a one to one relationship is marriage. Just look at the married couples around you, and make your own judgment.

But the problem in our society is not the one to one relationship, however problematic that may become at times, but an n to n relationship as it was required in our pre-historical hunting parties, and is called for in modern society.

The higher n becomes, the more the structure will crystallize towards a set of stacked "n to 1" relationships, like shown in Fig. 7.2.

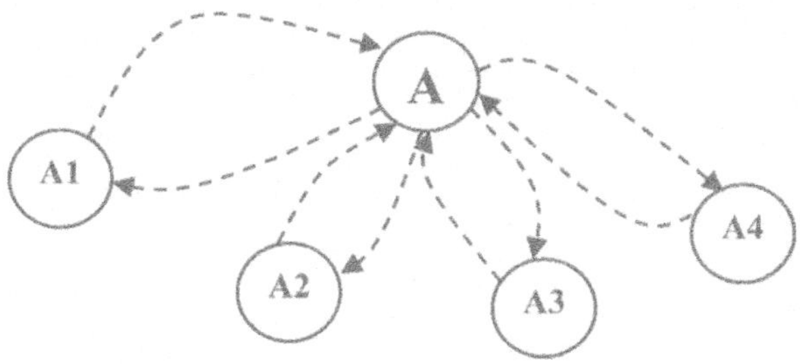

Figure 7.2

Why do we have to introduce hierarchy here? Why can't five grown up people work together on equal terms? History is full of attempts. Management by committee has been tried repeatedly. The Roman Empire, the French Revolution, and more recently, the Soviet Union come to mind. It never yielded anything but bloodshed. The modern equivalent of management by committee is the "self-managed workgroup". That is one of the most pathetic farces I ever saw.

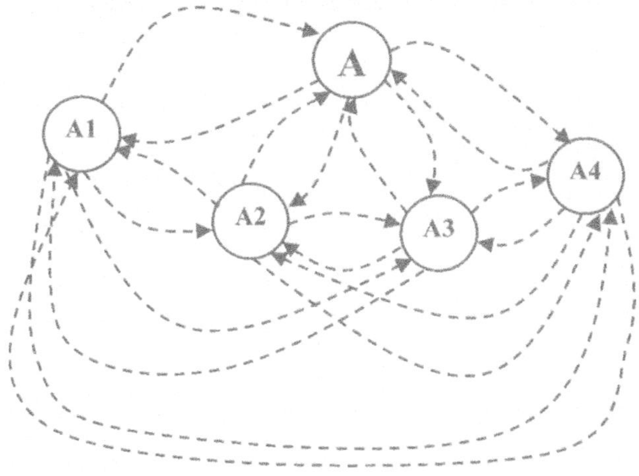

Figure 7.3

In reality, it is a team managed by an unrecognized, unsupported underpaid leader. But maybe that's the hypocritical purpose of the whole exercise. The fact is: collective leadership has never worked. I do not claim to fully understand the reason for that, but look at Fig. 7.3.

The relationship simply becomes too complicated, the amount of communication needed to keep it alive too overwhelming. Therefore reality will rather look like Fig. 7.4.

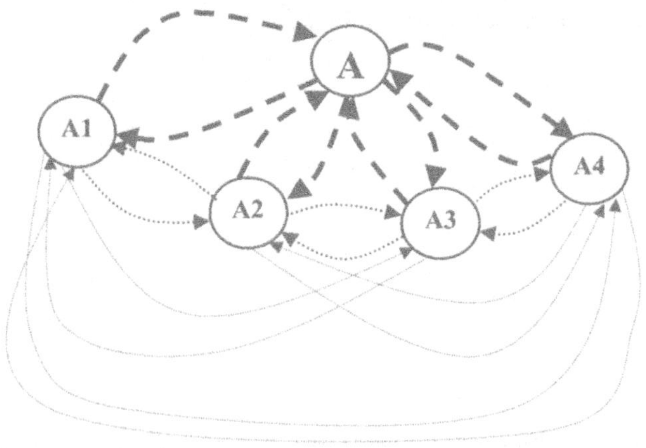

Figure 7.4

There are, need to be, relationships between the subordinate members of the group, but they are in total not as strong as the relationships with the leader. Should that ever become different, the leader is "out of touch" and revolution is imminent. As n grows, we see the structure of Fig. 7.5 emerge.

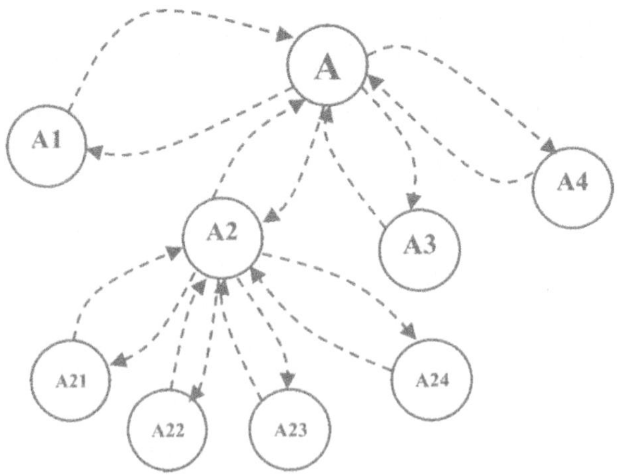

Figure 7.5

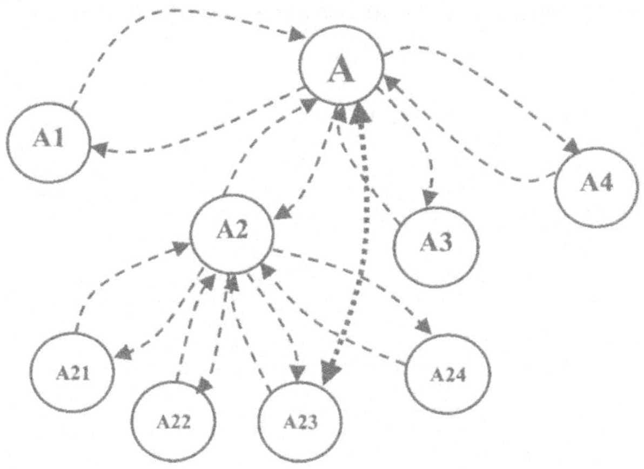

Figure 7.6

Even here, there can be additional relationships, like those shown in Fig. 7.6. however, if they become too strong and too numerous, they have a destabilizing effect on the system.

7.3 Control Span and Organizational Structure

Most large, modern enterprises have a deeply stacked version of the previously described model. Its complexity is governed by a magic number, called "control span", meaning the number of people one manager can effectively lead.

There is a quantitative relationship between:

N = number of people in an organization
C = control span
L = number of hierarchical levels.

Very obviously

$$N = \sum_{l=0}^{L} C^{l}$$

As all mathematical formulas, this one is uncontestably true and quite unrevealing. The gist of it is that, if you want to increase N, you either have to increase C or L. The difference between those two is that:

- If you increase C, you lose communication.
- If you increase L, you lose communication.

Let's play a bit with this. In Figs. 7.7, 7.8 and 7.9 we show different possibilities.

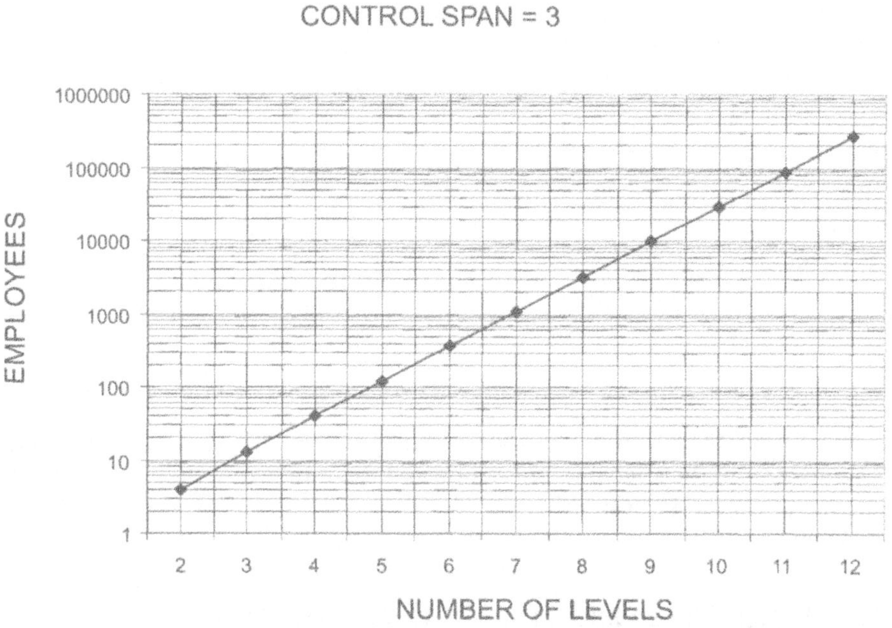

Figure 7.7

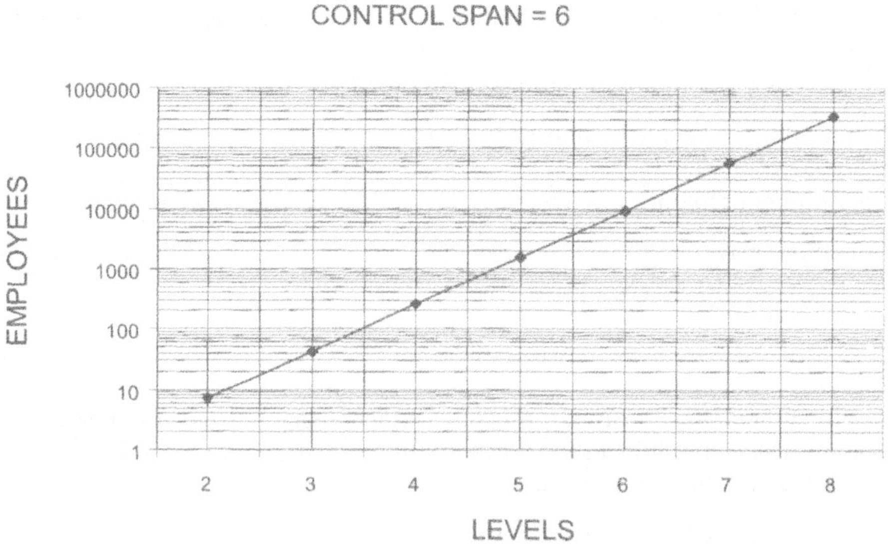

Figure 7.8

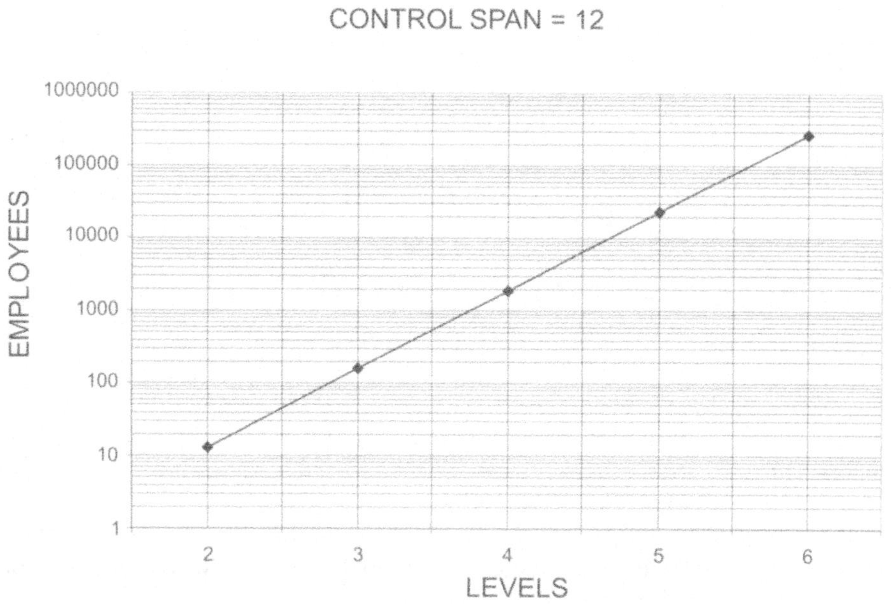

Figure 7.9

This means that, if you have an enterprise with 1000 employees, you can either have:

- 4 levels, and a control span of 12,
- 5 levels, and a control span of 6, or
- 7 levels, and a control span of 3.

What would you select? Well, maybe there is less to select than you think! There are serious limitations to all this. As you could already suspect, those are mainly in the realm of communication.

There is for instance the question: "How well can a complex task be divided in partitions that can be executed more or less separately?"

Let us assume that, within an enterprise, a number of entities (people, groups, organizational units...) need to cooperate and communicate to get a certain task done. Let's represent in Fig. 7.10 the necessary communication by arrows. The thicker the arrow, the more intense communication is needed.

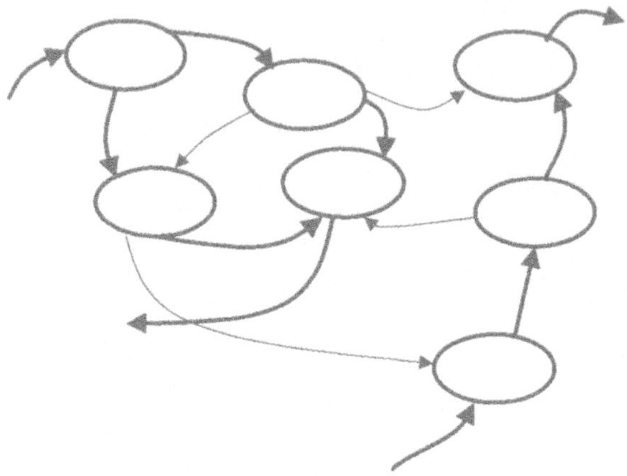

Figure 7.10

If we needed to divide this process in a hierarchical way, it is quite clear what we would do: we would avoid to cut thick lines. So we would probably do what is represented in Fig. 7.11.

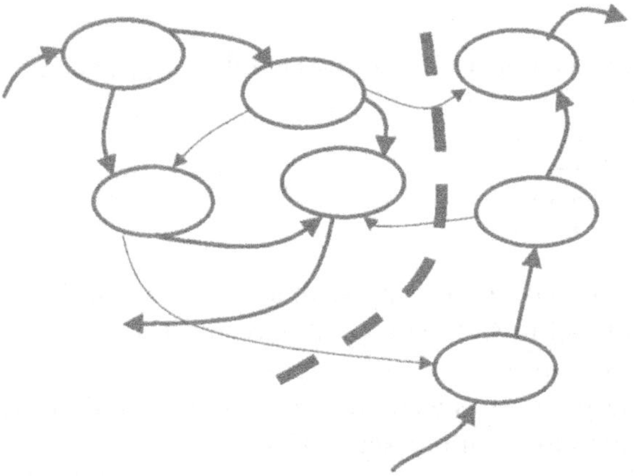

Figure 7.11

If you make parts and then assemble them into ever more complex units, this model works really fine. Those were the good old days of Taylorism: throw it over the wall into the next guy's cubicle and forget about it. Unfortunately in today's enterprise you find thick arrows almost everywhere.

There are other considerations as well. When you create a hierarchical unit, you create more than a work group. You create a living thing with a culture, a will and a purpose of its own. It is headed by somebody who truly enjoys to be "the boss", and is likely to use and direct its resources not just for the good of the enterprise, but for his own betterment as well. Further, hierarchical levels are powerful information filters. We all know them, those managers who have only one qualification, only one talent, and only one desire, and that is to be "the boss". Especially in the USA the term "reporting to" has to be taken quite literally. The bosses spend most of their time collecting, merging, massaging and bending information that comes from below, putting a favorable spin (for themselves, of course) on it. You do that through 6 or 7 levels of hierarchy, and what arrives at the top has nothing whatsoever anymore to do with the reality it originated from. When you consider that, you are no longer so amazed at how detached most of top management is from reality.

Then there is the question of control span. How much is right? Some people, especially in the past, used to claim that three is the proper figure. In reality, it all depends on things like the complexity, the integration, and the need for communication of the job at hand. We also have to factor in the leadership style.

If I want to control people, closely observe and direct their every move, I can probably not deal with more than three at a time. Although in most situations such a leadership style should be considered pathologically paranoid, there are certain occasions where it could be appropriate. I could think of extremely critical tasks in nuclear reactors or chemical plants as an example.

But in most situations, I had no problem with a dozen people reporting to me. After all, one of the most challenging tasks in the army, commanding an infantry squad, comes with 9 subordinates.

One rather severe problem is that decisions about organizational structures are only partly influenced by the practical considerations mentioned above. The unwavering desire of people to be "the boss", and the surrounding politics will in many cases be the more decisive factors. In 1995, I observed in a US company that had 16,000 employees some "tentacles" with an organizational depth of 14 levels. If that had been the uniform pattern throughout the whole organization, it would have meant a control span of two! Fortunately such madness was not the general rule, which only means that in those instances where we had indeed 14 levels, the control span must have been *considerably below two*. There is obviously no rational explanation, nor excuse for such a ridiculous construct, but it happens all the time.

But deeply stacked hierarchies do more than just waste energy on senseless report massaging. They do not only fragment the company's resources, they also fragment the company's image and goals. The odds that somebody on level 14 will not have the faintest clue of the visions and objectives that exist at the top level are overwhelming. There is of course an endless list of countermeasures that are supposed to mitigate the problem, from communications meetings to company newspapers and back. None of them work properly, and there is a reason for that. They are not even a remote substitute for the almost biological interaction within the tribe or hunting group that determined our social context many times longer than modern enterprise has so far. The employee will lose his identification with the enterprise. Literature calls this effect "alienation". But the residue of evolution makes people want, need and seek an affiliation of some kind with a group. The most likely candidate is the local group the individual belongs to. He will now identify with this group's goals much stronger, more directly and more clearly than with the mission of the enterprise. Before long, the competition that needs to be eliminated is the neighboring group. Ruthless "bosses" will exploit this to their own benefit. From there on, an enterprise will waste an astonishing portion of available energy and resources on something as futile as internal friction. I never saw this *not* happen. The only difference between organizations is the extent of the problem. This effect is probably one of the strongest limiting factors to excessive growth.

And it's not getting better! In the good old days of paternalistic leadership, there used to exist something called "loyalty", gluing the pieces of the enterprise together over and over, in spite of the constantly developing cracks. People, from the Chief Executive Officer (CEO) to the worker in the plant, had a perception of commonality, of intertwined destiny, of responsibility for each other. Top management at least *tried* to take good care of their people, and the employees *more or less* rewarded that. Today's buzzword is "shareholder value", *again* focusing all the attention on just one pinpoint aspect of the complex creature enterprise. The fad of the day is undiluted, unabashed capitalism. The result is that work force and management treat each other with increasing indifference. As the gap between propaganda and reality becomes ever wider, cynicism rises to unprecedented levels. Loyalty is dead. It is no longer seen as an essential value. Downsizing, outsourcing, contractors, consultants, these are the words that draw attention in the executive suite. They all mean the same thing: fewer employees and less cohesion with the few one is willing to keep. This is the "competitor" running amok. The situation is revealed with raw ruthlessness by cartoons like "Dilbert". When I was first exposed to them after coming to the USA in 1992, I considered them the destructive tasteless artifacts of a sick mind. I had to learn soon that reality caught up with them amazingly accurately. We have not seen the end of it yet. Quite obviously, the selection criteria that decide about the composition of the future leadership focus more and more exclusively on "competitiveness"! Of course we will some day mourn loyalty, and the next day resurrect it. Everything happens in cycles. Ultimately we will rediscover the fact that industry and trade are activities by humanity for the benefit of humanity, and that there is more in it for all of us if we are somewhat *less* competitive. But until then, immeasurable damage will be done.

8 The Enterprise and the World

About thirty years ago, I read an absolutely delightful book: "The Strategy of Culture", by the Dutch philosopher C.A. van Peursen[14]. If it becomes available again: highly recommended! In three of the chapters Dr. van Peursen describes how mythical, ontological and functional thinking have shaped the relationship between man and his world.

It is quite important to understand that these different schools of thought do not really supersede each other. Even today there are a lot of mythical aspects in our experience and understanding of the world. New views complement the old ones, and may move to the focus of attention for some time, but the old ones stay as well.

When I looked for the first time at how the creature enterprise understands itself in its relationship to the world I saw a parallelism with van Peursen's explanation for the evolution of culture that astounded me. That was probably mostly due to my limited insight. What else could we expect? Enterprises are populated with people, the same people that form culture!

Many years later, I read "Against the Gods", by Peter L. Bernstein[1]. What a marvelous wordplay: odds – gods! It is about the history of risk taking. Then it dawned on me that what van Peursen described was essentially the same. How do we cope with the uncertainty surrounding us, with the fact that we are obviously not the masters of our own destiny? Words like coincidence, chance and probability have a deep and mysterious meaning. They shout at us that we are not in control. But if not us, who is? The philosophical debate about these questions is not over. As a matter of fact it has not made considerable progress in the last couple of millennia. The very fundamental and so far unresolved question is:

Is probability a fundamental property of the universe or is it merely a crutch that we humans constructed in order to be able to reason about phenomena we do not understand on a mechanistic level?

Modern quantum mechanics seem to point to the former, but Einstein believed the latter *(God does NOT throw dice)*. Why does that one nucleus disintegrate right now while the other one does not? Maybe we just don't understand enough physics to tell or, on the other hand, things like frequency distribution might be basic properties of space and matter. A related issue is of course the uncertainty principle. Is that a basic property of nature, or is it due to the fact that our measurement techniques are too coarse? What if we could have, of course totally imaginary, perfectly unobtrusive measurement methods, would uncertainty then still exist? What is reality? Is it just the object or is it the system formed by object plus measuring equipment, maybe even plus observing subject?

I am going to ask you to put your imagination in overdrive for one of those fantasy experiments again. Here we go.

Throwing "honest" dice has always been the prototype of a stochastic event. Now let's have a closer look at this. The dice are made of inhomogeneous material. Their geometry is not perfectly symmetric. The surface on which they are thrown is highly inhomogeneous, almost impossible to model, especially if it is felt. The initial boundary conditions, determined by a human arm and hand, equipped with analogous control mechanisms sporting poor reproducibility do their worst on top of all that. The result is a "random" event.

But now imagine the following:

- We precision-machine dice from the most homogeneous material we can find. That will probably be some polymer.
- We polish their surface to perfection.
- Just putting the dots on the sides will make the dice slightly "dishonest", but I think we can live with that.
- We build the most perfect tabletop we can, probably highly polished glass, in which we afterwards etch a highly defined texture so that there be an understandable, reproducible friction between dice and table.
- We build a digitally controlled, computer driven robot arm. Very close tolerances and extremely precise controls are essential. The emphasis is more on reproducibility than absolute accuracy.
- In order to eliminate the influence from the surrounding atmosphere (temperature, pressure and moisture), we put all this in a vacuum chamber, and evacuate it to the maximum possible extent.
- We have the robot arm throw the dice under near perfect kinematic control; acceleration and deceleration, and thus the trajectory are preset with all the accuracy we are able of. In order to fool an unsuspicious audience, we could apply quite some fantasy to the trajectory. As long as it is reproducible, it does not matter.
- Of course we would have to put the dice in a known start position in the mechanical hand before casting them.

The question is: would under such circumstances the roll of the dice still be a random event? What do you think?

Now I happen to believe that I can make this machine throw whatever I want as often as I want. Probably not from the first time, although even then I am certain that we would see a serious deviation from the normally expected randomness.

The purpose of this mental exercise is not to lure you over to Einstein's side in a probably lost battle against quantum mechanics. The idea is to disseminate some doubt in the minds of the very certain. That is always a rewarding experience!

But there might be a practical application for all this. What if we used very regular dice and a very regular table, but we equipped our arm with acceleration sensors and computer controlled external feedback controls, some kind of restraints that would correct our arm movement so that acceleration as well as deceleration would be limited on the high side? Just let your muscles work, and the machine corrects by restraining you if they work too hard, or in the wrong direction. Of course, we could by no means achieve reproducibility by that, but we maybe could just shave off enough of the randomness to seriously cheat. Here is a promising business idea for you!

Please take your imagination out of overdrive before you do permanent damage.

I am of course aware of the fact that the whole previous exercise smells strongly like the positivism Auguste Comte[2] propagated. He believed that when we just would have learned enough about the universe, we would in the end be capable of understanding everything. Although positivism has been somehow out of fashion for about a century, I am not convinced that it was qualitatively wrong. It probably is rather unpractical. It deals with an asymptotic case. Those are notorious for being theoretically definable, but practically unattainable.

And of course, building such toys, as much fun as it might be, would do nothing to remove the immanent uncertainty from our existence. Even the nature of uncertainty itself is obviously... uncertain. It would do nothing to remove the threatening unpredictability from a universe that we do not even start to truly understand. It would do nothing to comfort us with the known finiteness of our lives in a world that we do not control. In fact only a deeply felt, very honest and unselfish religious inclination will help here. I saw very few people display that, but I saw some, my blessed mother in law, a woman of great wisdom and depth, being one of them.

But for those mere mortals among us other means are called for, and always were. So let's walk through the history of the understanding that man and his creations, such as the enterprise, have about their relationship to the world, and thus about themselves.

8.1 The Mythical View

In this stage, man is literally surrounded by the world. It is a world that is infinitely mysterious. Very little is understood. But there seems to be regularity. There seems to be causality. We tried to create some kind of structure by trying to imagine what *could* make the world tick the way it does. Gods or ancestors living on a mountain top. Spirits in every brook and every well. We always kept in mind that we were a part of the whole. Therefore, the frontier between man and the surrounding world was not rigid, but somehow permeable, as represented in the diagram of Fig. 8.1.

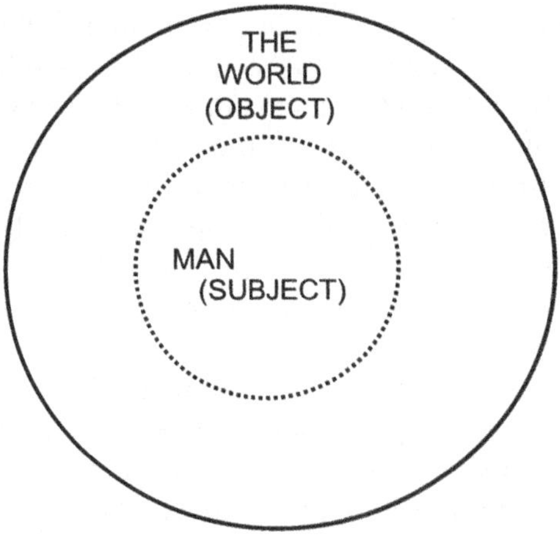

Figure 8.1

The mythical world is no easy world. The forces surrounding us that determine our destiny must be appeased. The equilibrium must be maintained. We used rituals and sacrifices to make sure that all the forces got their dues. Today's small business is not in a very different situation. Figure 8.2 shows that.

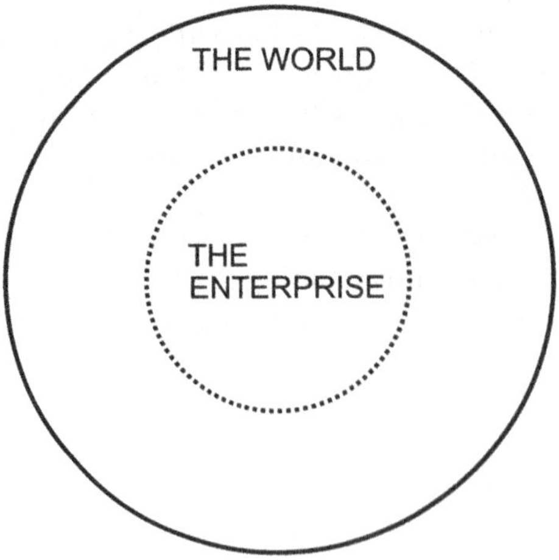

Figure 8.2

For them too, their environment is very much something that "just happens to me". A big production site in the neighborhood closes or a new development is approved; equivalents for famine and a good harvest in the old days. The question "Will that ship I invested everything in ever come back?" was not much different from "Will I get that breakthrough contract?" It does not really matter whether the Gods dwell on mount Olympus or in Washington. They can, quite unpredictably, do terrible things to you like increasing the minimum wage drastically, or mandate health insurance for all employees. And then there is "The Economy", that frivolous beast that seems to determine everything and totally eludes prediction, even more control! The small entrepreneur struggles with all that as much as the ancient mariner with the often-unfavorable winds. He does what he can to appease the deities and maintain the equilibrium. He creates reserves. He becomes a member of the local Kiwanis, Lyons or Rotary and of the local Chamber of Commerce. He makes a modest contribution to the reelection fund of his congressman. At the annual cookout of his church, he operates the barbecue. And then he hopes and prays.

How is that with large corporations? At a first glance, one might expect that there would be a big difference. That is not so. First of all, the corporation also is faced with the lack of predictability of the beast Economy. It sits there, towering over them, promising on one hand to make them fat and happy, at the same time threatening to eat them alive. Whatever move it elects to make, they know that they will be utterly helpless. There is no more certainty about the future in big enterprises. There are just more people who have read books about it. This is best illustrated by the planning exercises big enterprises go through. Let's talk about the so-called "hockey stick effect", as depicted in Fig. 8.3.

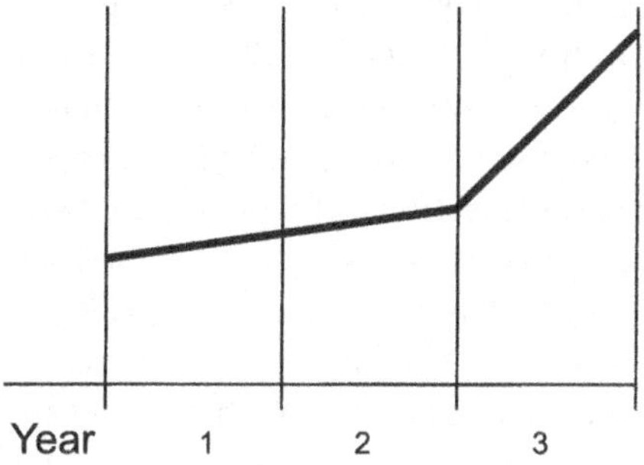

Figure 8.3

Year 1 and year 2 of the plan show modest (albeit often exaggerated) growth. But in year 3, we really are going to take off!

The "hockey stick" is of course wrong, but at the same time, in a strange way, right, because the next year, the prediction is going to look like Fig. 8.4.

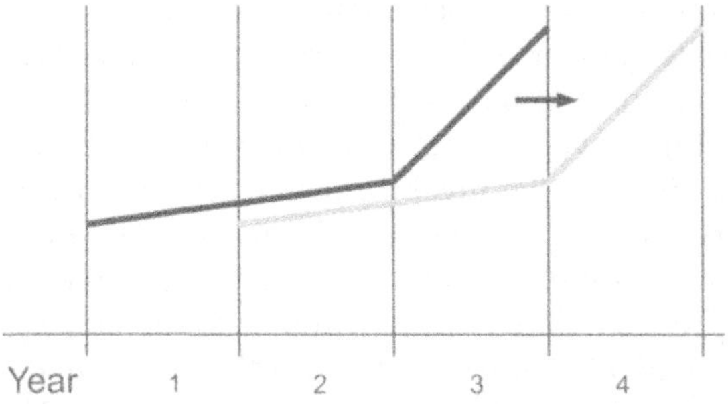

Figure 8.4

The narrative is going to say: "We did not quite achieve our goal last year, but now..." So the projected upturn was not a faulty prediction; it's just postponed for a year. The hockey stick is forever! There are a number of reasons for that:

- Next year is more or less "visible". Three years out is almost everybody's guess.
- My prediction for next year can be used as a yardstick for my bonus. Three years out mostly does not matter.
- I need to show optimism and a strong belief in the medium term prosperity of my business.
- After all: who knows? This might actually happen if we believe in it strongly enough!

This is a truly "mythical" approach to a world that is obviously beyond our control.

But there are other mythical elements in the large enterprise. Just think about the people that work there. They are either operating plants or warehouses (and in that case, they are truly blessed, although they will never know it), or they live in cubicles in corporate headquarters. Their gods neither dwell on Mount Olympus, nor in Washington, but in the executive suite. For the majority, thus the cubicle population of our large corporations, the people living in the top floor have all the attributes of Greek Gods. They are moody, unpredictable, revengeful, demanding, cruel and almighty. They can make or break you without any apparent reason in the blink of an eye. They must be appeased by the proper rituals and by the occasional sacrifice. They are at the same time feared and revered. They are surrounded by secrecy and by saga. Every once in a while, they get involved with mortal women in affairs that seem to have stepped right out of Greek mythology. Those things were always complicated, but today, they often have an ugly end in front of a court, or even the US Senate.

What the cubicle dweller does not understand is that top management's world is not much different from his. They just have different Gods to worship and fear, Gods the people in the cubicles have never heard of, but all the more very real ones. The Gods do not enjoy more security than the "cubicians": they only get kicked out of bigger, more comfortable offices. What the "cubician" does understand is that his dearest wish in life is to become a God himself. What he does again not understand is that, should such a thing ever happen, he probably would treat his fellow men just as capriciously and with no more respect than the leadership he came to loath so much. That does not make the existing leadership less responsible, but certainly less lonely.

People learn rather fast that acquiring and keeping the favor of the Gods has very little to do with things that happen in the actually existing physical world. All this is mythical, happening on a "higher level".

8.2 The Magical View

There is not a thing in the world or it has its pathologic aberration. The degenerative form of the mythical world-view is the magical one. The difference is that here, one attempts to get, and believes to be able to get, a certain amount of control over the outside world. There is, has always been, white magic attempting to heal or to protect, and black magic targeted at harming and destroying. Culturally, they are the same. Both believe that they can – *and are entitled to* – mess with the supernatural in order to shape the surrounding world, as depicted in Fig 8.5.

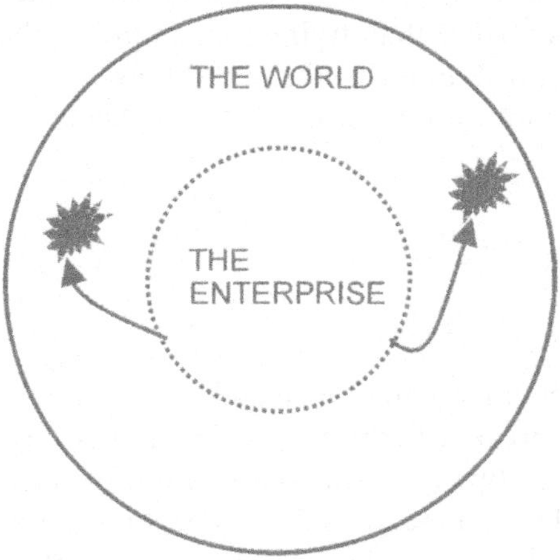

Figure 8.5

A mild form of white magic is superstition: the little dos and don'ts that are supposed to help you navigate the rough and uncharted waters of life. Even today some people carry the strangest things with them, not just coins, but up to a rabbit's leg.

Black magic is rather visibly destructive and repulsive. In the past, it often took recourse to sick and cruel ceremonies and it often was prosecuted by society with hardly less cruel brutality. Just think of the Voodoo dolls.

I don't know a CEO who carries a rabbit's leg in his pocket, although statistics almost dictate that there must be some. I also don't think that we have many Voodoo dolls in corporate America. But we have offices in Washington with full time generously compensated professional lobbyists. We have PACs (Political Action Committees) that can contribute money to the election campaign of candidates that we think to be sympathetic to our cause. Of course, in some cases the law forbids us to use company money to fund such ventures, but we can have our executives contribute to them. If they contribute 1% or more of their annual income, they become members of the "President's Club", and will have dinner with his majesty once a year. Given the deep ethical inclination of our business leadership, it is quite inconceivable that there would be compensation in the form of somewhat propped up bonuses or salary adjustments, but technically possible that surely would be! Now if that isn't magic!

And don't we call that very gifted CEO that seems to convert everything he touches into gold "a true magician"?

But the most crystalline pure expression of our magic behavior is in the complete and utter disregard we are willing to show for facts when they conflict with popular, officially adopted and supported doctrine. I often think that, if just the executive committee would declare the laws of gravitation suspended, a lot of people would gladly jump from the 20th floor. Well, maybe they would hesitate at the last step, but they surely would encourage their subordinates to take the plunge! This goes further than trying to manipulate the outside world. It is creating a new one, with other truths and different laws. Poor you, if you happen to be the one upon whom falls the duty to actually *say* that the emperor is indeed naked!

8.3 The Ontological View

The ontological worldview, as we saw it emerge in Greece and also in certain Indian philosophies is a quite dramatic break with the mythical period. As Fig. 8.6 shows, we are no longer encapsulated by the world. We have our own existence, our own platform to stand on. From there, we are now able to contemplate, to study the world. Fear is replaced by inquisitiveness. We see the enterprise go through the same evolution. Also, modern corporations study their surroundings with more curiosity than fear. We study our markets, the economy and the monetary system. We understand infinitely more about all this than even a century ago. But unlike the physicists, who truly thrive in the ontological world, and have been able to achieve remarkable predictability and reproducibility, we find that the economic world pushes back much harder in

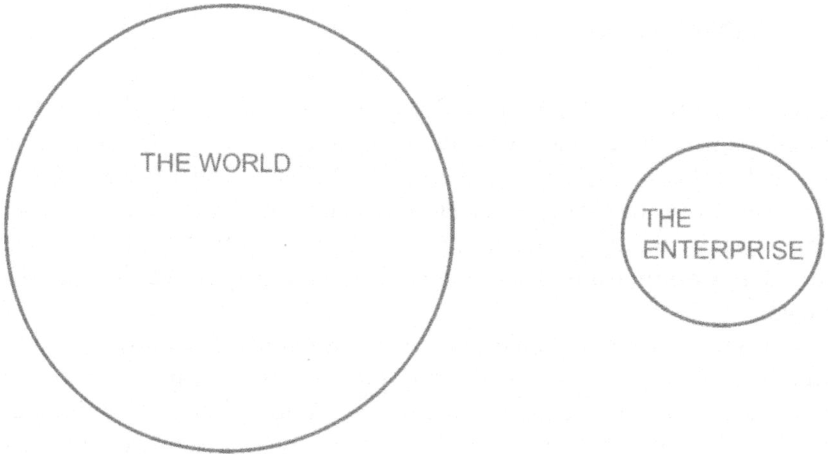

Figure 8.6

a much earlier stage of discovery than the physical world. There are understandable reasons for that. Physics is about things and the economy is about people. If you have truly figured out how one iron atom behaves in relationship to its 8 or so neighbors (and that might be hard enough), it is not all that difficult to predict how 10 billion iron atoms will behave. But even if you truly understood how a person is interacting with the 8 closest other persons (and you don't), you would have no clue about the behavior of a million people. People are *individual.* There are no two identical copies. Even "identical" twins will, due to their ever so slightly diverging life experience, show enough difference to put most, if not all bets off. Individuals have dozens, maybe hundreds of relevant attributes that show some kind of a statistical distribution. Those properties are not easy to measure, so we can't even be certain that they show a "normal" distribution, although that would be an obvious assumption. But even if we could measure all this, the precise modeling of such a complex system would be a daunting task, even for today's fast computers. I should know, because I tried, under the now known wrong assumption that we have the distribution! If I had been victorious, I would not be too shy to report it here. It's like trying to solve a differential equation describing mass hysteria.

It is thus still infinitely more difficult to reason quantitatively about the human world than about the physical world. Which is why the business community lags considerably behind the scientists in terms of cultural development. Business and thus the enterprise, has not truly made the transition to an ontological view. They just have their toe in the water!

8.4 Substantialism

We already mentioned it: there is nothing without a pathological aberration! Substantialism is the exaggeration of the ontological view. Simplified, one could say that this is magic on a higher level. The basic driver is the same: the lust for power over the world, over our environment. Substantialism tries to acquire power by isolating objects, and sucking them into the subject, so that in the end they disappear and at the same time, strangely start to have a life of their own.

Substantial means: being able to exist on its own without any context or surrounding. People like Descartes and Spinoza pointed this out. One very clear outflow of substantialism is individualism. The Latin word "individuus" (undivided) is a translation from Greek. When we go back to the roots, we find "atom". Substantialism is about isolating objects, in order to investigate them in a kind of vacuum. It puts more emphasis on the boundaries than on the core of things, more on separation than on unification.

Whatever is touched by substantialism becomes rigid. We see this in religion and philosophy: dogmas become fixed, impermeable. They can no longer be questioned or reviewed in the framework of a changed context. The context has been amputated. It is no longer deemed to be an element in the process!

In science as well, we have fallen victim to this phenomenon. By stubbornly pursuing isolated questions like: "What are the ultimate elementary particles?", we did not only spend billions on ever more powerful accelerators (that were not going to do the trick anyway and we knew it beforehand!) but worse, we restrained thousands of physicists for a lifetime from doing more useful things. For the same token, as a scientific method, isolating objects in order to study them is not necessarily wrong. If you want to measure the properties of a substance, you go to great length to purify it as much as possible first.

We see this rather often. An approach that is very appropriate and useful as a methodology in the lab can be quite wrong as a guideline for a more general philosophical view on the world.

Now let's see how the enterprise has been affected by this. Let's look at Fig. 8.7.

Like modern man, modern enterprise shows the quite fatal tendency to isolate objects, rob them of their context and suck them in. From then on, they become part of the enterprise, and are no longer connected to the outside world. They are no longer observed as parts of the world. They practically vanished from it.

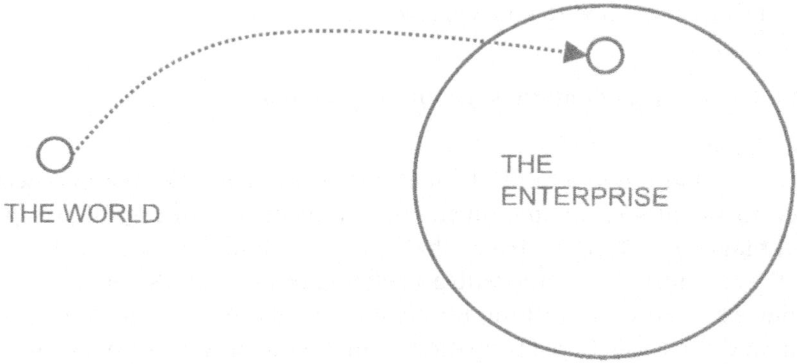

Figure 8.7

We do this to a lot of different objects:

- concepts
- markets
- technologies.

The most remarkable examples can probably be found among concepts.

Take one like "customer". It seems so clear when you look it up in the dictionary:

Customer *(noun)*

One that buys goods or services.

This definition suggests that we are talking about an "over the fence" operation. Goods or services leave the enterprise, money comes in.

Talking about a truly simple definition... Further, a customer is of such a fundamentally vital importance that it is difficult to see how there could be any confusion about a concept like this. But there is! Our businesses have seen fit to isolate the concept "customer" from the "over the fence" element, and have invented the notion of "internal customer". They use this in their dealings with corporate services for only one purpose:

- I am your customer.
- The customer is always right.
- When I say "jump", you jump.

This proves to be quite detrimental to the internal regulating mechanisms within the enterprise. By robbing the concept "customer" from its natural contextual elements like markets, competition, choice, legal framework, all we have left is a pretty crude power instrument. More importantly, this erodes the proper understanding for and dealing with the *real* customer, the one that actually pays over the fence. But like with everything touched by substantialism, there is no point in debating this. The concept just became too rigid, too naked and too strongly absorbed to allow for a meaningful discussion.

Similar things happened to concepts like

- cost
- communications (the modern word for propaganda)

and many others.

There is one more remarkable element. When you come from a mythical worldview to an ontological one, substantialism seems a quite logical extrapolation of that course. Coming from "that" to "what" and then wanting to see the "what" even more clearly and with a smaller granularity does not seem unreasonable. The really astonishing observation is that our business people, having great difficulty with the transition from the mythical view to the ontological view, effortlessly bypass the latter to move at once to substantialism.

The result of this "isolationist" way of looking at the world, sharply focusing on one aspect neglecting all others has one more consequence. A complex creature like the enterprise can only be understood and managed in a holistic way. Thus focusing on just one aspect is doomed to fail. But the latter is exactly what we do! It's almost like in the fashion world: the fad of the week rules without opposition! There were many of those:

- management by motivation
- management by incentives
- management by objectives
- quality (and of course the meaning of the word got perverted to such an extent that it is now completely remote from what really matters: the properties of our products and services)
- customer focus
- supply chain management
- supplier alliances
- partnerships
- shareholder value
- re-engineering.

Just be certain that there are many more to come. It may be interesting to note that we made a full circle through the whole set of stakeholders: employees, customers, suppliers and shareholders. But we looked at them one by one, in the typical way of substantialism, and in the end gained very little or nothing.

Thousands of books have been written and even occasionally read. Millions of lectures have been given. Then we find that the promises are – quite predictably so – not kept and we jump on the next bandwagon. These things slip through our hands like the beads of a rosary. This phenomenon seriously contributes to the increasing feeling of uncertainty that is plaguing our workforce. It also plays a role in the "selection machine". It is a good idea to display the books about the latest fad on the sideboard in your office. This shows to your audience (modern managers mainly have *audiences*) that you are "up to date" without necessarily brandishing you as an egghead. This often leads to amusing situations. One character had on his shelf this book "How to tell lies", quite visible for everybody. As if any of us would have believed that he needed such a guideline!

8.5 The Functional View

There is a very logical progression noticeable in all this. In the mythical worldview, we were concerned with "that", the world surrounding us, largely mysterious and threatening. We were trying to establish and maintain a kind of equilibrium with it. In the ontological culture, we were concerned with "what", defining things, giving them names, reasoning about them. In the functional school of thought, we will get involved with "how". We will try to understand how things work, function in their relationship to us and to each other.

One could also entertain the following thought. The ontological approach emerged as a reaction against the fears and uncertainty dissipated by a magical worldview. For the same token, it is quite natural that there would be a reaction against the rigidity and divisiveness created by substantialism. When you look at the following diagram (Fig. 8.8), you will notice that subject and object are no longer closed systems. The subject is still elevated a little bit, but they point at each other. Reality is only that what can be described in terms of its functional relation to the subject. This is a quite radical change, showing dramatic footprints in arts, religion and science as well as our understanding of society. It could not bypass our enterprises unnoticed.

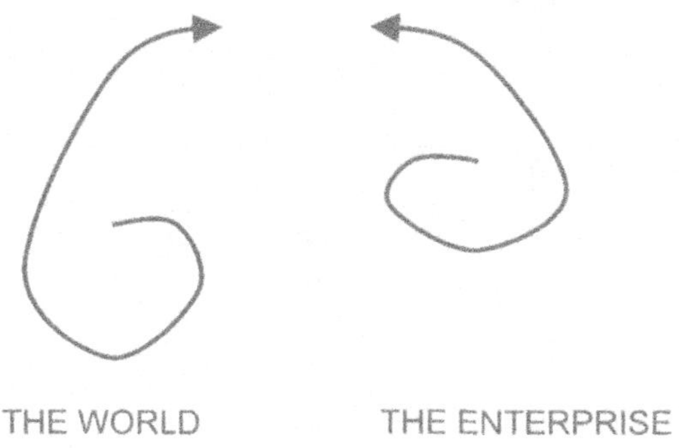

Figure 8.8

The most noticeable influence this worldview has can be seen in our language, especially if we expand the latter to encompass the total of symbols and formal systems we use to communicate. The "flow sheet" or process flow diagram is an important rather recent addition to our expression tool set. This is clearly a method of communication that focuses on "how".

Of course, functional thinking has existed in our culture for a long time. But it is only recently that it took a truly central position, slowly pushing back the older worldviews. In that respect, it is still young in our culture, and society does not yet feel totally comfortable with it. The incredible clumsiness you see when putting the workforce through these flowcharting classes is only a very logical consequence of that novelty.

8.6 Operationalism

You already guessed it: also the functional worldview produced a pathological exaggeration. Operationalism works much more subtly than magic or substantialism. What it really does is restrict the essence of things to the process by which they come into being. Van Peursen has in his book a glorious example: a diagram explaining how a snake functions. However helpful such a diagram becomes for understanding the processes, this definitely *is* not the snake. It is only one, albeit important aspect. Once we lose sight of this, and start to shout: "process is everything", we move into the operationalist world. As an example, let's look at the diagram below (Fig. 8.9), representing the quintessential enterprise.

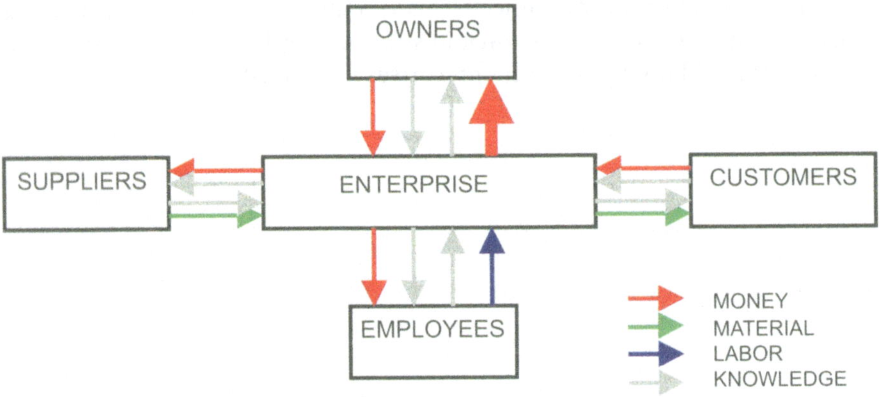

Figure 8.9

Such a diagram is certainly helpful to understand and reason about the relationships between the different components. It certainly overcomes and improves on the myopic focus on one of the elements that plagued the substantialist view. But to think that this diagram captures the whole essence, the life, the being of the object enterprise would be fatally wrong.

Process is *not* everything. *Nothing* is everything. We will have to learn that, but before we do, we will slide a lot further down the path of our next exaggeration: operationalism.

Up to now, we have been looking at "that" in awe, we have been asking "what?" and later "how?" It would be quite reasonable to expect the next question to be "why?" We are not there yet, although our increasing preoccupation with evolution will in the end drive us into that direction.

The emergence of the functional worldview is reason for hope. The inherent holistic, more open approach and the increased attention to the question "how?" offers promising inroads to the study of the interaction between society and the enterprise. What is the meaning they have for each other? Not only this question, but also many of the dislocations between humanity and the enterprise that need urgent repair can be better understood from a functional viewpoint.

We, humanity, can only benefit from that.

9 Commerce and Crafts

Every enterprise is engaged in two main activities: let's call them commerce and crafts.

- Craft means: I can *make* or *do* something.
- Commerce means: I *have* something that you want, and you *have* something that I want. Let's *trade*.

The conflict between the two is deep, even fundamental, albeit largely unnoticed. It does not make so much of a difference whether your craft is plumbing or biochemistry. The difference between trading in potatoes or derivatives is not that dramatic either. But between growing potatoes, and trading in potatoes, there are worlds.

Asking what came first, commerce or crafts is like the classical chicken or egg question. There is no reasonably secure answer. Both evolved in symbiosis, and the causality between them got lost in the mist of time. But it is still true that you had to *make, find, grow, hunt or steal* something *before* you could *sell* it. I do not believe that they had a very much developed futures market in the old days.

The fundamentally different viewpoints, from which business people and technicians (the modern operators of trade and crafts) observe reality, lead to enormous conflicts and tensions, mainly *within* the enterprise. We will need to address this issue.

In order to shed some light on the problem, I propose to look at advertisement. That may sound ridiculous, but I do not take advertisement lightly for several reasons. First of all, it plays a big role in brand name management, an art that has achieved astonishing things in the modern world. But more importantly, as advertisement is expensive, people usually do their homework before launching it. Therefore it is quite reliable as a kind of photo negative, representative for the mind set of the community it is targeted at. That is why when I travel to a country that I try to understand, I will watch TV commercials. My friends would not expect that from me, but it is quite rational. I will give you examples. The most important are the commercials about household goods, because they address the largest portion of the population. The rather unsubtle point behind many German commercials is guilt. Mrs. Mueller feels terrible, because she has used that indescribable (quite literally in Germany) no name washing powder, instead of Dash or Persil, and thus her family is not sporting the immaculate brilliant white their social rank entitles them to. Mrs. Mueller fell short as a wife and mother, and you bet that Mrs. Mayer is not going to repeat that error. The less renowned brands take another tack: they promote frugality, and make big displays of how much you can wash with only one drum of their product (example from a distant past: "Der weiße Riese"). Now Mrs. Mueller will be proud of herself: frugality is also a very precious virtue for a wife and mother. Basically, the Germans want to be confirmed in their social role, and that is what commercials target.

The French care much less about their social role. Falling out of it can make a person rather interesting. Guilt is not one of their focal points, because it is boring, unproductive, and, worst of all, it contradicts the supreme law of "savoir vivre". They care about comfort and ease of use. They don't want to be bothered. That's what French washing powder commercials target. You don't have to think. It comes out all right. You just buy our product, and we will do all the worrying for you. Which gives you time to "live", whatever that means! They occasionally show examples of the wrong outcome, and the inconvenience it causes for the poor victim. What a terrible waste of time and energy! If you just had bought our stuff, you would be at ease and sip a good wine, instead of dealing with this pull that magically lost its colors.

I do not intend to walk you through the whole European washing powder market and its implications for national character (although that might be interesting enough). I want to make the point that, in general, advertisement makes powerful statements about its target audience. More: advertisement addresses deep-rooted sentiments that are very seldom rationally described. Clever advertisement makes use of the subconscious! Look at that word: it suggests that things are happening *under* the level where cognition takes place. We will see: how sadly literally true!

So now let's look at typical headlines of advertisement targeted at the communities we try to understand here: scientists and business people.

The following ads come from "Science", November 20, 1998. "Science" is a good prototype for the kind of magazine the scientific community reads.

- Lower MDA's to Unprecedented Environmental Levels.
- Cytokines, Receptors & Adhesion Molecules.
- The Ecdysone-Inducible Mammalian Expression System, Proof that we are indeed control freaks.
- We see Genomics from your perspective.
- Get Power and Sensitivity Without PCR.

I don't expect too many people to understand what all this means, but take my word for it, it is all about things than one could do in the lab. It is about purer products, better instruments, less cumbersome techniques. Still, the fact remains that hardly anybody in the business community can decipher the ads targeted at the scientific community. In the opposite direction the technicians are very well able to understand, with contempt. The ads thrown at the commercial side do their part to shape the opinion both camps have of each other.

Now the other side. I was not so sure about the magazines business people read, so I bought two of them:

Forbes, December 14, 1998:

- The Ralph Lauren Purple Label Collection signifies personal achievement and great style....
- Business is the constant threat of storm.
- You never actually own a Patek Philippe. You merely take care of it for the next generation.
- At Hilton we can help you make forecast, a good impression, or history.
- Smart People spend hours figuring out how to use new technology. Smarter People figure out a way to weasel out of it.
- LIFE IS TOO BIG FOR CARS.
- Tiger Woods believes it. It's the smartest way to own a jet.
- Success is a direct result of ambition, connections, or a really good to-do list.
- Cindy Crawford's Choice... (OMEGA)
- Shirts for men who earned the silver spoon.

Fortune, December 7, 1998:

- Betcha this'll make her smile.
- Not just a face in the crowd.

Very much the same stuff, but there is one more example I simply cannot keep from you. This is an ad for Scotch:

Our drinkers are men of depth and substance, which puts our advertising agency at somewhat of a disadvantage.

Delightful, don't you think?

We never and we nowhere had a classless society. In classic Japan the pecking order (below the Emperor) was quite clear:

- the Warriors (and first and foremost of course: the Shogun)
- the Scholars
- the Craftsmen
- the Merchants
- the Peasants.

If you want to verify this: go to the Museum of Natural History in New York. They have quite convincing material.

I somehow like this set up, as you can imagine, but not enough to relocate to Japan.

Especially the relationship between merchants (business people) and craftsmen/scholars (the scientific-technical community) was always and everywhere interesting. The point is that they obviously cannot exist without each other, but they continuously wish that it were not so!

In medieval Europe, there was no science. The leading class was the warriors, often disguised as bishops, even popes, doubling as merchants in their free time, mostly by robbing full time merchants.

During the Renaissance, you wanted to project yourself as a scholar. Of course you had to be a merchant on the side, but you almost shamefully hid that. You also had to be a part time warrior. That was the pose you took when you wanted your portrait painted. At any rate you had to heavily support arts and sciences, in order to be a respected person.

During the industrial revolution, the merchants gained momentum. There was however still a certain amount of shame about the unchristian aspects of enriching yourself at the expense of others. This could be overcome by generous donations to the church, and/or sponsoring the sciences and the arts.

Today, the merchants (and in my classification, lawyers are a clean subset of the merchants, I am not going to give in to their claim to be scientists too lightly) are steadfastly on course for the top of the pecking order. They did not get to this point by their own achievements, but because the "competition" eliminated itself. I will not need to explain how the soldiers brought themselves in total discredit. The "scholars and craftsmen" (scientists and engineers), once promised quick solutions to all the world's problems. But it is perceived that they left us with an environmental mess and a pile of radioactive waste.

In 1999, it takes a certain amount of courage to admit that you are a chemical engineer. You can easily admit to be a stockbroker, and nobody will question your contribution to the bottom line of humanity. O tempora, o mores!

In spite of all fashions, the classes still need each other. Even the soldiers are needed, as the future will reveal, much to my chagrin but without any doubt.

Scientists understand the universe we all live in poorly. They know that and it irritates them. They relentlessly try to improve their understanding. They do this through very organized abstract reasoning, research, publication, peer review and debate. Therefore abstract reasoning is trained and honed over many years, in fact a lifetime long. There are of course just as many scoundrels and jackals among them as in the rest of the population. What matters here is the tool set different groups are the most familiar with to come to their judgements and beliefs.

Nevertheless, if you look at the advertisements addressed at the scientists, you will notice that they are about things one can *do* better, faster or cheaper. They mainly address abstract reasoning.

We know where abstract reasoning, the main tool of the scientist and technician, takes place in the brain. It is in the neo-cortex, the outer layer, evolutionary the youngest and newest one, where also our linguistic abilities are located.

Business people are quite different. What they understand eminently well, although mostly rather intuitively and on a purely phenomenological level, is basic human behavior. One could say that they are true specialists, who have accumulated a lot of awareness about a tiny subset of the universe: a very thin layer of the very upper life form evolution generated so far: the "R" complex of the human brain. The "R" complex is the oldest part of the brain. It is a mere prolongation of the spinal cord, and sits in the center of the later evolved layers ("L" complex and neo-cortex). It is the seat of the very primitive, but also very important life supporting brain functions. The main theme is self-preservation, as an individual as well as species wise. For that purpose, the "R" complex supports a widely varied set of functions. Sex is one of them: the obsession to replicate the own genes, and secure their survival in the world after us. You will indeed hear more "rowdy" jokes from businesspeople than from scientists. Fully logically (nature is eminently logical), also things that we would intuitively value "higher", like the care and protection of offspring are located here. Battle and aggression are controlled from this point. Ingrained habits, routines (ha, brand loyalty!) reside here. Group behavior has its seat there: the pursuit of power, competition, ranking battles, turf protection, secretiveness, group loyalty, ego, leadership acceptance, bonding, adherence to fads and fashions, preoccupation with appearance (ha: dress code), marching (or dancing) in lock step (we are going to do this as a team!).

That is why the kind of advertisement targeted at this fraction of the population always suggests that buying the product will promote your own self, make you one of the crowd, impress your superiors or your peers, or even better, it will in some obscure way immortalize you. Not the product's objective merit is highlighted, but the potential influence its purchase can have on your *relationship* with others.

Business people also have a fairly good grasp of the next brain layer: the "L" complex. That one is the seat of the emotions: anger, love, hope, hatred, fear, disgust, contempt, compassion ... That is why a lot of advertisement appeals at your fear. If you do not buy our product, terrible things may happen to you. You may become an outcast. Your boss will chew you out, etc.

I have observed that some business people display quite impressive neo-cortex (the seat of abstract reasoning) capability. But in all cases, the lower layers dominate. Is this bad? Of course it is not! Who says that the lower layers are the lesser layers? It is very much like with technology: without well and reliably functioning lower layers, the upper layers can never deliver their punch. But conversely, without the upper layers, the lower ones make very little sense. Further, all this is context driven. It would not be a good idea to approach a complex computer problem with the "R" tool set, but in a sales situation, too much neo-cortex may just get in the way. Further, there is no really good scientist without intuition, and there is no really good businessman without considerable reasoning capabilities. But on the average, they still lean to opposite brain layers. To make things even more complicated: "R" people can be extremely charming, on a deep and warm human level (that's the "bonding" thing). This is especially true if they also have a strong "L" component (compassion). More neo-cortex oriented people often come over abrasive, arrogant, uneasy. This is also perceived that way by the neo-cortex oriented people themselves. One probably should think twice before turning them loose on customers. To confuse things completely, we also have to highlight that there is hardly any correlation with the type of education one has had. I know people with business degrees that have quintessential scientific minds. I also know Ph.D. Engineers that are quite the opposite. In fact the most crystalline pure "R" person I ever knew was a Ph.D. Chemist, and could he be charming!

Social contact within the two groups is quite different. The "R" complex governs group behavior, and thus the business population will put a lot of emphasis on one's position within the group. This is a point of constant attention. The group judges the individual in a quite curious, subconscious way. Oh yes, there are the whispered bits of verbal information, given and received as if they were precious treasures, but there is more. "R" people are a lot more apt at nonverbal communication than neo-cortex people. Great writers, describing the business community and its dealings have captured this with a kind of smile that is at the same time contemptuous and compassionate. Thomas Mann[1] comes to mind as a superb example.

In the scientific community, the pecking order is shaped by more abstract factors like: academic titles, publications, official recognition (prizes in all sizes and shapes). Just in order to show once more that reality is not all that black and white: there are considerable group dynamics, with cluster formation around the ones that seem the most powerful. This effect has often helped to suppress scientific evidence for many years.

As you could easily suspect, the differences are much more in perception than anywhere else:

- The scientist perceives reality to be what can be proven in a way to survive severe peer scrutiny.
- For the businessman, reality is what the majority believes to be reality.

In spite of all the (partly artificially highlighted) polarization: there is no better and lesser; the whole point is to understand how the system "ticks", nothing more, nothing less.

---

[1] Buddenbrooks: The Decline of a Family by Thomas Mann
(Vintage International)
Vintage Books; ISBN 0679752609

Just in case you would start to think that this is all the product of an overheated imagination, let's look at a couple of examples.

Secretiveness:
What does one do after discovering something that nobody else knows?

- The businessman will try to keep it a secret, because he will try to exploit it to his economic advantage, and thus must make an attempt to deny its use to his competitors. This is precisely what the "R" complex would dictate.
- The scientist will try to publish it, because only the severe test of victoriously survived peer review will lead to acceptance within the scientific community. The latter is what the scientist needs as his reward.
- The compromise between the two is the patent, one of the more interesting "bridges" between science and business.
- Is the term "business secret" familiar to you?
- Have you ever heard about a "scientific secret"?

The battle analogy - business likes to use terms that are borrowed from the military:

- Attack and destroy the competition.
- We will defend our market share.
- We are beleaguered, embattled, ambushed.
- We will launch a major offensive.
- John Doe is leading the charge.
- Price wars.
- We are under fire.
- We will wipe them out.

I find it eternally amusing to hear this belligerent language from people that would almost certainly wet their pants if they were ever caught in a real combat situation. But nothing in this world seems to be real, so why this? Today it is "in" to quote Sunzi (The Art of War). That is, very significantly, a collection of platitudes on the level of Mao Tse-Tung's little red book, and never reaches the depth of a von Clausewitz or a Vuong N'Giap.

No wonder: war is just another form of business. It is about deterring or attacking an opponent, in order to increase one's "market share", or at least keep it. It is about seeking our own betterment at the expense of others. It is about heroism and mythos. It is about alliances, deceit, betrayal, victory … It is about demagogy, about controlling and guiding masses. It is waged by many at the expense of great sacrifice, for the sake of very few who run no serious risk – just like business.

You will not hear that kind of an analogy from the scientific community. What they will show you is an adventure, or a journey, or a quest, or a contest. The other scientist is no enemy. He is a companion in the quest for truth. He might very well be a perfect bore or something worse, but he is no enemy!

One argument could be that there are many cases of scientists becoming successful business people. This seems to weaken my thesis. But: I know no example of a successful business person becoming a great scientist (and please, do not propose Heinrich Schliemann!). If my polarization theory were completely wrong, these transformations should be reversible.

Take a closer look at cases where former scientists/technicians succeed in business. It is almost always in a niche they created by their scientific work. They had no or little competition, or such a technological advantage that there was no real competitive situation. They did not NEED to understand the competitive game in order to succeed. This was by the way the case for many of the chemical companies during a long time. It is still the case today for a lot of start-ups and spin-off enterprises in the neighborhood of elite universities. They have such an advantage in terms of technology that no "R" skills are needed. Once that changes, they will either acquire the "R" skills or go under. In some cases, they loose the tech skills in that process, and go under just as fatally (look at Apple Computers, and don't be fooled by their temporary recovery).

Let's agree that I made my point: "Business people are from Mars, scientists are from Jupiter." And that has serious consequences. When both communities look at the world, they will see something completely different. Especially when we will deal with the cultural aspects of the enterprise, that will become clearer.

Scientists will be more inclined to the ontological view. They will be in danger to succumb to substantialism. Some will show a tendency to embrace operationalism.

Business people very much dwell in the mythical sphere. They are very susceptible to magical escapades. If they move to the functional view of the world, they will have an inclination to glide down the path of operationalism.

It does not take too much imagination to picture what will happen when the two groups interact. We see flawed communications, mistrust and lack of mutual respect, even contempt flaring up everywhere. Being a technician living in an environment where your boss and most of your colleagues are business people is no fun. They understand each other so much more intuitively that you very soon are degraded to the status of "tolerated oddity" at best. Enormous amounts of energy are lost in this force field, even in those – exceptional – situations where people manage to deal with it in a rather constructive way. The very minimum price will be the necessity to pay constant attention to the different viewpoints and judgement strategies.

The two communities would indeed form one of the very few justified cases for "race segregation". But obviously that cannot be done. They cannot survive without each other. So we will have to find ways to peacefully co-exist. Should you happen to believe that we have found them, please let me know!

10 Leadership

We have our occasional flirtations with anarchy, but I believe that those stem more from frustrations with actual situations than from a fundamental rejection of leadership. Leadership is something very basic. It has been formed and shaped by evolution in the biological environment.

But let's first look what the dictionary has to say:

lead·er·ship (noun)

The position or office of a leader: ascended to the leadership of the party.

Capacity or ability to lead: showed strong leadership during her first term in office.

A group of leaders: met with the leadership of the nation's top unions.

Guidance; direction: The business prospered under the leadership of the new president.

I find these definitions extremely shallow, almost clinically sterile. No wonder: the concept has been watered down so much that the essence got completely lost. We nowadays talk about "cost leadership". This simply means having the lowest cost. We even have "leadership courses", as if one would actually be able to *learn* such a thing. The content of the word has been reduced to something like "being the first". In the process, we lost the drama, the heartbreaking tension that always exists between on one hand the superhuman demands on the incumbent and on the other hand his inevitably very human, often weak nature. The fact that we are again talking about something that happens between on one hand and then on the other hand suggests that we are dealing with a deeply human phenomenon. The excruciating shear stresses tormenting the people that are caught in this force field often delivered the material for great drama and poetry. From Homeros via Shakespeare up to modern times, the conflict within the leader between his enormous obligations and his all too human shortcomings formed the theme of many great dramas. King Lear, Wallenstein and Julius Caesar are as much about the perils of leadership as Romeo and Julia is about love in its losing battle against amok running competition.

Summarizing we could say that:

- Leadership is indispensable for our society to work.
- Leadership is a very problematic phenomenon.

- Its biological roots are poorly understood.
- The difficult and complex content of the concept has been considerably watered down. The latter clearly shows in our language.

We will therefore have to spend some time with leadership and its surroundings like the exercise of power and morality.

Whenever we humans think or write about humanity, we have the very understandable tendency to overlook a couple of facts. We are not very enticed by the idea that whatever we are and do has strong biological roots. A naïve understanding of religion has depicted us as quite unique in the universe, more precisely as God's spitting image, by far elevated above animals and the rest of nature. We came to like that situation a lot and we are very reluctant to explore any other viewpoint. It shows in our language. Being called "an animal" is not exactly a compliment. It also surfaces in the work of our philosophers. Descartes claimed that animals are machines without sentiment or emotion. He saw no problem with vivisection. No wonder that we have so much trouble to properly account for the influence of biology when we try to understand phenomena within our society!

Animals have leaders. They need them in their struggle for life. Not all animals though, but only the ones that have to perform rather complex tasks as a group. Evolution is eminently driven by *necessity*. The prime example is hunting. Whenever predators lack the strength or the speed to catch their prey individually, we see the development of leadership patterns. Every wolf pack has an α-animal. This animal determines the pack's strategy and tactics. It has privileges but also clear responsibilities. In the case of wolves, this is a male. Hyenas, with their unjustified bad reputation – they are in reality brave and intelligent creatures – show a pronounced matriarchy. Anyway, the α-animal's function is exactly the same.

How does one become α-animal? Quite simple: by defeating the incumbent. In order to achieve this, one needs a combination of physical power and intelligence that proves superior to the predecessor's abilities. This makes sense in terms of evolution. The group is probably better off with the new one and accepts that. It is cruel but quite effective. There is of course no guarantee that the new one will be the better leader, and there are mishaps. From an evolutionary viewpoint, also this makes sense. A pack that accepts a below average leader "deserves" to be exterminated, to have its genes taken out of the future world.

At any rate, the α-animal does not receive a "golden parachute". Deprived of its servants after the power shift it often proves to be rather unfit for life. Even while "in office", α-animals are often exposed to increased risks. When lions and hyenas, the archrivals of the savannas clash the male lion will hunt and kill the hyena matriarch.

As in the human environment, also in the animal world the struggle for the leadership position is often more determined by myth than reality. The leader is surrounded by the odium of invincibility. That is reflected in his behavior. The leader acts confidently. Challengers are intimidated and often restrain themselves for a long time after having acquired the necessary capabilities. It even happens that the stronger challenger loses nevertheless, because of the higher degree of confidence on the part of the incumbent. It is no surprise that evolution provided mechanisms to prevent a too frequent disruption of the power structure that could be harmful to the group.

It can hardly astonish that the closer species biologically are to us, Homo Sapiens, the more their power struggles resemble ours. In the case of chimpanzees alliances and the corresponding "small favors" that we know so well from human politics play an important role. In the animal world too, there is no more justice and equality than in our society. Talents, capabilities and opportunities are distributed as arbitrarily and apparently unjustly there as within our human species. But against the backdrop of evolution and over longer time periods, these things make as much sense there as they do for us. The problem is not that these mechanisms survive, essentially unaltered, in human society but rather that we have adopted an astonishingly schizophrenic position towards the phenomenon leadership.

On one side, the leadership will stubbornly reject the notion that their position has a clear biological basis. On the other hand, they relentlessly justify their privileges by "survival of the fittest" or "selection of the brightest and the best". That argumentation aligns seamlessly with the biological basis. If it ever occurred to them, it would come as quite a shock how much this reasoning resembles the justification of medieval rulers who pretended to govern "by divine grace".

The intellectuals see through the whole thing and distance themselves from the debate. The popular masses are not particularly interested. They are accustomed to be exploited by the privileged class, and they don't care too much who's turn it is right now.

As a consequence, there are a zillion books about leadership, but the core problems surrounding it remain strangely unexplored. The facts that we have neither any natural enemy left (apart of ourselves of course) nor depend on hunting for our survival any longer, have eroded the intuitive evolutionary experience of and justification for leadership. Obviously, even today at the verge of the 21st century we have to have to maintain supply. That requires management so complex that it makes prehistoric hunting look like a trivial hobby. Of course, such complicated undertakings require a leadership structure, even a deeply stacked one. But this situation is too new in our evolution for having been able to precipitate into the hard-wired part of our behavior. Our basic understanding of world and society could not yet be influenced by it.

It would certainly be exaggerated to claim that modern man is a total and absolute individualist. People volunteer to do lots of things together with others, even if these are no real essential necessities. They commit themselves in their churches and clubs for better than just selfish reasons. They underwrite this kind of engagement for a plausible reason: they *want* to do things, from music via theater to soccer, that they cannot do alone. In these cases, they accept leadership as a matter of course. It is not surprising that humanity does not instinctively reject the idea of being lead. Our tribal experience with leadership is too old and too deep for that. What people complain about - often rightfully - is the quality of the leadership.

Let's take our bearings and see where we are.

- Leadership is today as necessary as it ever was in human society.
- Its structure needs to be more complex and thus less transparent than in the past.
- The direct intuitive acceptance and justification of a naturally emerging leadership is gone.

We have no other choice than putting our relationship to leadership on a more rational basis. That will prove more difficult than one would assume. Leadership without the exercise of power is unthinkable. One may believe to find exceptions, but in those cases, a closer look will reveal that the applied power is just more subtle than usual. Power is a real problem in our society. I had it in all shapes, forms and sizes. I hated every minute of it. You cannot weasel out of it. Suppose you decided not to use your power. It's no solution! You are as responsible for the possible adverse consequences of that as for any other error in judgment. Nevertheless, for many people power is like a drug. They can never get enough of it. They will kill for it. It's probably the same like with crack cocaine: they simply do not understand what it will do to their system. Inherited wisdom claims that power corrupts, and it does.

Leadership always involves the submission of a group. The essence of leadership is that the group is guided by only one vision and one will. The potential effectiveness of such an arrangement is intuitively clear, but there are a number of questions.

What will and what vision is going to be implemented?

- The leader's?
- The ones offered by an advisor?
- The ones forced on us by a superior authority?
- The carefully evaluated collective will and vision of the group? In this case the leader will preside over the definition process.

What is the goal that we pursue with all this?

- The group's well being?
- The welfare of a greater collective (A superset of our group)?
- Personal benefit for the leader, either material or subjective?

 What means are utilized to achieve this?
- Brutal oppression?
- Deceit?
- Convincing and consensus?

We obviously are dealing with a broad spectrum of possibilities. Already Machiavelli has dissected them in a very intelligent and sober way, describing their pro's and con's. By the way, Machiavelli has been enormously and unjustly vilified. All he did was write "Il Principe"[9], which is no more or less than a handbook on the anatomy of power. He wrote it for Lorenzo de Medici, a rather young and inexperienced leader at the time. We have all reasons to believe that the net outcome of Machiavelli's effort was positive in the sense of lowering the over all suffering of mankind.

But no matter what, no matter how, no matter how noble the goal, we have to seriously question the legitimization of quasi taking away somebody's freedom to chose and to subject him to another person's will. I am not going to call Bakunin to the rescue. I don't think much of anarchy. My reasoning will, at face value, appear rather suspect: anarchy is utterly unpractical. We nevertheless are faced with a couple of difficult questions.

- Under what circumstances could it ever become justifiable to guide and control another human being's behavior?
- Where are the limits?
- What kind of "contract", written or not, explicitly discussed or not, regulates this relationship?
  - What can the one who is being lead expect from the leader?
  - What can the leader expect from his subordinates?

It will be terribly difficult, if not impossible, to find an abstract justification for leadership. The only promising road seems to be the "preservation of the higher good". We are now sliding down a dangerous path. We are going to define morality based on the circumstances! We have a name for that: casuistry.

What is the situation we in the Western World – and here we have the first of a number of debilitating limitations – find in front of us?

On a material level, we made enormous progress. Surprisingly, and certainly not intended, our progress has mainly benefited the lower classes of our society.

Average life expectancy went up dramatically. Sure enough we did not make any noticeable progress with the maximum life span of our species, but:

- Infectious diseases are all but eradicated.
- Under-nourishment is no longer a topic.
- The consequences of accidents can be repaired quite nicely in most cases.
- In Western Europe we managed to avoid war – at least among ourselves – for more than half a century.

Due to all these elements, the life expectancy of the underprivileged has risen quite considerably to almost the level of the leading classes.

In Western Europe, everyone who has the brains and the desire can get a first class academic education, even if he stems – like me – from a poor working class family.

A closely-knit social net protects every individual. Some of us argue that it is knit too closely. But even if some of the meshes were a bit wider, the whole would still be a formidable achievement.

Further, one could argue that today's popular masses enjoy a quality of life that is truly comparable to the one experienced by the leading classes of the previous century.

- Mobility:
  Hardly any of the 19th century's super rich had seen as much of the world as the German factory worker of the 20th.
- Medical care:
  I will rather be in a health plan today than experience what the pampered VIP of the last century had to go through.
- Access to information:
  No head of state of the 19th century had even remotely as much information about geopolitical processes as John Doe today. I am not going to claim that John Doe uses this information in a meaningful way, but he has it!
- Access to culture:
  When we think about music, literature, etc., there simply is no comparison possible.

All this obviously applies somewhat less to the United States than to Western Europe. Our American friends have some catching up to do in areas like medical care for the *whole* population and even more importantly access to quality education for all young people, irrespective their economic background. Nevertheless, it cannot be stressed enough how formidable these achievements are. We have elevated health, education, security, well being and self-actualization of our citizens to the supreme objectives of our states.

Are people happier for all that? Of course not! *Instead of peacefully perishing at age 45 from some kind of infectious disease or rheumatic fever, our 75 years old now lament about the possibility that social security might not be all that secure.* This was once pointed out by a German minister: Norbert Blüm. It was not received well, but it is the truth!

I believe that this question about the relative satisfaction of our population is quite irrelevant. Certainly contemporary people have more than ever the opportunity to realize what was written so nobly in the American Declaration of Independence: *"that all Men are created equal, that they are endowed by their Creator with certain unalienable Rights, that among these are Life, Liberty, and the Pursuit of Happiness."* But it remains their choice, subject to their free will whether and to what extent they will make use of these capabilities to shape their lives in a more meaningful way than would have been possible previously. That ought to suffice as motivation for those of us who are confronted daily with the thankless job to uphold this reluctantly accepted wellbeing.

But how could we afford this? Only a dramatically increased productivity in almost all aspects of human labor, starting with agriculture via industrial activity, research and commerce, up to the eternally unloved administration could set free the necessary resources to achieve all this.

The source of and the reason for the undeniable blessings of modern life are a gigantic unbelievably complex mechanism that we call "the economy".

One can have all kinds of feelings towards this contraption. One can love it, or hate it. Indeed the machine does not just work flawlessly. It does things to the environment that we could only morally afford ourselves in our period of innocence, where we had not yet understood the interrelationships between things to the same level we see today.

But no matter what, we cannot do without the machine. Even if we don't accept the status quo, because of its side effects, we cannot scrap the machine but only gradually improve it. This insight is missing in today's society. It is astounding what far-reaching judgments we are willing to make, based on a totally inadequate understanding. The European environmentalist who takes the tramway to work, and in exceptional cases does not own a car, believes to have solved the environmental pollution problem. Of course he makes a positive contribution, I am far from rejecting that. But has he found a *solution*? He does not think about the fact that the "clean" electrical power for his streetcar either comes from a nuclear power plant, and we know that there are a couple of unresolved problems with radioactive waste, or from a conventional plant burning fossil fuel. The latter has, as some of us know, unsolvable – as opposed to unresolved – problems with CO_2 and a couple of other small details. Of course, the tramway traveler generates somewhat less CO_2 than the person who drives a car. But to think of these things in terms of solutions! I really do not want to ridicule the efforts of the environmental activists, because the environmental movement today is as necessary as the trade unions were at the beginning of the 20th century. But dreams change nothing!

I am living in New Jersey, and some years we have rather harsh winters. After the 10th storm the question where to put all the snow that is removed from the street comes up as a real issue. On the ride to the airport, I heard my limo-driver explain the solution. We build a vehicle that instead of plowing the snow to the side sucks it up, melts and evaporates it. The steam can be used to power the vehicle. Somehow he figured that he would have excess steam – how right he was about that one – and as he saw no possibility to use that excess energy meaningfully, he was going to just blow the steam off into the air. I tried to argue with him. I quickly calculated that he would have to tow a tanker with about 30 tons of fuel oil, in order to "clean" just a mile of highway. He was totally unimpressed. Obviously, I had not understood the idea. Dreams do not only change nothing, they are also very resilient. Unfortunately, our pristinely clear dreams are often a more powerful guide for our actions than our messy, woefully incomplete picture of a reality that we don't like too much anyway.

About the economy, where we bump into relationships that are infinitely more complex than the superficial thermodynamics one has to understand in the case of the previous example, we find even more outrageously adventurous dreams and opinions. Many of us seriously believe that we can turn the clock back. That makes the problem of dealing with the fact that such a thing is utterly impossible only more difficult. It is a fact that saying goodbye to the industrial world as we know it today could only be done in conjunction with immeasurable suffering, decimating the population of the United States and Western Europe. As a consequence, the maintenance of the existing system is, if not the highest, then certainly a very high good. Nobody up to date has shown acceptable alternatives. Thus for us, the people, there will be no other choice than keeping the machine going, accepting its side effects, and very cautiously embark on a venture to prudently modify the machine towards a better long term compatibility with nature. In order to be meaningful, this has to be done as well within our more or less whole western world as outside of that.

The machine does not just run by itself. It needs machinists that at least have a primitive understanding of the complex interrelationships that govern the whole thing. One could also call them managers, leaders or even administrators.

The requirements are so complex, broad and deep that one layer of such machinists does not do. Many of the challenges require the cooperation of hundreds, even thousands of people. In that case, we bump into natural limits:

- limits in the ability of individual people to understand complex systems
- limits in our communications capability.

These limits are hard and decisive. We will not find a way around them. The only promising alternative is to partition the task in front of us in smaller parts. The trick is to build complexes that are within themselves consistent and sufficiently separable from each other to allow for clearly visible and defined goals and visions. What is narrated so casually here represents in reality the summit of the art of management. To proclaim that we have mastered this art would be somewhat optimistic. We see a lot of pathetic mishaps. But we have no other alternative than trying as well as we can. Once such a partition has been made, one can put a leader in charge and make him responsible for one of the parts. However, the mass is so enormous that we need to repeat this process several times. This leads to stacked leadership structures, and those are utterly unnatural. Primitive Homo Sapiens never needed nor knew such a thing. As a consequence, there was no time to hard-wire the necessary behavioral patterns into our genus. Now suddenly there is a need for abstract treatment of issues that used to be dealt with quite instinctively. Communication structures are put to a tough test. The question of trust emerges. The intuitive personal trust that resulted from the fact that the group witnessed the struggle for power and accepted the more capable contender as its leader can no longer be reckoned with. Forthwith, leaders are ordained from above.

On top of this, the daily work in a large organization does no longer offer a direct experience of its significance. There are worlds between hunting in a group and working on an assembly line. The sociologists talk about "alienation", and indeed, the contemporary world must look like a strange place to humans shaped by evolution. There simply was not enough time to absorb all this change in a biological sense.

One of the consequences is the emergence of an impersonal, even invisible leadership class. One procedure I always followed when taking charge of a new organization was to make sure that I talked to every single member. That takes time, even a lot of time, but I believe it was well invested. A standard question was: "When was the last time you talked to your immediate supervisor?" Quite amazing what responses one gets. Often it was months! I further can assure you that there is no significant difference between Europe and the United States.

We have a very obvious problem here:

- Leadership is more necessary than ever.
- Leadership is less direct, less biologically tangible than ever.
- Leadership is less intuitively acceptable than ever.

Evidently, we will need "Machinists" if we want to keep the machine running, and as described above, we have no reasonable alternative to that. It also is crystal-clear that we are dealing here with a class that is at odds with society like no one before. Nevertheless, I believe that the preservation of the "higher good", and that is the maintenance of our prosperity generating productivity not only justifies, but even mandates the acceptance of the obvious negative aspects – like submission – that come with leadership. But maybe our judgement about this whole complex is predestined to be irrelevant anyway. We are indeed talking here about the modern and admittedly hardly recognizable transformation of the leadership principle as it was originated and crystallized by evolution itself. Deeper layers of this world, closer to the core of our existence, supporting the platform on which also things like moral reflection rest, have already decided the issue.

We should stay aware of what we are about to do here. On the basis of the facts as described above and with, in the back of our head, the solid knowledge that people are not equal, we are ready to legitimate things like power, authority and privileges of one person over another! Such a thing can only work if a necessary amount of symmetry is preserved. Symmetry is anyhow an omnipresent principle in nature. It becomes the dominant principle when we deal with equilibrium and stability.

Tightrope walkers know this, and will only perform without the rod that allows them to control and correct small symmetry deviations if they are really very good. The latter simply means that they are able to preserve symmetry even without the help of the equilibrating rod. A loss of symmetry that cannot be immediately corrected will result in a fall. How can the symmetry idea be applied to our topic here? Of course not in the framework of primitive concepts like "left" and "right", or maybe in a metaphoric sense even that! Probably also morality is much closer connected to symmetry than we intuitively understand.

In the case at hand, leadership, we can observe a couple of bipolar force fields that need to be in equilibrium in order to guarantee long term stability of the system. Without any claim to completeness, I thought of the following:

Power	←→	Responsibility
Authority	←→	Accountability
Privileges	←→	Obligation

The principle "Noblesse Oblige" is older than the French Revolution, but was obviously not sufficiently understood. Otherwise, the latter would not have needed to happen.

Distortions within these systems do more than direct history. They also create immediate and local consequences wherever and whenever they occur. These are effects like productivity losses and thus further deterioration of the intuitive acceptability of the system. Those again are coupled with decreased wellbeing for the individuals that are within the range of those distortions. If such distortions are not detected and repaired by strong, system-immanent self-curing mechanisms, they will persist and expand. The inevitable final consequence is a collapse of the system. This has happened over and over again in history, and can be very clearly observed today. One could call this justice and a good thing if there were not every time a tidal wave of suffering drowning large numbers of mainly innocent people. Dialectic Materialism claims that such a collapse, with all the attached human suffering is nevertheless beneficial, because it means a step forward in the unidirectional and inevitable development of society. I do not observe such a thing. If I had lived in the later part of the 18th century, I too would have rebelled against the French monarchy. But one cannot possibly claim that Robespierre was progress compared to Louis the XVI. This "trade" was not worth the price! Is it ever? Was Cromwell more just than his beheaded king, Lenin more effective than the Zar, Pinochet better than Allende, Castro superior to Battista?

What do I mean with all this?

For a person that accepts in earnest, and with deep moral roots the obligation to serve his fellow men as a leader, it is probably much more effective to work with evolution than to contemplate revolution.

One question (at least) remains unanswered: what kind of leaders should we have?

The specification is really simple:

- The guts and stature of General George Patton.
- The humility and compassion of Mother Theresa.
- The reasoning power and vision of Albert Einstein.

There is only one small problem. Among all the billions of us, we are not going to find a single person that meets this specification. And if, against all odds, such a person should ever exist, I bet you that she would not even be interested in a worldly leadership position.

Like it or not, our leaders are going to be people, men and women with vices and virtues, talents and weaknesses. They will – oh horror – very likely be people much like you and me. With its incurable addiction to normal distribution, nature will arrange things so that most of our leaders will display a rather balanced set of the good and the bad, the glorious and the ugly. It would not only be utterly unfair, but also very ineffective to measure these very real people against the very unreal, totally abstract specification mentioned above. But that is what we constantly do to our leaders, from the president of the USA to our manager at work and back!

Leaders should try to internalize the true nature of their position: they are the first servants of the group they lead. They need an ever-present consciousness about their enormous obligations. They must understand the truly biological nature of leadership. They have to be ever cautious to preserve equilibrium. They should have an acute awareness of the fact that they are not just managing company assets, but that they are leaders of flesh and blood human beings, their fellow men. That means that they must have an interest in and accept responsibility for their people way over and beyond the work situation. Only then can a stable and robust form of leadership emerge, from which the enterprise and all its stakeholders will benefit. Our contemporary selection mechanisms are not conducive to such a form of leadership. That constitutes a serious destabilizing factor in our enterprise as well as our society. There is no simple way to reverse this, but even small improvements might work wonders.

What type of leader do I prefer? Clearly somebody who has seen and understood all of the above without ever reading this book, and therefore is able to experience his relative importance and unimportance at the same time. I want a leader that is truly human, and that includes seeing his own deficits and limitations. If that is a given, I will forgive and overlook even terrible shortcomings. But that's after all just a matter of personal taste, and thus by no means normative for anybody except me.

11 The Selection Machine

It is quite interesting to sit in one of these plush boardrooms of a Fortune 100 company, and hear the chairman say:

"Inwardly, we will take the position that ..."

But:

"To the outside world we will say ..."

It comes to mind that "Paleface speaks with forked tongue!" The really amazing part is that nobody is shocked. This *is* business as usual. The audience sits there in awe of the man's cleverness and in fear of the man's ruthlessness. He operates like that all the time, with the prudent caution of a snake and the ferocity of a tiger alternating as dictated for by the different situations life puts in front of him. If he says "A", he does not necessarily mean "A". He probably means "B". But what he wants you to understand and take away from the conversation is "C". He seems to enjoy it. Glad to notice that the system makes at least one guy happy! I don't think that he knows or feels that his behavior is wrong. A quarter of a century of struggle rising through the corporate ranks has thoroughly eradicated the notion of "right or wrong" from his consciousness. All he remembers is "appropriate", that means "effective in the given situation". This is a quite interesting phenomenon, and it deserves that we spend some time on it.

First of all there is the question: does he behave like this because of his position, or did he get here because of his behavior? This only seems like one of those "chicken and egg" questions again, because it clearly is mainly the latter. The selection systems in large modern enterprises assure that. We find here again one of these "strange loops", created by recursion:

- The selection mechanisms determine the future leadership.
- The present leadership defines the selection mechanisms.

Taking out the time dimension, that would lead to something like Fig. 11.1.

But of course, it is not that simple. The leadership is constantly subject to impulses that come from society as it evolves. The "material" that is fed into the selection process is individuals, equally shaped by society and its contemporary values. So Fig. 11.2 is probably a more complete picture.

Then, there is a *huge* factor in the selection process, that nobody really wants to acknowledge: coincidence. Being at the right place at the right time is a very powerful career catalyst.

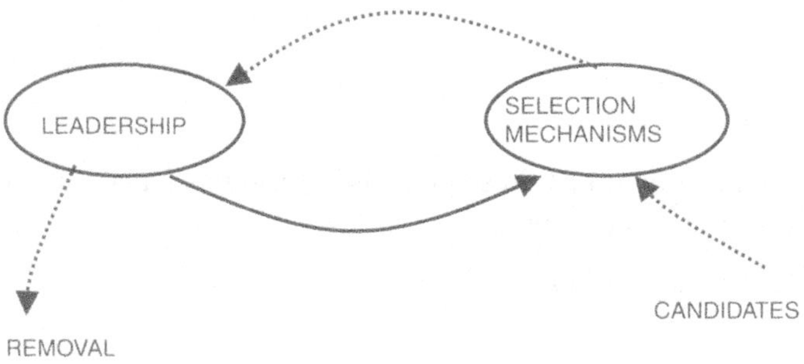

Figure 11.1

And last, but not least, as a subset of society, the enterprise will have its own, in some cases quite considerable influence on the evolution of the latter.

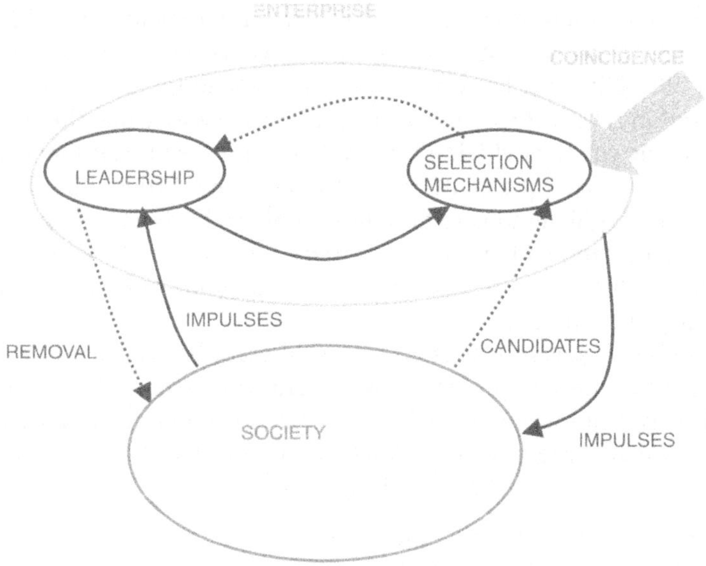

Figure 11.2

The "machine" we described so far would be complicated enough, but things become worse when we - necessarily - enter time. An individual evolves, learns as he rises through the ranks. The selection mechanism does not just act as a "sieve" it also is an educational environment. In the mean time, the surroundings evolve as well. Operating in this environment is like playing chess, with constantly changing rules.

This model, with all its complex, unquantifiable constantly changing feedback loops is of course not very helpful when the goal is to forecast a predictable outcome. But it still may be useful if we try to get a better understanding of the diverse influences.

11.1 Society and Values

"Values" is one of these words that are slowly changing and losing their content. For the sake of simplicity and clarity, we should agree on its meaning. I believe that "values" have to do with the resolution of priorities more than with anything else. What is more important to me, being competitive or cooperative, being rich or being recognized as a "good person", being happy or being successful, *being* something, or being recognized for it? What is going to define my world: beauty or truth, kindness or justice? We are all constantly confronted with choices that would, if extremely simplified, boil down to questions like the ones previously mentioned. It would be decisively too cumbersome to reason through each of them as they appear in front of us. So evolution has equipped us with an elegant shortcut. I believe that our so-called "values" are nothing more or less than a set of prefabricated – canned, so to say – answers to these questions, allowing us to keep our bearings without continuously unpacking our sextant.

It is fairly certain that a person's basic values are shaped during childhood and adolescence. There are a number of influences involved. There has been endless debate about the relative importance of genetics as opposed to environment. While there is not too much – yet – we can do about the former, we certainly do have some measure of control over the latter. Many entities, microenvironments come into play:

- the family
- school
- church
- the neighborhood
- clubs
- TV (a virtual community!).

As one consequence of the complexity of the value building mechanism, and the high number of parameters involved, the outcome should be about normally distributed over the population. Observations seem to support that. There are very few saints, very few absolute scoundrels, and a lot of people like you and me: a bit good, a bit bad, a bit strong and a bit weak.

I have no proof for any of the above, and I have little hope that I ever will. I am neither a psychologist nor a philosopher, just a guy that observes the world around him with increasing bewilderment, and tries whatever he can to make some limited sense out of it all.

11.2 The Selection Machine (User's Manual)

Now we put this material through the "selection machine". That is a multi-layered contraption. Let's represent it as a series of sieves as shown in Fig. 11.3.

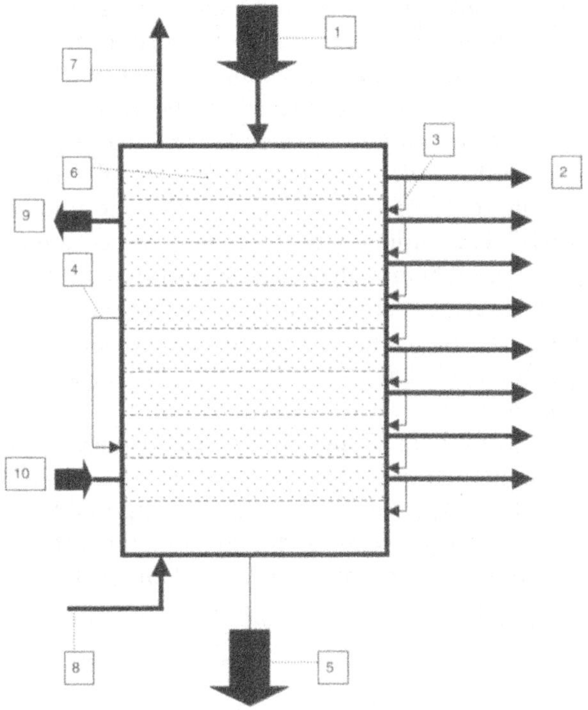

Figure 11.3

Let's look how it works:

1. Raw material, prefabricated by society, loaded with values, is fed into the system.
2. Coarse material is removed, and goes into a holding bin, normally for the rest of its useful life.
3. "Forgiving bypass". In some cases material that does not pass the sieve is bypassed to the next level nevertheless. There are "forgiving bypasses" in-

stalled on every level. This is a complicated process step that will be dealt with further.

4. Fast track bypass. In some cases material is bypassed around several steps.
5. Output: top management.
6. The sieve operates in "fluid bed" mode. Particles are rubbed against each other and can through that process eventually get small enough to pass the sieve.
7. Exhaust.
8. Stream of hot air.
9. Intermediary output (to a different selection machine).
10. Intermediary input (from another selection machine)

When thinking about this machine, there are a couple of things that we need to keep in mind:

- The mechanism has been designed and built by evolution.
- It is also operated by evolution.
- It is constantly being adapted and altered.
- There is no standard design. Although we will encounter the general principle everywhere, there will be significant differences in design from place to place. Also, in one place the characteristics may change quite substantially with time.

The first level we encounter is formal education. In the past this stage used to eliminate more than 90 % of the material. Lately there have been serious mechanical problems with this step, and the elimination rate is now much lower.

One can be forgiven for not passing the first stage, more easily now than in the past, but there always was a "forgiving bypass" installed, although it used to have a much smaller diameter.

All further stages are basically about pleasing people. This all-important ability is tested in a number of diverse environments. Sales, production, research, product management and so on. The paramount concern is always the same: "How do I please people one and two levels above me?"

11.2.1 The Forgiving Bypass

Now let's talk a minute about the "forgiving bypass". Almost everybody that wants to get to the top (or in our schematic the bottom) will need one at some point. How is it operated? There are a number of influences that can open the bypass for you.

11.2.1.1 Coincidence

If you asked me what the single most important factor in a career is, I would mention coincidence. One very seldom hears this, and there is a reason. Top management likes to view itself as the selection of the brightest and the best. They would like to think that they got where they are in a quite predictable, even unavoidable way by their extraordinary skills and capabilities. Even those that do not completely believe this themselves will be wiser than saying so in public. Creating or supporting doubt about the intellectual and moral superiority of the leadership, even questioning the meritocratic nature of top management is a mortal sin. It is punished by excommunication. No longer being "one of the boys" is the worst thing that can happen to an executive. It is the corporate equivalent of the death penalty.

Still, being in the right place at the right time is the single best thing you can do for your career. But of course you can't really control that. It is, for at least 99%, coincidence. I will give you some practical examples.

In spite of adamant policies, official statements, thick files and impressive databases that suggest the contrary, most modern enterprises are living in a permanent personnel crisis. It is somewhat difficult to see the retirement of a 60 year-old executive as a surprise, but for some of our modern dinosaurs even a couple of years of advanced warning is short notice. If you are, in a situation like that, the only one available with the right qualifications, and deemed half-way competent, you will fall upstairs. This will open the bypass for you at a moment where you got stuck with a bunch of superiors that would normally have blocked your passage through the next "likability" sieve. As long as they just say: "He is a really difficult person, but I do have to admit that he is competent," you pass. A high level of difficulty, considerable physical danger and high financial stakes associated with the job increase the probability of such an arrangement. I should know this, because it happened to me a couple of times.

Being in the right place at the right time has an inverse companion: being in the wrong place at the wrong time. Such an event can completely and permanently ruin the show. Of course, you can do very little about all this. As I said, it's coincidence.

Nevertheless, should you ever get lucky enough to be in a situation where you have some maneuvering room, some choices, then here follows the description of the ideal set up you should strive for.

The ideal place is:

- A business that has been poorly managed, and thus has a lot of shallowly hidden efficiency potential.
- A business that is far enough from the enterprises core business to show a different economic cycle.
- The business should be small enough so that top management is not fully aware of the elements involved in the cycle.
- The business should be big enough to make a noticeable economic impact.

The ideal time is:

- Succeeding a poorly performing predecessor. His performance should however not be so poor that it is generally noticed. Otherwise, that will be subtracted from your credit.
- The bottom of the economic cycle for that business, which as we already mentioned must not coincide with the behavior of the core markets.

I saw somebody wrestle with the selection machine for 15 years, making no noticeable progress in spite of undeniable talents. Then he got two "lucky strikes" in a row, and he is now at the top.

If you get into such a lucky situation, you acquire the omen of a magician, a person who can fix anything. This is part of the residual mythical/magical mindset in our enterprises. There is absolutely no rational basis. Especially in the chemical- and life sciences industry, the product pipeline is long. The products that boost you to fame and reputation have been invented and developed by completely different people, so long before you arrived on the scene that by now many of them are retired and forgotten. But you get all the credit! If all goes well you might go to the "fast track bypass". That is the career manager's ultimate bliss.

There is yet another way coincidence can foster your career. We will further see how important it is to get a sponsor. But for such a thing to happen, you need to be noticed. Again, there are certain things that you can do to that effect, but their effectiveness is limited. Being in the right place at the right time again is much more important. The occasion to meet the powerful person that will almost certainly propel you upstairs can come in many different forms. Ironically, dramatic mishaps, even catastrophes very often offer such an opportunity. An accident with casualties will almost certainly attract top management's attention. If it is not obviously your fault, and you can handle the situation properly, you will be noticed. Or if there is really big stink with a very important customer over a quality issue, and you can solve it, you may attract the attention of a powerful sponsor.

If my explanations about coincidence have made a cynical impression, I need to correct this. Quite to the contrary, we should be very glad that coincidence plays such a role, because it brings some of the original randomness that served us so well in natural selection and evolution back to the table. If that amount of randomness were not there, and the selection machine were totally and deliberately controlled by people, things would probably be much worse and for certain far more rigid.

11.2.1.2 Family Ties

There are dozens of jokes about this – one more tasteless than the other – but it still plays a role. Nepotism is, in this day and age, executed with much more care and discretion than in the past. There are a number of schemes:

- A works for company X and has arrived in high places.
- A fosters B's career, and thus creates an obligation on the part of B.
- A has a son, A_1.
- A_1 goes to work for company Y.
- A retires.
- A_1 now goes to work for company X. B who has in the mean time arrived at the top can easily arrange that.
- B now supports and sponsors A_1.

Or:

- A works for company X and has arrived in high places.
- So has B in company Y.
- A and B know each other, and get along fine. They have scratched each other's backs many times to their mutual benefit.
- A has a son, A_1.
- B has a son, B_1.
- A_1 goes to work for company Y.
- B_1 goes to work for company X.
- A supports and sponsors B_1.
- B supports and sponsors A_1.

It does of course also help to marry the "right" woman. But if that were the only reason for a marriage, I feel that the perpetrator has already punished himself properly before receiving any benefits. Unfortunately he has also punished the woman who may be totally innocent, but collateral damage seems to be one of the most pervasive characteristics of evolution.

I was in absolutely no position to ever benefit from nepotism myself, coming from a poor working class family, but I have difficulty sharing the general indignation about this phenomenon. First of all, one should trust genetics to some extend. Then I saw a couple of "sons" give a rather good account of themselves. Further, if being born and raised in a well to do family does not much to make you a better leader, it certainly also does very little to make you a worse one.

It used to be quite common to inherit power. Monarchy was the standard form of government. Monarchy has a couple of things going for it. One becomes king by being the king's son. One can be stupid or bright, good or bad, it doesn't matter. So in a monarchy you can either be fortunate or unlucky with your rulers. That's all coincidence. But the future king does not have to cheat or lie to get the job. He does not have to betray his friends or back stab his competition. He will become king, no matter what. Some monarchies had sequences of luck (Prussia). Some had a series of poor performers (France) that proved quite fatal.

So with a king, you could win or lose, but with the career politicians you have already lost!

Could it be that the leadership questions in our enterprises are not all that much different?

11.2.1.3 Social Connections

Belonging to the "right" club is important. What membership will foster my career and operate the bypasses at the proper moment? That differs from country to country and enterprise to enterprise.

Sports are always and everywhere important. It does help to play tennis with the chairman. Especially so if the chairman is a beginner and you are an expert and thus able to place the ball in such a way that he can get it. Golf is an important "contact enabler". Belonging to the right country club surely is a good idea. In some companies one must be a hunter in order to be really one of the boys. In the more casual ones it could be the bowling club that acts as the cradle and proving ground for the future leadership. I don't do any of those things. I play chess. That game requires strategic vision, intensive study, precise reasoning, concentration and audacious decision making. That's obviously not a game for the future elite, but rather a laudable hobby for the working classes.

The real important thing about all those activities is of course the social contact on the sideline. That immediately disqualifies chess. You do not chat or toast each other while playing chess.

The conversations are very different from country to country, and often pricelessly amusing. The British are the masters of cultivated futility. "Did you know that George played this course two under par?" "By Jove, I would never have thought him capable of that!" The French have quite different topics being deliberated on the sideline of an opulent diner: la chasse, les femmes, and then, the number one concern of the French nation: la digestion. One can address sensitive business issues, but only at a very specific point of the meal "entre la poire et le café". In Germany, there is a high degree of formality, with speeches and toasts. There are shy attempts at cultivated futility, especially in conjunction with golf, without of course ever coming close to the British proficiency. There is a lot of attention going to the creation of a harmonic atmosphere (Gemütlichkeit!). For the German it is extremely important to feel that he belongs to the group and exactly knows his place in it. That is celebrated very ceremoniously.

I don't know what the Americans debate in their country clubs. I never could bring myself to join one, but I bet it is their national obsession: money.

The result of all this is bonding, on a very fundamental biological level. If you can, as a junior but accepted member, truly belong to such a group, the more powerful members will not hesitate to operate the bypasses when you need them.

11.2.2 Social Skills

In order to become an accepted member of "society", you have to know how to behave, how to talk, how to dress and a zillion other thing of that kind. You have to establish your place and your balance within the group. This is a high intensity undertaking. You see people running with their engines full power. At least subconsciously, they know the paramount importance of "fitting in". Body language plays an important role in this game. The objective is after all to please those in power and to get an endearing relationship with them. The whole process is very interesting, even fascinating. It is as structured as the courtship rituals of birds that we know from animal movies. It also very much resembles what you read about the formation of the leadership in the chimpanzee family. This is not the contemptuous, even sarcastic comment you might believe it to be at the first glance. Something very fundamentally biologic crafted by evolution in thousands of years, something truly human is happening here.

The most stylized form of this behavior is displayed during big formal festivities. Nothing does more for bonding than the collective celebration of common victories. So we love to share the glorious feeling with pomp and circumstance.

I saw them glide over the dance floor in their tuxedos, holding these absolutely abominable women in their arms. I saw them radiate the good time they had. But with their gigantic egos and all their unjustified pride, they looked suspiciously like Honoré Daumier's sculptures, pitifully grotesque. The folds grooved in their faces by years of bitterness were only partially pasted over by their blessed smiles. Their body language, crafted to impress and subdue did not even now leave them. But if you looked closer, you could see that they were stressed. Intensely displaying a good time is quite hard work. And suddenly, I felt a deep sadness, and an infinite compassion for them. On the spot, I forgave them all their sins, all their arrogance and just silently wished them well, although I did not know where in heavens that wellness was to come from.

The youngsters learn the ropes. Some have a more intuitive grasp of the whole process than others do. The most talented ones do some pretty ingenious maneuvering in order to propel themselves on a certain collision course with the projected trajectory of a powerful personality. Even Nelson would have had difficulty to improve on the technique. Some are infinitely more at ease than others who visibly wrestle with the stress of it all. Some stay on the sidelines and just observe the whole process in continuous awe. I used to be one of those. As a non-participating outsider you have to remind yourself constantly that this is not an amusing spectacle. These are the mechanisms of life, of evolution itself. It is ultimately fascinating.

11.2.3 Sponsors

Having a sponsor, a powerful person committed to support your progression through the ranks suddenly gives you a whole bundle of tickets in the career lottery. This is clearly one of the most powerful career enhancing factors, so powerful that it even rivals coincidence. Why does a sponsor enter in such an alliance? There are many possible reasons. Some of those are more selfish than others. Even a very powerful top level manager needs people that he can absolutely rely on. Being sponsored often comes with a commission in somebody's "Praetorian Guard". Nepotism may play a role as well, and also the social circuit occasionally generates a sponsor, but I still think that in most cases, the sponsor truly believes to do something good for the enterprise. He has discovered some talent, and he is going to position it so that the company benefits from it.

There is however a problem with sponsors. By the nature of things, they are usually rather old. They thus have the ugly habit to either die or retire at the most inconvenient of times. That leaves a bunch of orphans. The wise sponsor makes provisions for such an eventuality. He will create a network that will catch his orphans if he were no longer there. Those networks are often real jewels, extending far over the borders of the own enterprise.

A very special form of sponsorship comes with what the Germans call "Seilschaft", or roped party. The term is borrowed from mountaineering. Try to see the picture. Here is this group of people en route to the summit, scaling vertical walls, going through unimaginable difficulties and hardships. They are not only absolutely relying on each other. Their fates are quite literally tied together, all at the same rope. Not one of them can fall without either the others holding him, or all of them going down in the abyss. There is powerful symbolism in this. They secure and trust each other. They must have absolute confidence in their point man that has to make the very critical decisions about the path that they will all take. One sees the equivalent of such roped parties quite often in the enterprise. People generally frown upon them. I cannot share such disapproval. I find this one of the more purposeful aspects of the selection machine. That group of people learns a couple of quite important things on their way to the top. They learn to trust and to support each other. They learn to share risk and responsibility. They practice intensive coordination and communication. They train cooperation and solidarity. They acquire the habit to compensate their mutual weaknesses, to settle their differences and disputes in a constructive way, to give and receive leadership. The experience of having surmounted obstacles, too difficult for any single member, as a team will certainly make them better men once they arrive at the summit. Roped parties have their own and very strict selection criteria. They cannot afford to carry dead bodies up the mountain. I see no reason to have less confidence in that kind of judgment than in any other.

11.2.4 Technical Competency

Enterprises *do* things, *make* things and *sell* things for a living. For the selling part, everything that has been said before under the umbrella "human interaction" is really important. But it will not be very helpful with the "doing" and "making". Completely different skills are called for here. The problem is that the two skill sets we refer to are fairly disjoint. Apart from the rare genius that has it all, people that are brilliant in one corner will usually be terrible in the other. As we will see, the "selection machine" has a tendency to produce a leadership that has inter-personal skills as its strong suit. The feedback mechanisms that we will discuss further will thus lead to a quite consistent, albeit unjustified, downgrading of technical skills. While blatantly visible technical ignorance can be quite fatal, competency normally does not buy you too many tickets in the career lottery. But here we meet coincidence again, together with the amazing capabilities of self-adjustment that we see everywhere in evolution. Technical skills are not in high esteem, so the ensuing frequent mismanagement of technical issues occasionally creates one of these strange singularities that abolish all the normal rules. A technical problem with a plant, a product or a customer can become so expensive, so bad that suddenly a usually only meagerly appreciated ability to resolve this kind of problem becomes the propellant that pushes one through the bypass. It will never suffice to reach the top level though.

Please keep in mind that no one of the elements mentioned above is decisive. All these components are intertwined and feed back on each other. The best analogy would probably be the lottery we already mentioned a couple of times, bringing in the coincidence factor. All the other elements, family, social contacts, competency, just buy you more tickets. Increasing the number of tickets you hold of course improves your odds. But on the other hand, if you had all tickets but one, you could still miss the prize. This can lead to quite traumatic experiences for the extremely ambitious ones. There you are, brilliant, successful, a true master of the selection machine, after having lived in it for some 20 years. You have this impressive pile of tickets in your pocket. You are certain: nothing can go wrong anymore, you are going to make it. And then, something terrible happens. Suddenly, out of the blue sky destiny strikes; that one crucial forgiving bypass refuses to open. All the sacrifice, all the effort, it was for naught. Some people despair at that, up to suicide. The selection machine is a cruel god; it devours its children with the cold indifference of a Moloch.

In some way the ticket thing resembles money. Tickets multiply themselves. Having some enables you to acquire even more. But at the time you discover that all the tickets in the world are not going to buy you immortality, it is mostly too late.

I have absolutely no moral issue with the "selection machine", and I have no proposal for a significant improvement. How could I, after saying that all this was crafted by evolution? But we need to understand what is going on there, because the output of the process is our future leadership.

11.3 The Effects of the Selection Machine on Its Tenants

Given everything that was said so far about the operation of the selection machine, one cannot expect its product – top management – to be a narrowly specified pre-defined subset of the general population. There is quite some randomness involved, and we will thus find the corresponding frequency distribution. On the other hand, even casual observation will show that there is in fact a significant difference between said subset and the general population. There definitely are characteristics and there definitely is behavior that favors safe passage through the machine. In other words: the machine does indeed work. The question is in what direction?

The selection machine does not just select. It also is an educational environment. One cannot expect an individual to *live* in the bellows of this contraption for some 20 years without being influenced. People learn to *deal* with their environment, they *acquire* the methodology that lets them pass sieves. On one hand, that is not bad. Being able to adapt to the, even bizarre, rules of a new environment is a very positive property for a leader. On the other hand, this fatally reminds me of the exams in university. There were those students that tried to master the material, and there were those who prepared themselves for the likely questions as derived from the history of a given professor. Both methods had their successes and failures: the former clearly with more substance and depth, the latter definitely with less effort and higher risk. Within the enterprise, one is facing the exact same dilemma. On one hand, there is work to be done. On the other hand there is the problem to pass the sieves.

Curiously enough the selection machine is a powerful competitor for its own enterprise. That seems difficult to understand, but please bear with me. As an individual moves through the sieves he constantly needs to pay attention to his environment. He needs to think about and do a lot of things that add absolutely no value for the company but just facilitate his successful passage through the next sieve, thus detracting attention from the *real* business. That attention drain is bigger than commonly understood, but the damage is not restricted to attention deficit. Other resources need to be shared between the enterprise and the selection machine as well. I have seen this in action.

Here comes an example from real life: Mr. X is a powerful man, and highly desirable as a sponsor. He has built this enormous house, sporting a daring architecture, a worthy trademark for his achievements in society. But as so often with avant-garde things: there are annoying flaws, like for instance endless leaks in the roof. The available craftsmen are at a loss, another characteristic that often comes with avant-garde constructions. We, with our infinite ability to concoct the strangest resins, can of course help. Our boss (let's call him Mr. A) is extremely ambitious, and really needs a sponsor on the appropriate level. Mr. X fits the bill totally. Luckily, at a recent social function, Mr. X lamented to Mr. A about his eternal problem to keep the abundant rain out of his mansion. Of course he was promptly assured that our technology was going to save the day. But as Murphy will always arrange it, at the same time, one of our customers has a problem. You now have one guess: where do you think our most competent technicians, under the hopefully visible leadership of the boss himself go first? The customer will have to wait another day. The kickback down payment that takes place here does not come out of Mr. A's pocket. It is simply paid for by the company. The price of making the customer wait may be quite high, in fact possibly higher than the cost of totally replacing Mr. X's roof. That does not bother any of the participants. The benefit of pleasing Mr. X is priceless. No cost is too high (as long as it is "just" the company's money of course).

The attentive observer, living in the selection machine longer than in any other environment, learns a couple of things rather thoroughly. If there is no sure recipe that will get you through, there certainly is behavior that will get you stuck. And there are things that, without guaranteeing ultimate success, will always work into the right direction. It is easy to derive a number of behavioral rules from this:

- Tell them what *they* want to hear.
- Never question their motives.
- Avoid bringing up difficult or controversial issues.
- Know the price of everything.
- Question the value of everything.
- Give brilliant presentations, if necessary about nothing. The way you say things is infinitely more important than *what* you say.
- Never forget to quote them. "On October 7, Mr. X in his address to the European Management Meeting pointed out that '...'. I started to think about this, and said to my team: 'Why don't we take this one step further?' Then we worked long hours, also weekends, and this is what we came up with ..." Such an infantile babble would make quite a good impression in most cases.
- Keep the small annoyances away from them.
- Appear flexible, even accommodating ... towards them.
- Appear tough ... towards all others.
- Show respect, even reverence, not only in your language, but also in your gestures. Appear humble.
- Pay supreme attention to appearances, as they are much more decisive than substance.
- Never use language that *they* might find difficult to understand.

- When *they* explicitly ask for something, be certain that they get it, like yesterday.
- If *they* ask for a personal favor, rush it in, like last week.
- Never confront them: especially not over moral issues. Do not annoy them with "matters of principle".
- If you *have* to disagree with them do it unobtrusively. Guide the discussion so that they can "discover" by themselves what you wanted to tell them.
- Ask for their advice.
- Pretend not to notice their deceit and occasional betrayal.

I could go on like this for several pages. But *think*: this is the account of somebody who deliberately decided some 30 years ago *not* to play the game. The fact that I was in spite of that literally sucked through two "forgiving bypasses" and, even more astonishing, one "fast track" comes close to a miracle and means nothing in terms of statistical evidence. Imagine the story a real "selection machine expert" could tell you (but *he* won't)!

The consequences are quite frightening. Depending on the nature and the strength of their values, people may decide not to play at all, to just go along, or to pursue a career with a passion and a vengeance. It does not matter. When the machine spits out its product: our future top management, the latter will be altered, even shaped by the above "rules". The rules dictate the worship of pragmatism, up to the abdication of morality. Who can be astonished for a second by the attitude of the chairman I described at the beginning of this chapter? He was conditioned to say just that, but then, he had to be *willing* to be conditioned! Confronted with the choice: my career or my company, the very ambitious ones will always go for the former. The damage the enterprise will suffer as a result is immeasurable.

On top of all this, there will also be an effect on the culture within the enterprise.

In general, extensive preoccupation with the selection machine pushes the culture towards:

- Extreme inward focus throughout the enterprise.
- Self-centered thinking and behavior.
- Destruction of altruistic patterns.
- Downgrading of morality as a guideline for practical behavior.
- Cynicism
- Low grade communication and information through stealth, secretiveness and "Orwellian language".

But there is still another way in which the struggle with the selection mechanism takes its toll. People used to spend their lives in one and the same selection machine, especially in Europe. That is no longer the custom. If I get stuck on a sieve and there is no bypass in sight, why bother? I can leave through the intermediate output, go to another enterprise, enter a machine that will be different at least in the details, and try my luck there. There even is the possibility that I can start in the new machine one sieve further!

Let's call this machine hopping. These days, it is a commonly accepted practice. The enterprise does not want to put great efforts into showing loyalty towards its employees, and does not expect anything of that sort from them either. There are those of us that believe such an interchange, such an osmosis to be beneficial to all. They may have a point, but I believe that they forget something. Everybody who leaves the enterprise takes some valuables with him: experience, know how and probably most importantly, a part of the company history. This needs to be replaced. That will take time and money anyway, but in some cases it will prove to be completely impossible and we will have a permanent loss on our hands.

So far, we did little more than describe the terrible price we pay for the operation of the selection machine. We said nothing about the value it adds. That is quite obvious: it provides us with our future leadership. Here we meet one of these strange recursion loops that seem to lurk just everywhere. Somebody thoroughly conditioned by the selection machine would at this point start to question its value, compared to the outrageous cost, quite abrasively. That would of course just be one of these futile mythical exercises. The real question is: what alternative do you have to offer? Let's look at the facts:

- We definitely need *some* mechanism to pick our future leadership.
- The product generated by the selection machine is not ideal. This is not the kind of people I would like to have as friends (but there is very little danger here).
- On the other hand, it is quite adequate. It does the job. Our leaders do not need to be scholars or saints. They must lead our enterprises. So far they do. Not perfectly, with terrible, often laughable mistakes, but on average adequately.
- Without having solid proof, but with some knowledge of history, I would venture that any alternative method of leadership selection has a high probability of being more expensive while producing an even poorer result.

It seems to me that we are stuck with the selection machine, as with all the other stuff that evolution dumped on us. We cannot invent a better one. Only the very naïve and uninformed among us could ever hope to do such a thing. But it might not hurt to understand it better.

11.4 Influences Shaping the Selection Machine

The official owner of the selection machine is top management. Top management has no easy life. They have to juggle a lot of different interests, which are at the first glance all mutually conflicting. Shareholders, employees, customers, suppliers, they all are constantly screaming for a bigger piece of the cake. There is however one thing they *all* want, and that is a secure future. Therefore protecting the long-term survivability of the enterprise is probably top management's most important duty. It also is the one issue about which, at least in principle, all the stakeholders agree. A well functioning selection machine is very instrumental in securing a company's future. Therefore the "better" top manager will pay a lot of attention to it.

But there are a couple of problems. First of all, your average top manager has a considerable ego. How could it be different? He made it through the machine against overwhelming odds. If you become a member of the 10 men board of a 100,000 employee company, it is easy to see that the probability for that to happen was only 0.01%. Isn't it quite tempting to say: "This can't be coincidence anymore. It *must* be that I am that good." Of course this is flawed reasoning, as those among us who still remember their probability courses will have noticed. But when did science ever come out as the winner in a collision with ego?

So the reasoning is the following:

- The machine produces a predictable high quality result (for instance me).
- All this talk about coincidence is largely exaggerated.

However, there still may be a need to fine-tune the machine:

- There undeniably still is some element of coincidence in the system. That should be pushed back by an even more structured approach.
- Some of the sieves clearly need design changes. I had trouble with them. As I know that I am the right kind of person to lead this company, the machine should be altered so that it will let a person like me pass with less trouble and in less time.
- Maybe the leadership we need tomorrow is different from the leadership that is good today. We may have to adjust some of the sieves accordingly.
- Society changes and so do the values. The people that enter our system today come with different expectations and values from the ones we had 30 years ago. That may require some minor changes to the machine.

I can hear the more alert among you shouting: "This is nonsense, we will never get anywhere that way." But observe this attentively and you see evolution at work again. The more people rise through the ranks, the more worldly wealth they acquire, and thus the more they have to lose. Quite consequently, they become more conservative, meaning more inclined to keep things the way they are. Even if they develop outrageous concepts about the world, they will only be prepared to follow through with *really small* changes. That protects us from *really big* mistakes. We need that kind of protection.

On the other hand, society is indeed changing. We are by and large becoming more materialistic and more hedonistic than previous generations. The – still existing – individuals that are willing to invest 20 years of sacrifice in order to then – just potentially – get into a position of power are becoming an ever-smaller minority. Today's generation demands faster rewards. They want it all, and right now. I already see changes being made to a number of selection machines to accommodate that trend.

Many people have the tendency to blame everything on the enterprise, to act and speak as if the enterprise were a kind of disease infecting the healthy body of society. In reality, enterprises are entities *within* and integral parts of our society. They cannot significantly deviate from whatever happens in society, in the good as little as in the bad. Through their particular form of activity and organization, they may amplify and expose certain aspects of society so that they are more readily visible. But it still is society that makes and forms the enterprise, much more than the other way around. The enterprise simply cannot afford to ignore any significant change that is going on in society.

The whole "political correctness thing" that invades society like a cancer these days is not very helpful. I believe it to have a quite detrimental effect on morality, by bluntly and publicly endorsing, even encouraging dishonesty. As despicable as things like racism and sexism are, hypocrisy, lying and cheating about them is worse, much worse. If you are a racist and openly say so, I can debate the issue with you. Maybe I can't convince you, but in most cases I can give you something to seriously think about. If political correctness makes you hide your standpoint behind a smoke screen, you are not any less of a racist, but probably just a more stealthy, vicious one.

Of course, people have always lied about their ulterior motives, but as long as systematic deceit had not yet received the stamp "politically correct" there was at least some form of shame or guilt associated with that. Now it is all sanctioned by society! Political correctness has taken over a large chunk of the selection machine, and that is not for the better.

Fortunately, all these changes are slow and small. We are well advised to keep it that way. One does not outpace evolution with impunity.

12 Decisions

Enterprises need to *do* things, and the first step required in such a process is a decision. One might be tempted to believe that this is a real simple issue. It should go about as shown in Fig. 12.1.

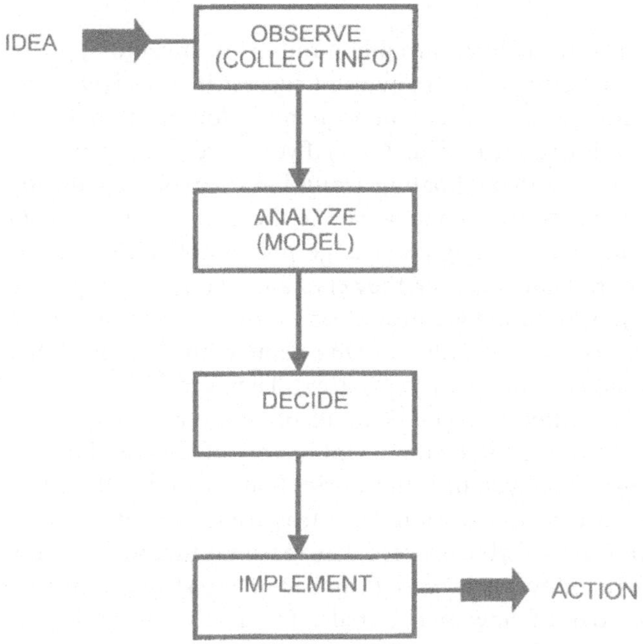

Figure 12.1

The short story is that an idea is converted into action.

It seems so simple. The first thing you need to do is to collect information about the surroundings where the idea is going to be carried out. It is like collecting maps and literature about an area that you want to go visit. Then you analyze the data, preferably modeling them. That usually leads to alternatives. Once you have a good quantitative grasp of all the alternatives and their possible consequences, you present this picture in front of a decision making body. One of the alternatives (and that absolutely can be: do nothing), is picked and will be supported. The rest is pure mechanics: project scope, schedule, budget, resources etc.

Unfortunately, this description stems much more from wishful thinking and operationalism than from reality. Maybe it happens like this in small, family owned and managed enterprises, but certainly not in the Leviathans of modern industry. They will absolutely claim that the process as described is followed to the dot. They also dearly wish that it were so. They even have strict procedures and gigantic bureaucracies with no other goal than enforcing this kind of decision-making. I have seen these mechanisms at work during my 30 years in industry, and I can assure you that here again reality deviates so much from doctrine that it is hard to see any resemblance between the two. The reason is of course that *people* do all this *while they are crawling through the selection machine.*

Let's start with the idea. Ideas have variable numbers of inventors, going from zero to a dozen, depending on their apparent success in any given stage of execution. In reality, an idea is very seldom born in one lonely brain. When you think about the genesis of a great idea, it is as if you were looking at creation itself. The components are there, floating around in a percolating, inspiring atmosphere. They are passed from one person to the next through discussions, literature and symposia. Through a strange process of self-organization, somehow the parts gravitate together, they crystallize and suddenly there is our idea, freshly born. A lot of the greatest ideas ever were born out of the careful emotionless observation of failures. One wanted to do one thing, struggled with it and could not find a way to progress. Then suddenly, one *saw* that something completely different could be done, often quite easily.

Like everything else in this world, the hindsight history of ideas and inventions is considerably bent. When you hear the stories that are told in the aftermath, you would almost get the impression that ideas are the result of a very organized, deliberate and controllable process. The reason is that we have this longing for a rational, structured world, and it can become so strong a longing that we pretend not just to our fellow men, but also to ourselves to have such a world. In reality, I know that I cannot provide a clean reconstruction of the genesis of any of my patents. I just know that I had the massive benefit of pre-existing knowledge as well as discussions with colleagues. This is not just the fate of an average person like me. Even the genius Goethe stumbled over it. He doubted the pure originality of any of his ideas. He even included his studies about color, the part of his work that he was immensely proud of, in these considerations.

But even if an idea has many fathers, it still needs *one* champion. That is somebody willing to pick it up and run with it, shepherd it through the labyrinth of corporate bureaucracy and protect it against the wolves. In the end the champion will almost in all cases believe that this is, was and will forever be *his* idea, and in a certain sense he is right about that.

But why at all should we pursue an idea? I saw an astonishing variety of reasons. Let's group them according to what I call "motivation class".

Class A, for the objective good of the company:

- We simple have to do this if we want to continue business. This applies to legal requirements, infrastructure, environmental and the like.
- It will make a good return on investment.
- It will strengthen the company's strategic position.
- It will lower our exposure to all kinds of risks.

Class B, for the subjective good of the company:

- It will annoy/discourage the competition.
- It will send a strong signal to the market place.
- It will enhance our prestige.

Class C, for objective selfish reasons:

- I own the patent. If this thing gets built, I will (at least in Germany) receive a generous "inventor's compensation".
- This will attract attention from the top level. I will get noticed.

Class D, for subjective selfish reasons:

- This is going to be my monument. I will be remembered by it.
- This will enhance my standing with the local government.
- This will make me famous.

And why should we *oppose* an idea? One good reason is that every project costs money, the company's money. So if I don't see a believable class A motive, and if I don't see a class B motive that ultimately can be converted into a class A gain, I have to work against it.

Projects never are proposed with an honest class C or D label. Their proponents will always disguise them as A or B. But people may be able to look through that, and find that they have their own selfish reasons for fierce opposition. Competitiveness and jealousy are powerful drivers here. This game can become quite bizarre. I even saw class A projects opposed, because of the suspicion that there could be a class C side effect benefiting somebody else!

The enterprise knows all this and continuously tries to keep it in check. The armament build up is impressive:

- thick guidelines
- forms to be filled out
- whole departments doing nothing but compile an "independent" economic evaluation
- complicated approval procedures
- committees

- expert opinions
- audits.

The effort is absolutely enormous, the mass of bureaucracy unbelievable.

The amazing thing is that in my whole career, I never saw *one* obviously stupid project avoided by all these checks and balances. This may be an unfair statement as people may have decided in some cases not to come forward with their proposal, deterred by the prospect of extreme scrutiny. On the other hand, I saw fairly stupid ideas sail through the process and into realization without as much as a hiccup. The most blatant example was a palatial headquarters building for a division that was losing money by the $100 millions.

Buildings are always suspect for a number of reasons. First of all they elude normal profitability analysis, as you would apply it to production equipment. And when you are a manufacturing company, your systems are totally geared towards production equipment, which makes them quite unapt to come to a clean judgment about something like a building. That relieves you from the obligation to present a class A justification. Buildings also are the most suitable objects for a class D attempt. Further they can very easily be disguised as class B. For all these reasons a "building project" is almost never presented unless vigorously supported by a powerful personality. The latter in most cases believes that this is going to be his monument, his mausoleum. His attachment to the project is accordingly strong. In most cases it is not his idea though. Probably some ambitious serf cooked it up and served it to him in a very palatable kind of arrangement. The more he thinks about it, the more he starts to like the idea. Here we go, and from now on there is not much standing between us and a $100 million graveyard.

What can one do to prevent such a project from actually being built? Certainly, one cannot simply unveil the fact that this is class D. That would be the corporate equivalent of suicide bombing. There are rare exceptions where reasoning helps. I gratefully remember one occasion where I could stop such a thing in its initial stage, by saying to my then superior who had already swallowed the bait: "Boss, *you* do not need such a thing. You are a great scientist and a man of impeccable moral quality. That is how we will remember you. The last thing you need is a monument. Don't let them pull you down to that level." It worked! But as they say in TV commercials: "Don't try this at home!" The reason why I could get away with it was that the man was *indeed* a great scientist of impeccable moral caliber. On top of that, he had a keen sense of humor that allowed him to see the relativity of his own person and position. I mourn his death until this day.

So by now we have understood that a gigantic bureaucracy will not safeguard us against bad investments. But if it doesn't help, then it probably doesn't harm either. In such case the damage would be limited to the quite substantial cost and the paralyzing effect on the enterprise. Unfortunately, reality is worse than that. In a strange way the bureaucratic hurdles *foster* bad decisions. This must sound strange, so bear with me.

Please put your imagination in overdrive again, and follow this fictitious story.

Suppose that I am the champion running with a large petrochemical project. It is going to cost hundreds of millions. What do I need to do apart from making the paperwork look attractive? Well, I need to engage in quite substantial lobbying efforts. I cannot just appear in front of the appropriations committee and take my chances. I need to prepare that event very carefully. If I don't, I risk a eclat that might not only bury my project, but possibly also my person with it. So I go visit every single member of the committee, all of them highly placed executives. I give them a carefully prepared precisely choreographed "personal briefing". At the end of this, they have hopefully all seen the light, and will be on my side during the session, which will be no more than the solemn celebration of a consensus that was already achieved. But I cannot just restrict my efforts to the high and mighty. There are a number of people writing "expertise's" and "independent opinions" about my project. I need to make sure that what they are going to write does not conflict with the story I told the powerbrokers. Ultimately, the committee members are going to read their write-ups, and poor me if someone discovers an unexplained discrepancy. So I am going to visit these experts, offer them my "technical assistance" with the papers they need to write, and make sure that they acquire a sympathetic attitude towards my project. Those people are after all just... people and if I can alleviate their work burden, they will be grateful and believe my story without too much inquiring. They are further rather flattered. I outrank them considerably, but I have very long discussions with them, always preserving a very humble posture.

All that will be a quite intensive full time job for several months. But the rewards will be worth it. Six weeks prior to D-day, the frantic activity comes to a halt. The papers are filed. Everything is well prepared and nothing left to coincidence. The dreaded session will be no more than a ceremony, with the committee members falling over themselves showing off their in-depth understanding, and supporting my case. There is no doubt about the outcome, and that's how it should be. Unless...

Destiny strikes. Four weeks prior to the session, I discover new information. Well, it's not exactly *new* information. It was sitting out there all the time, and I should have had and considered it, but I didn't. In the light of that new information, my project does not look good at all. The return is going to be much lower, not only than the figures quoted in my paperwork, but also lower than the threshold we normally apply for capital projects. This might turn into a quite substantial financial disaster. What am I going to do now?

The honorable thing would of course be to call the whole project off. The problem is that I have other, more important concerns than this project, namely my progression through the selection machine. In the selection machine, the "honorable thing" does not pay off. I learned that many years ago. I have now done all this lobbying. I cannot simply recall my propaganda as if it were a faulty automobile. Stopping the project now will set me up with a major credibility problem. It shouldn't, but it will. I have this gigantic bureaucracy marching in lock step with me, and even at their unimpressive speed, their enormous mass accounts for a lot of kinetic energy! I cannot do a 180° turn without creating serious disruption. This cannot be stopped anymore. Precisely at this moment, with this project, my prospects for higher office are looking really good. Shall I do the honorable thing now and throw it all away? Of course not! I will do the following:

- Dig in.
- Prepare a believable line of defense, just in case somebody else stumbles over the same explosive piece of information.
- It will take three more years for the terrible truth to materialize. During that period, I need to get away.
- If I am promoted high and fast enough, the "criminal investigation", if there ever were such a thing, will not point in my direction, but harass my poor unfortunate successor, or even better *his* successor. Too bad, but it can't be helped.

And so on…

Before you take your imagination out of overdrive, please accept my assurance that I never did such a thing. On the other hand, I never came into the embarrassing situation to be faced with such a predicament. On yet the other hand, I always did my homework very seriously, so that the previous statement might be based on somewhat more than just pure blind luck.

But you see what happened. The enormously expensive machinery that was intended to prevent stupid investments is not only failing on that account. Much worse than that, it is even contributing to my inability to correct my own mistake!

Throughout the corporate world, I found that on the average there are serious flaws in the decision-making mechanisms. That is of course not limited to investment. The decisions in other fields are of no higher quality. The ones about personnel probably are the ones that are the most damaging in the long run. In almost all cases we find that:

- The preparatory homework is not done sufficiently thoroughly.
- In a very early stage, the process becomes personalized. Mr. X (a powerful executive) *wants* this.

- Flexibility and adaptability get lost early in the process and are replaced by a kind of stubborn rigidity.
- In most cases there is no accountability. If anybody is punished in the aftermath, it is mostly an innocent bystander!
- The amount of *real* scrutiny is inversely proportional to the importance of the project.

Especially the last point may raise some eyebrows, but I saw one billion $ projects sail through the board in minutes. I also saw them have fierce debates, lasting for hours about… dress code. The reason for that is simple. What can you say about this enormously complex, enormously expensive high tech venture? Just express your concern and fear will not look too good, especially not in this stage any more. On the other hand, everybody can come to a sound judgement about the bicycle stall, or about dress code for that matter.

One of the problems is that the term "decision" means quite different things to different people.

When we look in a dictionary, we find the following:

- The passing of judgment on an issue under consideration.
- The act of reaching a conclusion or making up one's mind.
- A conclusion or judgment reached or pronounced; a verdict.

That is obviously a very ontological explanation.

If you asked me, I would say:

- A decision is the switch that starts a new project or a considerable course change.

This would probably be a more functional view.

Now ask our power broker. What he will see is:

- *MY* prerogative.
- *MY* instrument to control the world around me.
- The symbol of *MY* status and power.

That is obviously an understanding that has its roots in the mythical, maybe even more the magical world.

Because of the way our enterprises are organized, the latter definition is the most influential one. The rest is history.

How can we get away with this? The fact that everybody is more or less in the same situation *allows* everybody to just live with it. I suspect that in smaller companies, the situation is somewhat better, but that is offset again by the intrinsic advantages of being big.

There is one important thing to remember here. The fact that our own "selection machine" is the enterprise's most fierce competitor, not only for attention, but also for action is at the basis of a lot of these deficiencies. If any large enterprise should ever be able to overcome this handicap, then they will have a formidable competitive advantage.

13 Excellence and Mediocrity

The leadership truly believes to be the selection of the brightest and the best. Are they? As we have already discussed in the chapter about the selection machine, they definitely are not. They are the result of a selection process, crafted and operated by evolution itself. The latter should give them quite a platform to stand on. But they do not claim to be just that. They think of themselves as a kind of intellectual and moral elite. Now that is definitely stretching it too far! They are neither of those things. They lead our enterprises, and do so more or less adequately, but to see an elite here would simply outrageously contradict the facts. Quite contrary, they are neither the smartest, nor the most morally inclined nor the bravest ones. They are what they are: our leadership put into office by evolutionary mechanisms. At face value, they are quite illiterate and corrupt.

The relative illiteracy of our leadership is one of our worst problems. I recently read "The Loyalty Effect"[15], a very intelligent book by Frederick F. Reichheld. It deals with the fact that loyalty between the enterprise and its partners, customers, suppliers, employees and owners, is a generally largely underestimated but quite important factor for the economic success of an enterprise. The book has been published by "Harvard Business School Press". Its intended audience is clearly corporate leadership. The book itself is obvious testimony for the qualifications of the author. It deals very profoundly with the subject, does so in a very sensitive way with a lot of respect and understanding for the reader. Further, it shows that the author must have a vast experience with the American corporate universe.

Now *that* author, with *that* kind of background and experience, deems it necessary to go to great lengths in order to explain something as trivial as the net present value of a sequence of future cash flows! That says something about the author's expectations towards his audience. Given everything we have so far said about the man, we have reasons to fear that his assessment is quite accurate. That casts a devastating judgement over the intellectual abilities of corporate leadership. My own experience unfortunately totally confirms such a pessimistic view. I do of course realize that I owe an apology to the many intelligent, well-educated business leaders that I was fortunate enough to know. But on the other hand, they will be the first to recognize that they cannot tilt the average. There was for instance this one EVP (Executive

Vice President) of a Fortune 100 company. He went to great lengths to hide that he had a Ph.D. in chemical engineering, in spite of the fact that his position and function full well required such a knowledge and education. I once asked him: "Bob, why are you so shy about your Ph.D.? I read your thesis, and I just wished I could have written something that brilliant. If I were able of such a feeling, I would envy you!" The answer was very revealing: "If they knew, they would just classify me as 'one of those egg-heads'. I would never be able to be 'one of the boys'. That would seriously limit my effectiveness." There is not a shred of doubt in my mind that he was right.

The sad truth is: many of our business leaders today have an ego like a supertanker, an intellect like a matchbox, and a conscience like a pinhead. They certainly are clever, even shrewd, but they have a very limited understanding of the world, mainly because they are not particularly *interested* in what we call "the world". Their world is the enterprise, and cleverly dealing with internal competition, internal critics and internal supporters is the name of the game. They will even proclaim the importance of *external focus*, if such a statement is likely to meet an *internal* positive resonance. They are driven by fads and fashions, which they change faster than shirts. They live in their plush quarters, guarded by fire spitting dragons called secretaries, and they shun contact with the real world as much as possible. They have only one paramount concern: their position within the class they belong to. To be or not to be for them means to belong to the leadership, accepted and vested with credibility, or to become an outcast, a nobody. This all-important and illusive "credibility" is a really strange animal and absolutely prone to misunderstanding. Instinctively, we would connote it with things like truth, or repeatedly verified correct predictions. In reality it means nothing of that kind.

When we look it up in the dictionary it is described as follows:

The quality, capability, or power to elicit belief: "America's credibility must not be squandered, especially by its leaders." (Henry A. Kissinger)

This very obviously is something completely different. I saw blatant samples of that. We once had an EVP who was a catastrophic business leader. He must have cost the company at least half a billion $ in terms of very visibly predictable bad decisions. He was a great fan of personal luxury, at the company's expense, and the true caricature of a leader. Of course his favorite topic when delivering his brilliant charismatic speeches was – leadership. I saw him do that in front of the collective upper management of a Fortune 100 company. He loved to bring examples from American history, especially the civil war. A number of times he quite blatantly misrepresented historic reality, just so that it would suit his story. He could get away with that without a trace of worry: his audience simply was too uneducated to ever notice. They just sat there in awe. If I had ever tried to put him on the spot, it would not have mattered: the man was eminently "credible".

Credibility is like an award, given or denied to you by the "old boys". It will be given to those who say the easy, agreeable, soothing things and denied to those who forward statements that are difficult or painful, as essential as these may be for the wellbeing of the company. Which is why "credibility" now has a strange negative connotation for me. It sounds like charlatan or con artist.

The careful observer smells a dense stench of exalted mediocrity everywhere in America's executive suites. Mediocrity is the #1 requirement. Intelligence, conscience, social responsibility, all that must be mediocre before anything else. Only ambition and ego can, in some cases, grow infinitely with impunity. People seem not only to have a tendency to tolerate quite visible excesses in those fields, but even to admire them, and to surround them with endearing myths!

Mediocrity has its own standards and its own vocabulary. You will encounter the word "professional" quite often. It is considered as a compliment but it means: "conform to the expectations." Conformity is the overriding concern in the executive suite. But as there can only be conformity with the majority, it also means mediocrity. That puts "professionalism" right next to "political correctness". Even excessive stupidity is tolerated in the executive suite, if it is sufficiently balanced by political correctness and conformity.

Such excesses like academic brilliance would of course immediately violate the supreme law of mediocrity. Some leaders manage to get by in spite of them, very much like Gorbachev managed to rise through the Soviet ranks, ever careful to conceal their intelligence, ever cautious to hide their considerable knowledge and understanding of the world. But the companies that ultimately wake up to find this kind of people in command are just plain lucky. There is no mechanism that guarantees such an outcome, and it therefore remains the exception.

Mediocrity is an interesting phenomenon. It is much more than just the absence of excellence. It has a life and an identity of its own. It displays extraordinary self-preserving and self-organizing abilities. I saw them at work in a number of enterprises. They lead to what I call "institutionalized mediocrity". There is nothing that mediocrity abhors more than brilliance. Whenever and wherever excellence emerges you see the institutionalized mediocrity mobilize with a vengeance. If you would not know better you could have the impression to see the flawless execution of a well-designed, even rehearsed plan. The whole thing develops with the eerie precision of a fish swarm's movements. Have you ever observed a fish swarm? Have you ever wondered how it is able to change direction as if it were one body? What fish took the initiative, for what reason? How is the intention communicated? To me, this is one of the great wonders of nature. The self-organization that develops with a lightning speed within mediocrity at the faintest smell of excellence shows striking similarities to this and it is not a bit less mysterious. I saw it happen several times, but I am far from pretending that I understand the exact mechanisms. Nevertheless, there seems to be a pattern.

Let's say that this happens in the research environment a big multinational corporation. Big corporations are a quite accurate sample of society. Their inhabitants show in almost every respect exactly the same normal distribution as the general population they emerge from. It is quite reasonable to assume that in such a system, just by coincidence and from time to time, a set of extraordinary capable people will get together. A generally observed uneasiness with the current state of affairs and a wide spread sentiment that things could and should be done better, plus the presence of an inspired leader at the top level are conducive to such an event. Then a new organizational unit is created, and a highly committed leader is picked to run it. The top executive has known him well for a number of years and has absolute confidence in his abilities. The unit leader is in an ideal position. He has been chartered to address the problems in a new way that he fully endorses. He does not inherit a team. He can pick one. He does so with great care and discriminating standards. A lot of the more inspired people within the company have seen since a long time that there was an urgent need for change, and they jump at the occasion. It does not take much convincing to make them join the new team. There is a budget for about 100 professionals, but the leader operates cautiously: quality before anything else. The result is a slowly growing team with qualifications and capabilities that are significantly above the company average. That is not enough to satisfy the leader. He does not just want a new level of competency but also a new level of commitment and cooperation. To that end, he jettisons everything that does not add value or is likely to get in the way. Dress code goes over the side immediately, so do a lot of useless status symbols. Working hours are not regulated. The contribution is important, not the attendance. There is very little hierarchy, and whatever is needed is kept as unobtrusive as possible. The team becomes highly motivated. When you walk past their building, you see lights until very late in the evening. It's not that there is a lot of top down pressure. People are so interested in and captivated by their work that they simply forget to go home at night. First results materialize. They are promising, interesting and intriguing. They also came very, very fast. All this works quite enticingly on the universities with which our unit is setting up cooperations. After a rather short time, we can effortlessly pick the cream of the crop among the alumni. We don't even have to place ads.

This is the moment where the "institutionalized mediocrity" wakes up. They have had an uneasy feeling about this whole thing from the very beginning anyway. First of all, it was unnecessary to create the new unit. If the company had given them the additional head count instead, they would easily have been able to do whatever was necessary. But the deviation of budgets is not the worst insult. Those people are strange! They have no interest in our gossip. They make no attempt whatsoever to find their own place in our pecking order. They are not even interested in the most fundamental bonding. They simply ignore us. They seem obsessed with their work and highly convinced of themselves. We could even call their attitude arrogant. All that could be endured, because of the assumption that this new unit will be short lived. This will go away by itself as so many other novelties top management has sprung on us before. But now the newcomers start to present results, exactly in those areas where we have been wrestling for years. That cannot be real of course. We don't even have to look to be certain of that! If it were that simple, we would have cracked it ourselves years ago. The problem is that top management might buy it. We could become second class citizens forever.

And then they start to talk, or rather gossip. With deep furrows of concern in their brows they mention to the business people the outrageous waste that is ultimately going to be charged out to their cost centers. Do you believe that they had a *party* on company expenses? They are just enjoying themselves *playing* with all their sophisticated toys, they are not even interested in your day to day problems. What good will it do your business when they go give lectures in universities? Do you know that Dr. X never shows up before 10 a.m.? (The fact that Dr. X never leaves before 11 p.m. of course escapes observation.)

There are so many of them all babbling the same messages that this gossip, however stupid, however remote from the truth creates a quite audible murmur throughout the company. Our top-level executive sponsor gets aware of that. When he comes to visit our department, and after being presented with a brilliant solution to a problem that has been bugging him for years, he takes the department head to the side and confesses: "We are in trouble. Your people are too brilliant. The general population is not going to accept that." The mediocrity party steps up its efforts. Their strategy is simple and effective: encircle and asphyxiate. They communicate with the organization much easier than we do, and that is only partly because they have more time. They simply operate on the same wavelength. Old relationships pay off. The pressure increases. The unanimous recognition we get from the outside world rather hurts than helps. Badly outnumbered as we are, we decide not to fight, but to fully concentrate on our job instead. In the end, results are going to be what counts! That's what we think. We are wrong. With all our technical brilliance, we have no clue about the world.

Lightning strikes. Our sponsor leaves the company, and goes play big boss somewhere else. The hallways buzz with whispered innuendoes. Finally, top-management has understood that this creation of that new unit was a very bad move. That was the final cause of disagreement that finished the man. The pressure increases again. The allegations and the mockery become even more perky and primitive than they were to begin with. Mediocrity senses victory to be within reach. They were already very skilled in talking their defeats into victories, now they learn that they can just as easily talk our victories into defeats. However adequate, even brilliant the solutions we develop are, we find less and less people in the company willing to try or even touch them. The majority cannot be wrong.

From now on the question is only what form the inevitable demise will take. There is of course always the option of reorganization. That however could be just a trifle too obvious. There are much more elegant methods. A world scale petrochemical company once had a chemical engineering research lab in the San Francisco bay area that was truly outstanding. Their patents are still benefiting the company, and in the meantime earned many times whatever the operation might have cost. But mediocrity was victorious and the lab had to go. They simply decided to move the operation to Texas. Most people predictably decided not to come along! Problem solved. They were back to normal.

You may have guessed it: it did happen to me. As a matter of fact, I went through this no less than three times in three different countries on two continents!

We can of course not just sit here and lament about all this. We must try to understand.

First of all, in spite of all our disappointment, there may be some aspects we have missed. If a considerable part of society can, without any organization or structure, self-organize and then act out something like a precision choreographed ballet in such an awesome way, it would be absolutely stupid not to suspect a deeper sense. I will try to address this possibility through a couple of questions.

- Mediocrity *is* the majority. Should the majority not have a major say in important decisions?
- Would it be appropriate for a bunch of people sitting on one extreme end of the normal distribution to decide what is good for everybody?
- Is the amazing self-organizing ability displayed by mediocrity possibly one of the defense mechanisms evolution created to protect us from the perils of "big leaps"?
- We know what happened, and that disappoints us, but we do not know the alternative world that would have emerged if things had gone the other way. Would it really and consistently have been a better world?

When you look at it this way, something that started out looking absolutely and abjectly horrible begins to make some sense.

But on the other hand:

- Don't these mechanisms impede improvement and progress quite massively?

And on yet the other hand:

- Who determines what improvement and progress look like?
- Are there objective, defendable criteria for such a choice?

But still:

- Aren't there are a lot of historic examples where, although final proof can never be obtained, it would not be unreasonable to assume that the majority *was wrong* with quite detrimental consequences?
- Would it not be the duty of management to carefully determine where and when we need excellence, then build it and defend it with their lives?

However:

- How could they do this, intertwined in the network of mediocrity as they themselves are?

You see this problem take place between "on one hand" and "on the other hand", which only means that it is part of the core of our life.

We could be disappointed that top management does not take a more courageous and visionary stand on these issues. But then, how should they? After all, they were picked from the general population by a selection machine that does everything to discourage bravery and altruism. They are, in their own way mediocre. The sad truth is that it might even be better that way.

As you can imagine, I never was a very happy inhabitant of the executive quarters. As a matter of fact, I successfully refused to relocate there, I wanted to be close to my people. That in and by itself was another mortal sin, offending the brotherhood. I have no regrets whatsoever. I had only a few friends on the top floor, but as a kind of compensation, they were – and are – very good friends.

14 Courage and Bureaucracy

"Errors are a natural component of every complex system."
John von Neumann

If anything in this world is certain, it is the continuing trend towards increasing complexity around us. This phenomenon alone would have been sufficient for a serious identity crisis. Contemplate the following:

No more than a century ago, the majority of the population worked on farms. They were surrounded by nature, animals and tools they truly and fully "understood" within their still rather mythical context. They "knew" how they could manipulate their environment. Much of their knowledge came in the form of inherited traditional rules. "Never plant vegetables before St. Medardus day." It worked in most cases. Even the scientists dealing with subjects that could not be experienced as directly and intuitively were in a completely different position compared to their contemporary colleagues. A man like Maxwell had a pretty solid overview of the sciences of his time. Nobody today can even dream about that!

Today, we are surrounded by "black boxes". We all, including the few remaining farmers, routinely utilize equipment so sophisticated that we don't even start to understand the scientific principles behind it. One should fear that this would drive us crazy. Thank God for the functional worldview! As long as we understand, more or less, what the equipment does and how we can operate it, we are at peace with it.

The situation does irritate us though. Although we have infinitely more control over our lives and our environment than the farmer of the last century, we do not perceive it that way. For the farmer, unpredictability was an integral and accepted part of nature. For us, unpredictability is a threat. We know that it will generate events that we perceive as "errors" and therefore we fear and abhor it.

How does this play within the enterprise? The amount of complexity and uncertainty around us constantly forces us to take risks. The only way to avoid them is to do absolutely nothing, which in the end will nearly always prove to be the biggest risk of all. Hundreds of books have been written about risk taking and risk management, but we never really came to terms with the problem.

There obviously needs to be a kind of equilibrium between cost and benefit. In many simple situations, this equilibrium is immediately visible, as depicted in Fig. 14.1.

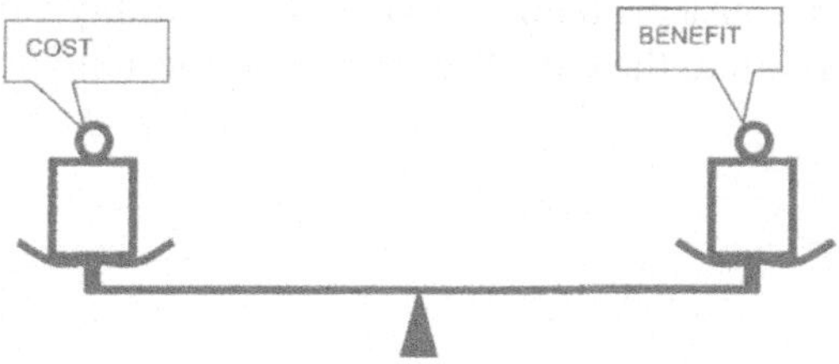

Figure 14.1

It is also immediately visible under what circumstances we would decide for some kind of action: if the scale clearly tips to the benefit side. This is shown in Fig. 14.2.

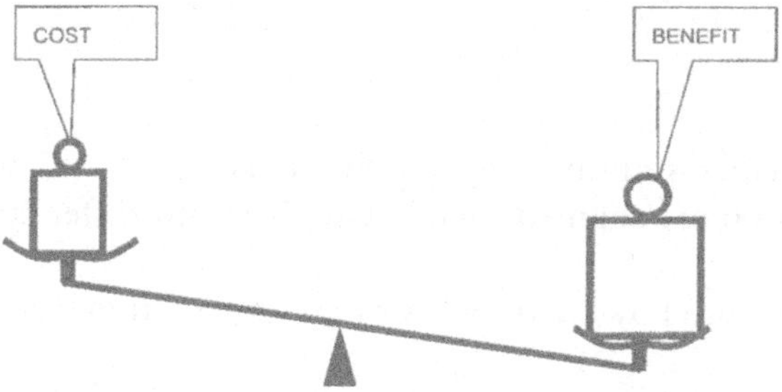

Figure 14.2

But what happens if uncertainty enters on either the cost side or the benefit side?

Let us say that there is a huge benefit *potential*, but it is not quite certain that it will materialize. Let's take this quite impressive benefit in Fig. 14.3.

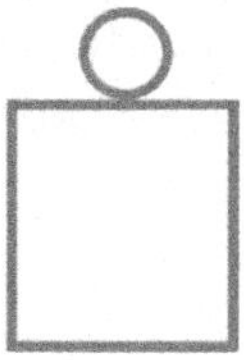

Figure 14.3

Theoretically, there is no problem. Insurance companies have been in business for centuries now, and they have refined the methods needed to judge this kind of situation to the point where further improvement seems almost impossible. As long as you know the probability of all the events involved, you can come to a straightforward and defendable conclusion.

If this huge potential benefit has a 50% probability to occur, we simply cut it in half for the purpose of comparison to the cost. We see the solution in Fig. 14.4.

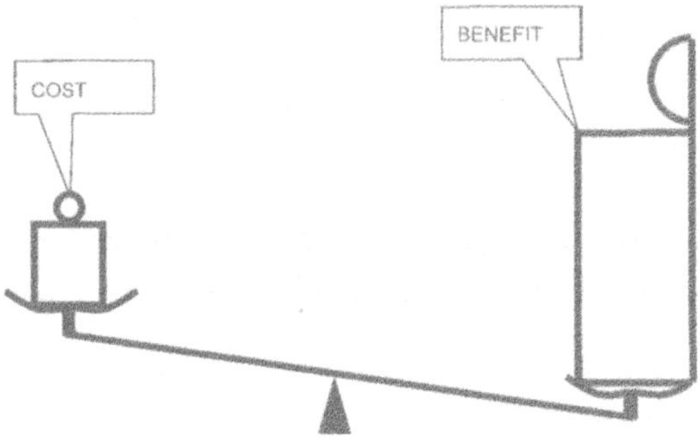

Figure 14.4

You clearly see that our balance still tips over. We should go ahead. What insurance companies do is a bit more sophisticated but not basically different from what I explained before.

By now, you must be pretty bored by the triviality of my explanations, but please bear with me!

From the enterprise's point of view, the situation is really clear. That is why they all will *verbally* encourage risk taking. The problem is that the people that operate the company on different management levels have other concerns than just maneuvering the enterprise into a favorable position. Let us look at our Mr. John Doe, VP (Vice President) with Manufacturing Corporation again. How does he approach this problem? He obviously sees the same picture we do. After all he is not stupid. It's just that he has a couple different and more important concerns. He is on his way up through the hierarchy of the organization, and he will rather be damned than jeopardize his chances. He has already invested too much in his plan to become an Executive VP to even give that possibility as much as a thought!

For Mr. Doe, the important issues are:

- What is the probability that this will work out?

And here stops the last piece of common ground he had with the company. From now on it's all about Mr. Doe:

- How big an achievement will this appear to be?
- How much of the credit am I going to get?
- How much of the blame am I going to get if this fails?
- Last year I had this debacle with Adventure Inc. Mr. X is watching me. If this goes wrong again, I will be perceived as foolhardy.

You can extend this list almost infinitely.

Let's represent Mr. Doe's hopes and fears as little suns and thunderclouds, the difference with the previous weights being that the latter suggest a lot more substance.

First of all, there is the question of credit. It should be BIG, but the company optics are no precision instrument. There are distortions and thus the credit will be artificially shrunk. We see this represented in Fig. 14.5.

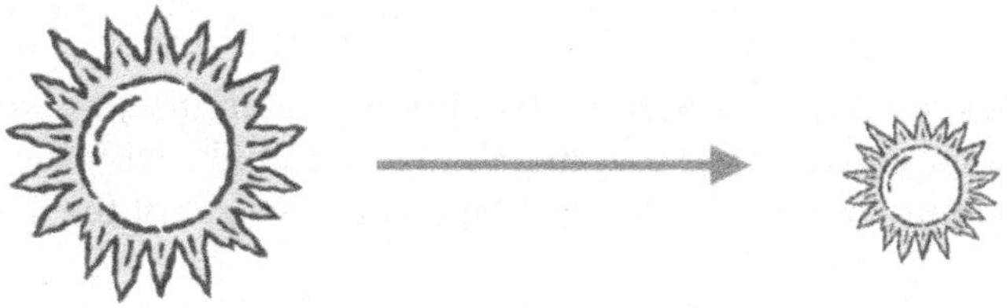

Figure 14.5

Count to that the 50% probability of success, and you get Fig. 14.6.

Figure 14.6

But *if* everything goes just right, Mr. X will claim a share of the credit, which leaves even less for me. That is represented in Fig. 14.7.

Figure 14.7

Something similar, but in the other direction is going to happen with the potential blame. We already observed that the company optics are distorted. Credit is always miniaturized, blame always amplified. We see that in Fig. 14.8. The reason is what the general population would call bad character. We don't grant our fellow men too much!

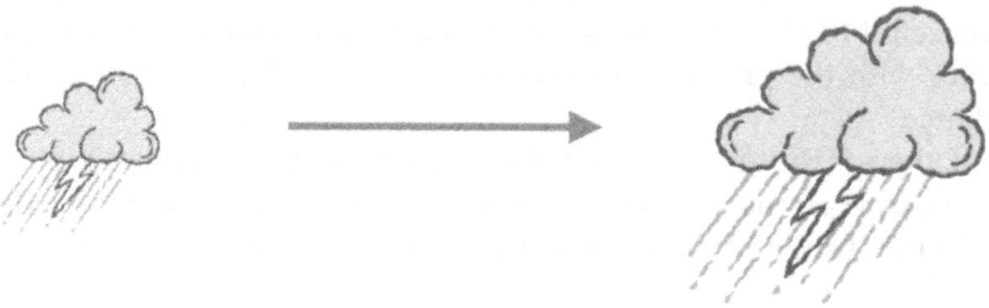

Figure 14.8

Of course, the blame too has only 50% probability to materialize, so we might naïvely believe that we could cut that in half too. But unlike with success, sharing the blame miraculously does not diminish the weight of the individual portions!

Now Mr. Doe is going to see Fig. 14.9.

Figure 14.9

And we have not even added the additional risks of having to brave Mr. X's criticism and the reputation of not being prudent enough! You know how it will end: Mr. Doe is not going to touch this thing. The net result for the company will be a lost opportunity, but there hardly is any penalty to be expected for that.

We mentioned before that our corporate vision is out of whack. One result of that is that we will be much more preoccupied with *not making errors* than with *doing the right thing*. We can hardly blame people for that. In spite of all the slogans an error is always punished much more severely than an equivalent success is rewarded. All our measuring systems show the corresponding aberrations. To stay with our metaphor, our weigh scale is in reality looking like Fig. 14.10.

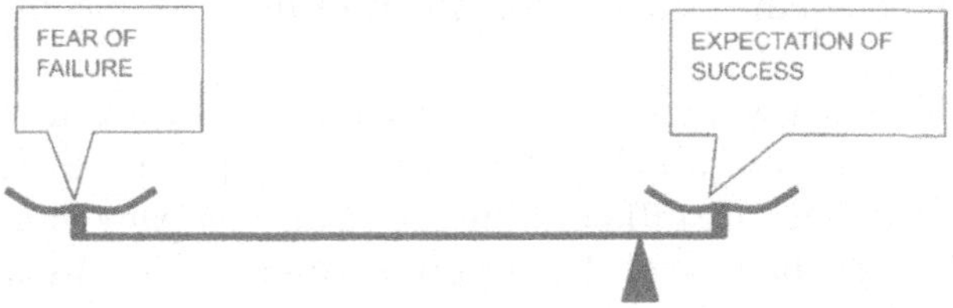

Figure 14.10

You can hardly call this a precision instrument, but that's what is used in our day to day decision making in the enterprise.

All this means that we will go to great lengths in order not to expose ourselves to the risk of making an error. We are willing to put much more effort in this than in our pursuit to do the right thing. Remember: the right thing will only benefit the company, but the consequences of failure will be on our own head. There is however a small problem. What do we need management for, if not to make the judgement calls in questions that are not mechanistically determined? So how does our executive John Doe weasel out of the most important reason for his presence in the company? He tries to mechanize the core portion of his job! The desire to do this is so pervasive among management that the company will launch considerable collective efforts in this direction.

The most blatant example is the performance appraisal. Performance appraisals are a very important instrument, because they influence the quality of our employees, which will be one of our most critical success factors. But this is also a very tricky thing to do. You have to cast a judgement over another human being, and however hard you try, to a certain extend this will remain subjective. Even for the most noble and brave among us, that is a quite frightening thought! You could be terribly wrong, find out after it is too late to correct anything, and have to live with the guilt. John Doe is not too worried about this aspect. He has different concerns. First of all, he has no use for any commotion in this area. If there were any, his boss, Mr. X would get involved and be less than pleased with the distraction. Secondly, employees today are no longer totally defenseless. If push comes to shove, they can go to court, and even without the dreadful prospect of eventually losing the case, that is not a nice experience. But things would not even have to go that far in order to become very unpleasant. Just having to face the feisty Mr. Y and explaining to him the reasons for his not so favorable appraisal is something John Doe is not looking forward to. What will he do now? There is a whole host of possibilities:

- Give everybody about the same rating.
  This is dangerous. If Mr. X notices, there will be one of his temper tantrums. It is almost certain that Mr. Z in Human Resources, who hates his guts, will draw Mr. X's attention to this.

- Go out of his way to ratchet up the rating of potentially difficult people into the no danger zone.
  That is already much better. It will take a fine balancing act but it can be done. To the top performers, from which he has to steal the "points" to do this, he can always say that these are difficult times, that the company must apply more severe standards than usual. Their performance and loyalty in times of need will not be forgotten though!
- Ask help from the Human Resources department.

That is the solution! Throw the hot potato over the fence! If he could just get HR to issue very strict guidelines, almost narrowing his own discretion to zero, he would be totally off the hook. He will go visit the head of HR, deep furrows in his stern face, and explain his concern that this appraisal thing is handled very individually in different parts of the company. A very diverse set of criteria is applied. That opens us up to a whole host of risks. There is an urgent need for some form of standardization. The best thing would be a computer program. If anything went wrong with that, he could always blame IT and that is a very popular standpoint. It may be too late for this year, but for the time being he can get by with the previously mentioned approach.

In most cases, the HR people will take the bait. They have been so frustrated for so long by now, that any chance at a spark of visibility becomes irresistible. Pretty soon the appraisal process is totally mechanized, highly reproducible and, if needed, defendable in front of a court. In the course of events it has lost something: relevance to the value of the subject employee for the company. But then, everything has its price!

The next thing to happen is that Mr. Doe will give a well-received presentation in the upper management meeting. The title: "Increasing bureaucracy – a concern for all of us!"

You see what is going on here. As soon as our leaders lose the courage to stand up in front of anybody, be it top management or a court, and say: "This was my decision. I took it after a great deal of deliberation and I assume full responsibility for it," a cataclysmic void opens that bureaucracy is all too willing to fill. This is not restricted to appraisals. It happens in all kinds of decision situations, e.g., about

- hiring
- firing
- investment
- projects
- changes in budget or plan.

Those are only a couple of examples.

Unfortunately, courage is one of the properties that are weeded out radically by the selection machine. Courage means exposing yourself, while having the opportunity to dodge. You just do that often enough and you will be hurt, statistics will take care of that. The supreme wisdom of the selection machine environment *requires* ducking instead of bravely standing up. Consequently our top management's courage is well below that of the average citizen. That again makes silly, resource consuming, decision deteriorating bureaucracy quite inevitable.

15 Pleasing the Stock Market

Today's fad is shareholder value. But why do I call it a fad? Isn't it important?

Shareholders are our *owners*. The only reason they give us their money is their expectation that we will provide them with a higher and/or more secure return on their investment than the zillion alternative opportunities they see in front of them. It would not be a good thing to consistently disappoint them. It would be neither morally justifiable nor wise. It would not even be clever. It would not really benefit the other stakeholders, suppliers, customers and employees either.

The contemporary totally myopic focus on the shareholder however ignores the fact that the enterprise is a fairly complex value-generating machine, with many groups of stakeholders. We never seem to be able to come to terms with the holistic nature of the thing as we here see it in Fig. 15.1.

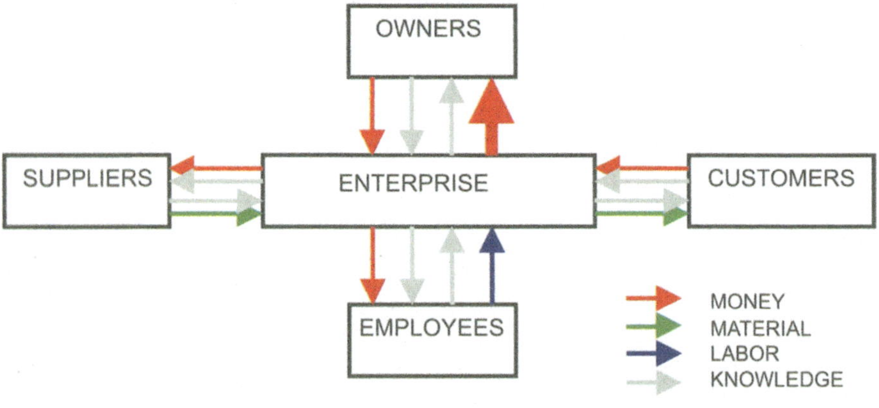

Figure 15.1

In the course of my career, I saw the focus shift. I experienced periods where all of the attention went to the employees. Then the customer was discovered as the center of the universe. Now shareholder value is all that counts. The suppliers will have their turn, too. There is a lot of talk today about supply chain alliances and such.

The truth is of course that our value-generating machine can only exist by the grace of symbiosis, cooperation and mutual understanding between the different stakeholder groups. Focusing on any one single group is wrong, must be wrong! That is a somewhat difficult concept for the following reason. If you shrink your time perspective to let us say one day, the thing is basically a zero sum game. One can only spend a dollar once, so ... every penny you give to one of the stakeholders has to come from the other three. Does a time perspective of one day sound ridiculous? Look at the trends around you. Everything points to a faster pace and ever shrinking time constants. Quite soon, with Internet trading and shrinking fees, it will be very well possible to hold shares for just one day *for everybody*. The Wall Street trading floor is going to expand worldwide!

In the contemporary context it is thus quite understandable that the captains of industry succumb to the temptation to take sides, and mainly foster the interests of one of the groups, for the time being the shareholders. The problem is that this is not good for anything, and in the end, over a longer period of time, nobody is going to benefit from this, the shareholders as little as anybody else.

I strongly believe that industry is *not* a zero sum game, and that in the end either all or nobody will benefit. It is of course top management's duty to make sure that the former happens. I also strongly believe that for such a beneficial situation to emerge, a balanced treatment of all the stakeholder groups is of essence.

Let me formulate a number of questions here:

- What kind of shareholder do we need and want?
- Are we willing to go the extra mile to keep that particular one?
- What kind of shareholder are we willing to deter?
- How do we manage our shareholders' expectations?
- How do we tell them where the limits are?

In the contemporary context, these questions must sound truly ridiculous, like the bad dream of a European socialist. But wait a minute. We constantly ask these questions about all the other stakeholders, or don't we?

The problem is that there are shareholders and shareholders and then, there are analysts. Just like there are employees and employees and then ... trade unions. Let's try to classify our shareholders in two opposite types: A and B.

15.1 Shareholder Type A

She most likely is a housewife. Many years ago, she has started to prepare for old age. It actually was her husband's idea. He said that he had this business that he hoped and believed to become successful, but one just never knows, and he would feel a lot more secure if she had some funds of her own. She bought the first couple of our shares 40 years ago. She did not need an analyst to pick us. From her kitchen window, she could see our smokestacks, thick black billowing clouds of less than healthy exhaust. In those days however, that was not yet a problem. It rather was a symbol of prosperity. The image we projected was one of strength and stability. Nothing could destroy us. We would certainly survive her. That was the whole point. For her first 5 shares she paid $20 a piece. At the end of the year, we offered a dividend of $6, a meager 6%. We failed to disappoint her; it was still more than the government owned Post would give on a savings account. She bought 10 additional shares. With time our dividend went up. That was nice. But also the share price went up, keeping the return on the magic 6%. She religiously did not only reinvest her earnings, but also her additional savings. The fact that our share became more expensive from year to year rather irritated her. She had to pay more for her additional shares from year to year. But on the other hand, she also got more dividends and she found out that this more or less balanced. Then Aunt Wilma died, and left her a quite handsome amount of cash. She immediately invested it in our stock. The bill amounted to an appalling $100 per share, but considering that last year we gave her $8 for everyone of them made it look quite reasonable. When she calculated the total value of her holdings she was pleased and almost started to feel rich. When she looked out of her kitchen window, she could still see our plant. The smokestacks were gone. All that we emitted was a plume of snow-white steam left and right. But for her, the picture radiated still the same old confidence. It was about that time that she religiously started to study our annual reports. She worried with us and she hoped with us.

Today, she is in a nursing home. One could call her a wealthy widow. Our share is quoted at $250. But our dividend last year was a meager $12. Her grandson believes that to be totally inadequate and urges her to sell and reinvest in some Internet stocks. Those show of course an even more miserable earnings to price ratio, but as opposed to our share, they are supposed to skyrocket in the near future. His grandma just smiles; she knows better. She believes that $12 per year for shares that she originally bought for $20 is quite a performance. We made her wealthy and she will never abandon us. She is, of course, just as mistaken as her grandson!

15.2 Shareholder Type B

You cannot really call him bright, but he certainly is aggressive. "Hey man, the money will not come running to you, one has to go after it!" That's about the highest level of intellectual sophistication you will get from him. He never heard about the tulip onion drama that happened in 17th century Holland. He would not know what to think about the theory of "the greatest fool", although he is a prime candidate for the position. He never cares about dividends. It is of absolutely no importance that he grossly overpays our shares, because he just believes that tomorrow, another fool will pay even more for them, and then he will be out with a nice profit. He knows nothing about our company. He picked our stock because a Wall Street analyst recommended it. He found out via the Internet. The analyst projects a $9 billion profit in the year 2000. The fact that I, a senior executive, do not remotely know where such a profit could come from would not disturb him even if he had that piece of information, but of course, he doesn't. Wall Street analysts are infinitely smart and credible. I am obviously not. The fact that even if such a profit would miraculously emerge, his shares would certainly not earn the same return he could get from a profane CD (Certificate of Deposit), does not seem to be a problem either. He is not particularly interested in our dividends. Granted, our result *may* influence our stock price, but so will a report from some analyst. He just wants to ride the stock market wave and sell with a profit. He is going to watch us closely. Or that's maybe the wrong statement. He is going to watch *the stock market's opinion about us* very closely. The only thing he is really interested in is his money, for the time being sunk in our stock. At the least sign of discomfort he will sell, and so will thousands of others. For shareholder B, the stock market comes close to a miracle. It is a machine that creates money, wealth – more specifically *his* money and *his* wealth – from nothing. It is nothing less than the medieval dream of making gold coming true. He too is badly mistaken!

While I could probably find some practical life examples for both types, they still represent the rare extremes of the spectrum. Real investors exist somewhere between them.

15.3 Polarization

The polarization is obvious:

- For shareholder type A, owning our stock is a higher form of saving. You only need to pick a good performer, become an owner and stay that way.
- For shareholder type B, playing the stock market is very much like the horse racetrack. You only need to have some insider knowledge, so that you can outsmart all the others playing the same game.
- Shareholder A feels very much connected to our enterprise.
- Shareholder B could not care less.
- Shareholder A will keep our shares for a lifetime. She would have emotional problems parting from them. She just hopes and prays – in vain – that her grandson will do the same after inheriting her estate.

- Shareholder B will probably not hang on to our stock for more than a year. In the mean time some new "hot" tidbit of information will make him focus on a different enterprise.
- Shareholder A judges us by our dividend as it evolves over the years, and by nothing but that. That's how she expects to make money *in the long run*.
- Shareholder B judges us by our stock price right now, and by nothing but that. That's how he expects to make money *today*. His whole attitude reminds me of a hippie slogan I saw painted on a wall in Matalla on Crete: "Life is today! Tomorrow never comes."

But the concerns of our two extreme types of shareholders are not totally unconnected:

- A high dividend, shareholder A's biggest concern, will also ratchet the stock price up. So that's good for B as well.
- An excessive increase in the cost of our share will greatly please shareholder B. Shareholder A, while reinvesting will feel that she has to pay more and more for the same chunk of our enterprise. She will not like the fact that her return is going down.

Institutional investors represent a large number of shareholders. Interestingly enough, without really owning a dime of our company, they exercise more influence than any single shareholder. Their behavior will necessarily fit somewhere between A and B. There is in fact a broad spectrum. Pension funds will usually take a more conservative posture, much closer to our shareholder type A, although they will never develop anything that even resembles loyalty. "Aggressive Growth Funds" will be closer to our shareholder B, although they will operate on the basis of much better information and more thorough analysis.

And then, there are of course analysts. Now there are analysts and analysts, and some of them are absolutely conscientious people that just try to understand how our company ticks, in order to be in a position to give intelligent recommendations to our potential shareholders. But there are others as well and they all have one thing in common: the need to be noticed, to make a big splash. It suffices to read the prose generated by the Wall Street gurus to understand what I mean. It reminds me of my childhood. Every once in a while, as a reward, I could accompany my mother to the market in our village. There was this one guy who sold shoe polish. He not only managed to scream louder than all other salesmen, he also somehow made shoe polish – more specifically *his* shoe polish – appear spectacular. The loudness of it all is only outdone by the shallowness of the thoughts behind it. As an example, on May 19, 1999 Dell took a beating. They had committed the crime to come in with fiscal first quarter earnings of only 16 cents a share. They fell 4 5/16 to 39 3/4. Now watch the explanation.

The world's biggest direct seller of personal computers reported fiscal first-quarter earnings of 16 cents a share after the market's close yesterday. While that matched analysts' estimates, some analysts had predicted Dell would rebound from last quarter's slowdown in sales growth with earnings as high as 18 cents a share.

"Dell's revenue was a little bit light compared to expectations," said XXX, the head of U.S. equity research at YYY in Geneva. "We prefer to see companies beating estimates."

That's a real profound comment, isn't it?

And then there is a minor detail: 16 cents per share at today's price amounts to a 1.6 % annual rate. 18 cents at yesterday's price would have meant about the same thing. Even if Dell managed to triple their profit – and how should they do such thing? – that would still yield less than a CD! Nobody seems to get nervous about that. The world is measured against analysts' expectations, and nothing else. This is big time speculation, and the only thing it can do is catastrophically fail. But maybe in that light Mr. XXX's comment is not all that shallow and stupid after all. Once we have totally surrendered to the idea that this is all about appearance and expectation and about nothing but that, it starts to make an eerie kind of sense.

Normality – as much as shareholder A appreciates it – is not a rewarding subject. It does not produce the limelight you need in order to become one of the real BIG gurus. Further, shareholder B loves the spectacular. He makes his money only if somebody is rocking the boat. Analysts not only have the ability to rock the boat, they are also keenly aware of the fact that the center of gravity of shareholder behavior is shifting rapidly towards B. They can effortlessly hype a share up by heralding exuberant profit expectations, and then hype it down again when these expectations are – quite predictably – not met. If our Mr. B pays sufficient attention to this game, he makes a ton of money in the cycle, much more than Mrs. A in many years!

The clearly observable trend towards B behavior is not the only destabilizing factor in the system. Internet trading will do its worst to aggravate the situation. Not only will it dramatically shorten the time constants of the system, thereby fostering even greater volatility and wild exaggeration, it will also admit a high number of poorly informed players to the game. The latter will totally depend on information from third parties and that will further increase the influence of a new breed of analyst. I mentioned with some contempt that for shareholder B his involvement with the stock market resembles betting on racehorses. For our cyber-shareholder it will be like a video game! Bang bang bang ..., but it's not the alien space ship that explodes, it's a real life company with *people* in it for God's sake!

15.4 What Should Our Poor CEO Do About All This?

There are a number of considerations here.

If our share price became unreasonably low, a corporate raider could appear and just buy us. The risk for something like that to happen would considerably increase if we had prudently stashed away substantial reserves for a rainy day. The first thing the raider would do is of course fire the whole board – and that would include the CEO – and replace it by his own loyal ones. He might do a lot of other outrageous things after that, like ripping the company into pieces and selling the parts. Of course nothing of all this could be remotely as horrible as firing the CEO of Manufacturing Corp.

If we need additional capital and we want to emit more shares, a high share price is going to generate more money. That's what we are going to tell shareholder A: "Listen, somebody pays $300 to match the share you once bought for $20. We are going to invest those $300 and generate a profit that he and you will evenly split. Not a bad deal for you, is it?" Of course, should we ever get into a situation where we have more money than good ideas, and believe me, that happens nowadays, this reasoning would be totally invalid. But who is ever going to admit such a sorry state of affairs?

An excessively high share price will severely diminish the return on investment for our new shareholders, no matter how hard we work to optimize our profit. One would hope that then free market mechanisms would kick in and gently regulate the price to the appropriate level. Alas, that is not how the stock market ticks. Torn as they are between greed and fear, especially our fast growing lot of type B stockholders will have a fatal tendency to overreact. When they get concerned, they will hardly stage a retreat, much rather a full-scale flight. I saw instances where a company was struck by adverse circumstances like a lost lawsuit. If you calculated the net effect on profit, and converted that to share value on a constant return level, a decrease in value of $1.5 per share seemed appropriate. But the shares fell $20! The stabilizing factor in this game is stockholder A, but she is shied away by poor returns. Thus stockholder B behavior becomes the dominant force.

And then there is something else: stock options. Our poor harassed CEO has some genuine self-interest here. With my unlimited faith in his unwavering moral integrity, I would never suspect him of doing anything bad to the company out of self-interest, but more cynical people might see that differently. Recently there has been some criticism towards the outrageous compensations CEO's rake in nowadays. Such criticism inflames especially if he receives in a given year an amount larger than the loss he made with the company he is leading. Ill feelings about such a thing can only come from shareholder A.

The existing system is totally aligned with shareholder B's interests. It will therefore not change.

If you were Manufacturing Corp.'s CEO, what would you do? You have several options:

1. You could totally commit to shareholder A's interests.

What does this mean?

- Assemble a powerful team. What you are going to attempt is too big for one man.
- Work your assets to the maximum. Focus on long-term sustainable profit, which will translate in the only thing A is after: dividend.
- Do not waste your time talking to analysts. If they try to contact you, send them a copy of our annual report.
- Cancel all press conferences.
- Go visit your customers instead.
- Decline to give interviews. You might make an occasional exception for the newsletter of the local boy scouts.
- Serve nicer meals at the annual shareholder's meeting.
- Buy a nice bouquet of flowers and go visit Mrs. A.
- Strengthen research.
- Focus on expanding business with the existing workforce.
- Show up on the factory floor – often.
- Renegotiate your deal. Reject stock options. Try to get, on top of a very basic salary, a decent percentage of the average profit the company makes over the next five years. Further, have a pension plan tied to the profit the company makes in the three years prior to your retirement.
- Implement similar compensation structures for all management personnel of Manufacturing Corp.
- Insure yourself. Negotiate a succulent golden parachute. Unfortunately, you will need it.
- Go for it.

Where will this lead?
First of all: you are my hero. But that doesn't buy you much.

- The analysts will be the first to notice. They will be shocked. They are accustomed to see big ego CEO's practically cower in front of them. You however don't seem to take them seriously. Their vanity will be hurt. The mildest punishment you can expect from them is that they are going to ignore us. But we probably will not get that lucky. They have subtle ways to hurt us: a little condescending remark here, a couple of whispered rumors there and soon our "credibility" suffers.

- The next one who will notice is shareholder B. He pays a lot of attention to the remarks, however casual, the guru's make. He now considers us a hot potato and sells our shares immediately. The problem is that there are a lot of shareholders B. Our stock quotation will suffer. It will lag behind the general market if it does not slide down right away.

While the previous effects materialize almost immediately, the beneficiaries of our new policies will need a lot of time to realize what is happening and to understand that it is good for them:

- shareholder A
- our employees
- our customers
- our suppliers.

They will first of all be confused and suspicious. It will take them a year, maybe more to muster the insight and courage to come over to our side and strongly support us. On the other side, the mobilization of our opponents is swift and strong.

At the shareholders' assembly the still remaining bunch of type B shareholders raises all kinds of hell. They will try to elect another board. They threaten with a class action suit against us for deliberately and willfully having inflicted losses on them. They announce that they have opened discussions with Mr. X, a notorious corporate raider. If only Mrs. A were there to come to our defense. But that's another problem: A types seldom show up in the general assembly.

From here, various different outcomes are possible:

- We may be able to fend off the attack. If we had secured the support of a strong block of type A shareholders, that possibility exists. The defeated B shareholders might decide to wait and see. We then would have the opportunity to shape Manufacturing Corp. into a really great company with a sustained strong profit, loyal stakeholders and potent innovation capability. In the end everybody would benefit, also the B shareholders if they stayed long enough.
- More likely, the revolution will succeed. A new board and a new CEO will be appointed. They will initiate a drastic course change and totally focus on their type B clientele. A regime as described under number two will emerge.
- Equally probable, the defeated B shareholders will desert en masse. The stock price will slide even lower. A hostile take-over is the next step.

In the last two cases, you will need your golden parachute. Bon voyage!

2. But you could of course also take the other extreme and totally commit to shareholder B.

What does this mean?

- Don't get too preoccupied with your management team. This is very much a one-man show anyway. You will need some serfs to prepare your slides and stuff. Pay attention to their artistic abilities.
- Totally focus on the share price (as opposed to share value). This will translate in the only thing B is after: short-term profit.
- Do not waste your time talking to employees, customers or suppliers. If they try to contact you, send them a copy of our annual report.
- Schedule regular press conferences at nice places. Make sure that you always break some spectacular news:
  - A restructuring program eliminating 3000 jobs.
  - A new product line (the name cannot be flashy enough).
  - A big new contract.
  - A new marketing concept.
  - A possible merger with gigantic synergy potential.
  - Medium term profit expectations.

  In fact, anything goes, as long as it is spectacular, colorful and loud.
- Schedule regular information briefings with the most important analysts, combined with golf. The Greenbrier would not be a bad choice. Approach analysts respectfully, always with a humble posture. Study their scientific backgrounds, beliefs and habits, so that you can tell them things that they subconsciously recognize as their own take on the world. This will also enable you to present your facts and figures in a format condoning their habitual methodology. That will make you all the more credible.
- Give as many interviews as possible. Whenever Manufacturing Corp.'s and of course your own name appear in the media in a not completely negative context, that is a good thing. The main issue is not to be forgotten or ignored.
- Hire a competent coach to work on your dramatic performance on stage. Everything is important: voice, facial expression and body language need to be refined in order to maximize the effect you have on your audience.
- Identify a senior executive that does not completely agree with your viewpoints. Fire him in a swift and dramatic action. Hold a press conference to announce his departure. This will give you an opportunity to portray yourself as a strong, hard driving hard-hitting executive.
- Drastically downsize research. Research is about tomorrow. Life is today.
- As a matter of fact, downsize everything that is conducive to reduction.
- Never waste time on the factory floor. Those people are not important for the outcome of your battle.
- Renegotiate your deal. Request stock options. Try to get, on top of a very basic salary, *really big* stock options that mature in two, maximum three years. Further, pay attention to possibilities like re-pricing, but I don't have to tell you about that.

- Implement similar compensation structures for all management personnel of Manufacturing Corp.
- Insure yourself. Negotiate a succulent golden parachute. We both know that you are not in it for the long haul.
- Go for it.

Where will this lead?
First of all: in spite of some contempt, I do not really hate you. After all, you are just an average guy.

- The analysts will be the first to notice. They will be elated. They love to be courted by big ego CEO's. You seem to take them very seriously. Their vanity will be duly caressed. The least reward you can expect from them is that they are going to pay a lot of attention to us and to you personally. But we probably will even get luckier. They have subtle ways to help us; a little endorsing remark here, a couple of whispered rumors there and soon our "credibility" skyrockets.
- The next one who will notice is shareholder B. He pays a lot of attention to the remarks, however casual, the guru's make. He now considers us a hot commodity and immediately buys more shares. The beauty is that there are a lot of shareholders B. Our stock quotation will strengthen. It will at least keep up with the general market if it does not outperform the competition right away.

While the previous effects materialize almost immediately, the victims of our new policies will need a lot of time to realize what is happening and to understand that it is threatening them:

- shareholder A
- our employees
- our customers
- our suppliers.

They will first of all be confused and suspicious. It will take them a year, maybe more to muster the insight and courage to come to some kind of an organized resistance. But even then, they will be hopelessly fragmented. On the other side, the mobilization of our supporters is swift and strong.

Our profits start to go south. That is easily enough explained. We had to take an extraordinary charge because of our restructuring plan. Only Mrs. A starts to worry.

At the shareholders assembly you do of course seize the opportunity to make a couple more of your patented strong statements and you receive a roaring standing ovation. If Mrs. A were there, she might have some critical remarks, but nothing to fear: A-types seldom show up in the general assembly. The board is confirmed.

Our restructuring plan does not produce the results we promised. Our profits do not improve. But then: does that ever happen? We have to launch a serious diversionary maneuver. Starting to work on a substantial merger, acquisition or divestiture would be a solution.

From here, various different outcomes are possible:

- This just merrily goes on for another year. Nothing to worry: you cash in on your stock options.
- More likely, your extreme popularity with the analysts and the press will lead to a situation where Gargantuan Corp., the market leader in your field with a revenue 5 times bigger than Manufacturing Corp., offers you their CEO position. You accept, because this comes with even more succulent stock options. You are going to do exactly the same there. The only problem is not to get stuck for five years!
- For some strange reason, you don't get away. After a couple of years, the damage you have done starts to surface. You have indeed permanently debilitated Manufacturing Corp.'s earning potential. Your glorious predictions do not materialize. The analysts start to ask critical questions, cautiously at first, then ever more assertive. The recommendation about our share goes from "buy" via "hold" to "sell". Your most ardent supporters, the B-shareholders, start to feel confused and insecure. They only have one way to express their doubts: dump our shares! The stock price suffers. They let you get away with the destruction of the company's profit capability, but this is a cardinal sin! All this will take time, several years in fact, but sooner or later you too will face a hostile shareholders assembly. Don't sweat it! That's what golden parachutes are made for. Bon voyage!

The two approaches we presented are as extreme as opposite. You will very seldom find them in their pure form, although even that does occur every once in a while. Real life happens somewhere between them. It is nevertheless useful to look at them. If you wanted to study a complex mixture, you would also begin with isolating and crystallizing the components.

There are interesting differences.

A casual observer may believe that the two extremes show some kind of symmetry, that they are perfect opposites. That is not the case!

The first approach has a very slim chance to succeed, but if, against all odds, it does, everybody wins. If it fails, it did not do damage to anybody while it was still afloat. During its demise, there will be damage, but that is then basically due to the transition to the second approach.

The second approach will most likely work. The question is only how we define success. If we agree that the objective is to make the CEO pretty rich pretty fast, success is almost certain. But the CEO is going to be the *only one* taking some benefit away. All other stakeholders are going to lose. One might be tempted to believe that this is not true, because those among our B-class shareholders that were smart enough to jump ship in time took away a substantial profit. While that is true, one has to factor in that they basically took the money from *other* B-shareholders that just speculated on the wrong side, not even to mention Mrs. A who is going to be hurt by substantially lower dividends. As a total class, the shareholders lose as much as all other stakeholders.

The biggest loss of symmetry is in the sequence. It makes a huge difference, which one of the approaches comes first.

If the first approach fails after an extended period of time, and is then succeeded by the second approach, the two complement each other really nicely. The first approach creates the ideal boundary conditions for the second one to succeed easily. If the order were reversed, things look completely different. The second approach ruins everything that the first approach needs to succeed. While the first approach is always an uphill battle with poor odds, if one has to do this after a period of second approach it becomes near to impossible.

Now watch our real life average CEO. He is neither a saint nor a complete scoundrel. He is no hero, but also no total coward. He is smart, clever even shrewd. He has a natural talent to manipulate people. He has an above average interest in and talent for self-preservation. He is a deal-maker, a compromise artist. He abhors extremes. He will almost certainly select a course between the two approaches. Some will be more inclined to the first approach, others to the second. The distribution shifts with the social context and the latter changes in time.

Today, we see a clear bias towards the second approach.

The increasing number of B-type investors, lower time constants and higher volatility in the stock market, induced by technology, will further drive the center of gravity to the second approach. All this is quite inevitable.

The only thing I can say is: "Fasten seat belts, and did you check your insurance lately?"

16 The Almighty Bonus

We now have the leadership that the selection machine produced for us. It is deeply hierarchically stacked, but otherwise astonishingly uniform. No illusions, no altruism no idealism. Just stone hard pragmatism with a powerful shot of selfishness. And of course the ability to superficially appear totally different: responsible, compassionate, dedicated and so on. The problem is how to mobilize and unite this bunch of self-centered maniacs behind the objectives of the enterprise. We believe to have the answer: the almighty bonus.

The ideology behind this is truly simple. We know that idealism, loyalty and altruism don't exist. The only way to make thousands of egocentric individuals act with the desired common goal and purpose is to arrange things in such a way that the goals of the enterprise and their own selfish expectations coincide. A miraculous tool called "management by objectives" achieves this. It works as follows. First, we define the objectives we want to achieve next year as a company. We gradually pare this down according to the hierarchy in ever smaller and more detailed packages. The objectives must preferably be quantitatively measurable in order to limit arguments at review time. Finally, every person in management has his own personal package of goals for the coming year. All we need to do further is to tie a substantial part of that individual's income to his achievements towards these objectives. The higher up in the hierarchy, the higher the "variable income" – or bonus – portion of the total revenue is going to be. We will skip the mechanics here, because they are not essential for the point I want to make. We now have achieved something quite remarkable. We have eliminated the need for altruism. In future, we can do without it. Whatever is good for our VP John Doe is also good for Manufacturing Corp. In that way all of John Doe's quite substantial selfish energy will be directed towards the good of the company.

But there are a couple of problems. Don't you have a strange déjà vu feeling? Didn't we have this saying: "What is good for General Motors is also good for the United States"? Did we buy that one?

16.1 Problems

It is indeed far from certain that the result of Mr. Doe's ardent attempts to optimize his personal income will make a contribution to the maximization of Manufacturing Corporation's profitability. There are serious problems of time and scale.

We will address scale first.

Let's say that I am a plumber, and I have one employee: Bob. I promise Bob that as a bonus on top of his salary, I will give him 10% of the after tax profit we make in the next year. How is that going to influence my employee's behavior? Quite obviously, he is going to try to maximize profit. He will try to be frugal with material and get as much work done as possible. The question is whether this will be unequivocally good for Gerard's Plumbing Services. If Bob sees his future with my little company only short term, he might focus too much on short term profit maximizing. He may cut corners in the quality area and by doing that erode our customer base. Even if he wants to stay for many more years to come, he may misjudge the interrelationships of the many parameters that determine the success of our plumbing shop. But other than that, there will be a quite nice congruence between his goals and mine. In this case, the bonus will work.

The possibility that our employee may misjudge the interrelationships between the elements of the game deserves some closer attention, because we know that there is a kind of inherent opaqueness in complex systems and it matters! We know this kind of problem from statistics.

Let us say that we have a quantity F that we want to optimize. F could be profit, return on investment, DCF (discounted cash flow) rate or whatever else we select. We also know – or believe to know – that F depends on n parameters X_1 through X_n. The real interesting information would be *how* this dependency works quantitatively. What many people will do in a situation like that is the following.

Move X_1 through number of values while keeping all other X's constant.

Register what this does to F.

Repeat the procedure with X_2 through n.

This allows you to determine the coefficients $a_1, \dots, a_n$ so that

$$F = a_1 \cdot X_1 + a_2 \cdot X_2 + \dots + a_n \cdot X_n \tag{1}$$

We are happy. We can now quantitatively control F. Well that might be the case, but only if reality had the courtesy to exactly behave as modeled by equation (1). All the X's are independent from each other. You can change any single one without influencing the others.

The problem is that reality almost never behaves like this. Let's take objects like inventory and customer satisfaction. Inventory has a negative impact on our profit. Customer satisfaction obviously will have a positive one. *But the two are not independent.* They clearly interact by something we could call "order fulfillment capability"! Using the method described above, we are not going to see the interactions at all, and ignoring them can do just anything to our model, from making it unreliable to even totally wrong.

So, equation (2) is probably a better model:

$$F = a_1 \cdot X_1 + a_2 \cdot X_2 + \ldots + a_n \cdot X_n + a_{1,2} \cdot X_1 \cdot X_2 + \ldots + a_{n-1,n} \cdot X_{n-1} \cdot X_n \quad (2)$$

There are ways to find the coefficients in this case, too. But who guarantees us that this is the right representation? There might be higher order interactions involved.

The more complex the enterprise, the more complicated these things get. I would not expect any Fortune 100 company to have an even remotely accurate quantitative model.

Luckily for John Doe, our Vice President in Manufacturing Corporation, his world is a whole lot simpler. His bonus is going to be determined by something like equation (1), and being an honors graduate of the selection machine, he doesn't particularly care about anything else. Manipulating equation (1) will be difficult enough as such.

Look what we now have. We have about 1000 equations like (1) that are going to be the driving force behind our enterprise. Not only that there is no guarantee that the result will be a move towards the company's optimum, the odds are that we will move in the opposite direction. Why that?

16.2 The Definition Problem

The way objectives are defined is our first pitfall. Due to the connection between bonus and objectives, the latter are losing their content. Normally "objective" would mean the definition of where I want to go or what I will try to attain. In this context, it means fixing a number so that I can maximize my bonus. There are a number of techniques I saw deployed.

16.2.1 Sandbagging

Let's assume that my net cash flow is the target. I expect that my business group can do 100 million this year. I try to get 80 in my objectives. I can probably get away with that, because last year I made 75. If things go as planned, I will *exceed* my objectives by 25% and that will translate in a nice amount of money. Unfortunately, I cannot have discrepancies between my objectives and the business plan, so the latter will also be based on my knowingly wrong number. That will have quite some adverse effects. The CFO (Chief Financial

Officer) for instance might now feel compelled to borrow the missing 20 million $. We might miss opportunities for additional discounts on our long-term purchasing contracts. We may have to rush in additional production and storage capacity at higher than necessary prices.

16.2.2 Calling It a Different Name

We are in one of these phases where the main focus is on reducing head count. I promise a stiff reduction. My boss is going to like that, because he can add this up to what he is going to write into his proposed objectives. I also have a workable plan to carry this out. I identify parts of my activity that can be subcontracted to third parties. I have contracts signed to that effect. I then lay off the 30 people that used to perform these tasks. This is going to enhance my bonus quite substantially. Unfortunately, the out-sourced activity does not come any cheaper. The severance we have to pay to our employees is thus a net minus. And we don't even start to think about the less tangible damage I did to morale.

Obviously, neither of these examples will benefit the company. The contrary will happen. But my bonus is looking good! These are only two rather superficial scenarios. In reality we often see much more sophisticated schemes.

16.2.3 Negotiations with Our Own Company

I can artificially inflate my net cash flow in a number of ways. Let us say that I am making and selling product A. My main raw material is product B, produced by a different division of our company. If I drop my price, I can increase my volume. If I now can put sufficient pressure on my colleague who produces B, so that the transfer price for B is lowered to the point where my per pound margin for A remains constant, I come out a winner! There will be a price. Net cash flow for Manufacturing Corporation is almost certain to decrease. But as long as I have the benefit and the company pays the price, I can live with that.

16.2.4 Excessive Bickering About Allocations

In almost every corporation the cost incurred by the functional units is allocated to the businesses. This is an eternal bone of contention. Monstrous amounts of energy, attention and time are spent on this subject. Ever more complicated keys, increasingly complex and less informative, less transparent accounting systems, lengthy and vicious negotiations, a climate of mistrust and suspicion, a tremendous waste of IT resources are only a couple of examples. The enterprise does not get one penny back for the substantial cost. In the end, it's all about money going from the left pocket to the right pocket. Why do we then do this? Theoretically, it is about cost transparency. It is about knowing precisely what the cost of each activity is. Theoretically, we could then compare that cost to the benefit, and make better decisions about what we do and don't. Even theoretically, one would have to subject this technique to the same kind of scrutiny the method itself suggests for other activities. One would have to ask how much such knowledge would be worth, and compare that to the cost. But there is no cost control on cost control! This kind of thing is simply taken for granted. Allocations are the ideal battlefield for the bonus artist. Shoving over some of the cost to a neighboring business group may not do anything to the company's result, but it goes directly to *my* bottom line. This is going to improve my bonus without the hard work that is needed to invent or improve products and conquer markets against serious opposition. Further I can go about it with a vengeance and ruthlessness that, should I ever try anything like that in the outside world, would get me in front of a court and losing. My colleagues are after all the only people that I can deceive and cheat without having to fear a lawsuit! The damage done by this kind of attitude is far higher than just the cost of the enormous efforts. This poisons the wells, impedes cooperation and distorts the company's view on profitability. But it is done and it is effective. Why does top management tolerate this? There is the very naïve view that the shrewdness one needs to play this kind of game is going to benefit us in our dealings with the outside word. My experience does not confirm this. It's like with the tiger. Once tigers have experienced how easy it is to kill a man, they will not hunt other game anymore. The fact that this habit will ultimately get them killed is as remote to the tigers as it is to our Mr. Doe. But there are the exceptional cases where this works as intended, and where people successfully apply the manipulation techniques rehearsed internally on the external market place. We then wake up one morning, finding a half billion settlement with the justice department on our hands, not even to mention the collateral damage. I would not call that a great success either!

Once our bonus artist has found out how easy it is to rob his neighbors, he will devote more of his attention to that, and less to the outside world, where it would really matter.

But maybe the top managers have an ulterior motive. They did not exactly get where they are by altruistic behavior. They did this themselves, and therefore it must be good.

In case of the bonus, like with many other things, we observe that a basically good idea, perverted by opportunism, turns in the end against the enterprise. This is especially the case if the bonus comes in form of a cash payment. If it comes in the form of stock options that can only be exercised in the intermediate future, things usually develop *somewhat* better.

17 The Cost of Cost Cutting

17.1 The Mechanics

If you want to be "in" these days, you need to talk a lot about cost. There are more corporate slogans with "cost" in them than I care to recall. There is a lot of effort spent on calculating the cost of everything to the penny. As a matter of fact, we are rapidly approaching the point where we will know the cost of everything and the value of nothing. As you can imagine, there are a couple of problems with this.

Cost does not matter all that much. Neither does profit.

You do not have to say a word more than this to become forever an outcast in every executive suite on five continents (in certain parts of Africa you might still get away with it, but not long anymore). The problem is that it's true! The bigger problem is that at this point 99% of all executives will cry in outrage that it is not. What happened? Rather simple: we lost sight of the core purpose of the enterprise. Please bear with me.

The purpose of the enterprise is to create value. But value comes in many very diverse forms and therefore we need a common metric. That common metric is money. It is far from perfect, but we have no better one. When we say that we need to compare apples to apples, we really mean dollars to dollars.

Unfortunately, almost every venture starts with spending money, thus cost. We do this in the expectation that we will generate enough revenue in order to retain after all expenses a surplus over a number of years, after which the product or the equipment is obsolete, and we can close the books on this cycle. Only *then*, it will be possible to show beyond doubt whether this *was* good or bad business (please notice the past tense). We do this by determining the "discounted cash flow rate" or DCF rate.

My experience tells me that few people understand what this means, but even fewer will admit that they don't. So let's explain it short and sweet.

C_n is the cash flow in year n.
i is an interest rate expressed as a fraction (6% would be 0.06).
Then, the DCF rate is the value of i for which

$$\sum_{n=0}^{N} C_n \cdot (1+i)^{-n} = 0 \quad (1)$$

For those of us who like it better in a narrative form, I will do my best, but I am not good at this.

Suppose you had a time line of cash flows. The first two years are negative, because you are building your business. Then you hopefully get out of the red, and your cash flow becomes positive for a number of years. Then you have to close the installation, and after all activity has subsided, your cash flow gets to zero. What you now have is a number of cash flows at different points in time, so you cannot really compound or compare them. In order to be able to do that, you need to convert everything to *one* reference point in time. Let's agree that we will take year one of the venture (that means this year) although any other year would do just as well. To do this, we have to agree on an interest rate, let's call it i. Let's say that I have a revenue in 2003. It's pretty easy to calculate the capital I would have to place today at that interest rate, in order to have it grow to the expected revenue in 2003. I do this for the expected cash flow in every single year. Also for the negative ones that represent net expenses. I then make the sum of all these numbers, and what I have is the Net Present Value of the cash flow array. The problem with this is that I have to assume an interest rate, and I could be terribly wrong about that. So there is a more elegant twist. I do the same calculation with a number of different interest rates, until I find the one for which the net present value is zero. This very long story tells about what is represented by expression (1).

But what is the practical merit of all this? Simple, it helps with the apples to apples concern. It means that if a bank would give me a certificate of deposit (CD) at an interest rate equal to what I calculated as a DCF rate, I could save myself the trouble building the company. The CD would generate just the same financial result, with a lot less effort, a lot less risk and a lot less headaches. When you expand that thought a little you will understand that it essentially means: somebody else can do this better, let *him* do it. So you want to build that gigantic petrochemical plant. You calculate a DCF rate in the order of magnitude of the interest you get for your checking account, but nevertheless, you go ahead with it. You may not exactly go out of business *yet*, but you certainly are a prime contender for the world stupidity award, and for going out of business in the very near future as well.

Truly, the DCF rate is all that matters, and it is poorly understood. Very often, projects with a known bad DCF rate are justified by "Strategic Benefits" or "Securing the Future" promising gains in 10 years or so. Reality is different.

Gains, even substantial gains in the distant future do not do anything significant to your DCF rate. Simple arithmetic dictates that. Let's illustrate this a little bit with an example.

Suppose you are a member of the appropriations committee at Gargantuan Corp. You get the following proposal on your desk:

- We invest $100 million this year.
- For the next 30 years we make a net cash flow of $4 million annually.
- The risk is extremely low.

The champion who wants this might argue that he is going to give you $120 million back for your $100 million investment. You will not go into the trap, because you will intuitively feel that $4 million a year represents just 4%, so this cannot be all that great. In fact the DCF rate would be 1.2%, so that it is more advisable to leave the money in the checking account.

But the champion is not stupid. He knows that he will have to offer a more juicy bait to lure you over to his side, so now he adds a real goody:

- After 30 years you can sell the facility for $200 million, guaranteed!

The champion will probably argue as follows. Not only do we get the $4 million cash per year, we can even resell the facility with a nice profit of another $100 million! In reality the DCF rate of this venture would be 5%, so we better go buy CD's instead. You would be amazed at how many people have bought that kind of bridge though.

Consistently making decisions that lead to poor DCF rates is the surest way to ruin a company. That cannot exactly be called "Securing the Future", by any stretch of imagination, can it?

Even some of those that have followed me this far will say: "Wait a minute, in order to get a good DCF rate we need high profits, and in order to get high profits we need low cost." Granted, but that makes reducing cost to *one of several means to the end* and not the single-minded goal it is mistaken for these days. "We reduced our cost by 20%", is often the last message you hear from a sinking enterprise. Even the message "our profit went up 20% from last year" can in essence be fairly disastrous. The only thing that matters in the end is the DCF rate. Only by *consistently* making decisions that lead to competitively high DCF rates will the enterprise be able to generate substantial value for *all* its stakeholders: shareholders, employees, customers and suppliers over a substantial period of time. Only that will provide the survivability we are all interested in more than in anything else.

Do things like profit and cost play a role in that? Of course they do, let's have a look.

Profit is a complicated animal, especially in its relationship to cash flow. First of all the issue is clouded by our accounting practices. There are a lot of reasons for that, the most important one probably being tax regulation. Let's not get caught up by this. It still remains true that it will be quite impossible to have a good DCF rate if profits are consistently low. So we better do whatever we can to get and keep them high.

Further, profit is from a mathematical standpoint a very fragile object. It is the relatively small difference between two rather large quantities: revenue and cost. Especially physicists fear this kind of thing. They know that even moderate margins of error for the big quantities will lead to wild uncertainty about the difference:

Profit = Revenue - Cost

We immediately see that there are two ways to improve profit. You either increase revenue, or you decrease cost. Those two have a quite different quality.

Decreasing Cost

This is what obviously comes to mind first. It is a quite natural reflex to comb through your cost elements, take every single one under the magnifying glass, and ask yourself: "Do we really need this?" Unfortunately, this is not as straightforwardly positive and effective as one might think. There are a number of reasons:

The core problem is that this method has limits. You can only decrease cost so much. The lack of insight in this matter leads to quite curious situations. In an enterprise, the so called "business people" spend a considerable amount of their time and attention to lament about the "functional cost" that is allocated to them from the central corporate services. The following statement is repeated endlessly: "If those allocations were just more reasonable, we would not show that woefully low return on assets." But I saw a number of cases where I could neatly substantiate the following reasoning:

"You say that functional cost is the reason for the inadequacy of your returns. Well, let's assume that we would find a way to provide all these services (accounting, tax, treasury, information services...) at zero cost. Don't look so shocked; the way I hear you talk suggests that you must believe such a thing to be quite possible. But look here, when I restate your return on assets under such an assumption, guess what: it's somewhat better but *still* woefully inadequate! Doesn't that suggest that there must be something else, something bigger rotten in the State of Denmark? But with all the attention you focus on functional cost, you are not very likely to find it, even less cure it. And that's the only problem I have with all that noise you are making: it is in the way of a *real* remedy."

Again, don't try this at home, especially not if you *have* rock bottom proof, unless you do not care about your career anymore. But in the latter case, absolutely go ahead. It is the greatest favor you can do to your enterprise.

Finding the *real* cost elements is not as easy as it could and should be. The relentless *internal* bickering about allocations, transfer prices and charges has lead to an insane level of complexity in our accounting systems. That is not very conducive to straightforward analysis.

The prime target should be the pure, senseless waste, the kind of expense that certainly will not benefit the company. But think for a moment what kind of waste that could be. Cost cutting is always a top down initiative. But in order to succeed it needs bottom up support, at least cooperation. The relationship between "top" and "bottom" of the organization is best described by paraphrasing Rudyard Kipling. "Top is top and bottom is bottom, and the twins shall never meet."

In the cost cutting case: the top doesn't know and the bottom doesn't want.

In the ensuing melee, it is likely that valuable activities will be cut, and useless, wasteful ones conserved. The outcome of an "efficiency improvement program" will much more be determined by a struggle of personalities and egos than by objective criteria. Unfortunately, activities that are aimed at the future will almost always find the weakest support. Nobody is going to be immediately hurt if those disappear. The champions that adamantly advocate them are mostly eggheads without real power. We can steamroller those with impunity. And there goes, in 1999, our capability to develop electronic commerce out of the window!

Farmers have known for thousands of years that it is not a good idea to eat the seedlings. Somehow that knowledge has been forgotten by the modern enterprise. The Germans have a saying: "The more intelligent one gives in." But there is a collateral statement: "That's why stupidity rules the world!"

Efficiency improvement programs are like bombing raids:

- They make a lot of noise.
- They do a lot of collateral damage.
- They encourage the opponent to dig in, to go underground.
- Their effectiveness increases with the quality of intelligence, which is usually miserable.
- In most cases they totally miss the *real* target.
- They are almost never decisive for the outcome of the war.
- And when you then happen to bomb the Chinese embassy nobody believes that it was an accident.

This will sound very strange, but we do not do efficiency improvement programs *in spite* of all these characteristics, we do them *because* of those.

More often than not, the initiative for such a thing comes from an executive in charge of a business in trouble. If he does not see a spectacular immediate cure, he knows that he needs to deflect attention away from his woes. That might buy him the time to find a solution. So any kind of smoke screen is welcome. The more noise the better. He has learned this during the long years he spent in the selection machine. This reaction so much became a kind of second nature to him, that he might implement it intuitively, without really consciously thinking about it. From now on the battle rages. But he is sitting there as the chief prosecutor, and not as the defendant. That is so much better that it warrants some collateral damage!

Intelligent cost cutting requires a delicate balancing of cost and benefits. But our management has been educated to be very aware of the cost and very skeptical about the value of everything. Part of that education is experience. They have bought a couple too many bridges in the past! It is infinitely easier to precisely quantify cost that to put a dollar amount on value. Confronted with, on one hand, opportunities to cut hard costs, and on the other hand soft – thus debatable benefits, there is an increasing tendency to opt for the former. That even is the case where the benefits appear to by far outweigh the costs. "Soft benefits" almost became a dirty expression in our corporations. Quite understandably so: the concept has been abused too often. That does however not mean that it wouldn't exist!

Activity based costing offers promising inroads. It is interesting however that it achieves this by changing the problem definition. Instead of saying: "We spend too much, we need to save," it states: "We spend our money on the wrong things, we need to rearrange our business." We do indeed misuse our resources (and not just our money!) pathetically on the wrong products, the wrong markets, the wrong customers and the wrong production sites. If we could prune away some of that waste, we would benefit much more than from any efficiency improvement program. Actually doing this proves devilishly difficult.

Cost cutting can be expensive, especially if it is done in a naïve way. The money we save buying less paperclips can easily be more than offset by the cost of the measures we need to take to that end. In most cases it is a question of timing again. When we trash a capability that we will only need 10 years down the line, we probably actually save money, even if we have to rebuild in 8 years what we destroy today. But if we scrap something that we will need two years down the line, we will lose our shirt!

Soft costs exist as really as soft benefits. If cost cutting is done in a vicious and thus clumsy way, the already existing mistrust between the top and the basis of the company will grow even bigger. The damage this does may be quite extensive but as it never shows up in the income statement, the number magicians that are at the corporate helm will often ignore it. In such an operation the ones that are the most loyal to the company, and thus the most readily willing to sacrifice, the ones that have *not* accumulated fat reserves for a rainy day will be hit the hardest. The message does not get lost on the rest of the population. The consequences for the corporate culture are so clear that they need no further explanation.

All this does not mean that we should not go after cost reduction. It is a fact that modern enterprises waste fortunes on futile, useless stuff. But we should keep things in perspective. We should see the limits and the dangers of naïve cost cutting. And most importantly: we should not believe or say that cost cutting is a kind of snake oil that is going to cure all our problems. There is after all another way:

Increasing Revenue

This is the high road. It is at the same time infinitely more promising and more difficult. *If* you can do this, you truly win the grand prize! Look what you achieve:

- The one priceless advantage of this angle of attack is that it does not have the natural boundaries cost cutting shows. There is no obvious theoretical upper limit!
- You break the classical paradigm that shareholder, employees, customers and suppliers are locked in a zero sum game. If you can increase revenue, there is indeed something in it for *everybody.*
- You can restructure your existing resources to do more with the same. That is quite dramatically different from doing the same with less. Especially if you can let your workforce fairly participate in the increased results, you will find them willing *and eager* to cooperate in such a restructuring.
- This might be the only setting in which re-engineering truly works!

The problem is: where should the increased revenue come from?

- Market growth? That may work in some well-isolated niches, but for a large, diversified company that is more or less tied to the total economy it will be too little and too slow.
- Market share? That means taking market away from your competitors. It would only work smoothly if they were sitting on the fence, interestedly watching us do this. In reality things don't work that way. Conquering market share is always a bloody and expensive operation, even if you happen to have a tangible technological edge.
- Innovation? That means developing products that did not exist so far, but that answer a very real need or want from a large portion of the population. It can be done and it has been done, but innovation is not something that you can suddenly pull out of your sleeve the moment you notice that your balance sheet is out of whack! Innovation capability has either been in place for many years already, or you cannot count on it for the intermediate future.
- Buy a competitor? Some people do this, slaughtering the poor victim's workforce and exploiting his market while preserving the own organization. The massive disruption of long standing relationships between sales people and customers is only one of the very negative aspects that makes the idea not look so great after all. In the end the real winners of such a deal might be your remaining competitors.

In spite of all this pessimism, there are of course always things that can be done.

- Our sales force could be more on the ball.
- Our tech service engineers could be more creative.
- Our marketing people could find additional applications for existing products.
- Our logistics people could make it less of a nightmare to buy from us.

But in the end, the only promising avenue is to have a consistent climate of innovation, so that this can become a constant and reliable source of growth. As we already mentioned this is not something that you can create within a couple of years. It can only be the result of a long sustained effort that has deep roots in the company culture.

Just thoughtlessly trying to increase revenue will prove as futile and counter productive as naïve cost cutting.

17.2 The Core of the Problem

There is an enormous amount of waste in the bureaucracies of our large enterprises. We do things in pathetically stupid and wasteful ways. But, unlike your consultants, I do not believe that we can easily improve this, certainly not in one decisive blow. The reason is obvious: our sub-processes are *owned* by people. I am not even so certain that they believe themselves that what they are doing is optimal, but I am willing to give them the benefit of the doubt. At any rate, what they are doing today is their livelihood: it pays their bills.

Just suppose one moment that I am right when I claim that things are being done in a terribly inefficient way. That in itself means that "improvements" are going to threaten the jobs of the people at the base of the pyramid. They will not look too fondly upon that. And how about the managers? They are in many corporations subject to the Hay system, one of the worst self-defeating schemes I have ever seen. Managers are actually *rewarded* for having large budgets and staffs. So they will try to keep those. And how about the executives? They have so many things going on that they don't want to rock the boat. Occasionally, they will make a symbolic gesture, getting tough on irrelevant, but easily measurable, things like the "travel and entertainment budget", but other than that, they want to be left alone.

People are very seldom enthusiastic about change. Change is a nuisance. It is at least going to make their life harder for the immediate future, and most likely far beyond that. But if we *really* wanted to introduce efficient and effective business systems, we would affect the lives of thousands of people on all levels in the organization rather dramatically. The conventional wisdom is that this is all just a matter of "change management". Please, tell me a better joke! As long as our people are mediocre in their competence, morality and loyalty towards the company, and as long as the leadership is mediocre in its competence, morality and loyalty towards their people, things like "change management" will never become more than a thin, fragile, perfectly useless gold coating over a rusted beam. I do not say "let's forget change management," because it helps ... somewhat. But it does nothing to alleviate the core problem.

Cost cutting is not something that can be done intelligently in a crash action and it's definitely not a job for consultants. If you come to the conclusion that you need consultants for this, save the outrageous fees and start working on you corporate culture. If you want it to happen, you need a deep-rooted climate of continuous improvement. That means constant questioning whether what we do and how we do it still makes sense today. You need a really broad participation for that, which can only come together with a visible job security. Only a person that knows that he will still have a job, maybe even a better one, is willing and able to eliminate his own position.

There are enormous reserves slumbering here, but mining them will be a tedious and complicated task. The quite popular pipe dream of short-term painless gain will only cost you dearly.

18 Employees

Let's face it: they come to us because of the paycheck. There is nothing wrong with that. Our loyal shareholders come to us because of the dividend. There is nothing wrong with that either. But is that also the only reason why they stay? I don't believe so, neither for the shareholders nor in the case of the employees.

Employees are of immense importance for the continuous wellbeing of the enterprise. All enterprises I know pretend to understand this. They write reverberating statements about this on their billboards, in their vision statements and public relations folders. Some present the warm and trusting relationship, the absolute unity of vision they claim to have with their employees in their TV ads. All this looks good and it feels good, but it is far from reality. The relationship between the enterprise and its employees never is and never was as harmonious and unproblematic as propaganda would like to make us believe. Does that make the brains behind the propaganda nothing more than liars and cheats? If the world were only just that simple! Although the picture they project has very little to do with reality, it has everything to do with what they would so dearly like to be reality. I do know that there also are a couple of absolutely ruthless cynical bastards around, but statistically those don't count.

We deal with the core problems surrounding leadership, organization and cooperation elsewhere in this book, but we need to mention some points that specifically pertain to the employee status.

There are a number of factors that seemingly conspire to complicate the relationship between the enterprise and the men and women that operate it.

18.1 The Employee Community

- The nature of the employee community.
  We were of course just looking for hands, and later for brains. Luckily, we always found them somehow. But unfortunately, they always seemed to come with something attached to them: a human being. Had we realized this earlier, we would probably have driven automation of our businesses forward with much more momentum. Human beings are awful. They are capri-

cious, greedy, disloyal, unreasonable and unreliable. You don't have to do anything more than read history, or if you consider that too boring, the works of the great authors of the past and present to find solid proof for this statement. Deplorably, human beings are just like you and me. You can't even assume up front that they are bad. Some of them aren't, and in some respects all of them aren't. Everything you can measure about them is rigorously subject to normal distribution. Probably everything else is as well. This makes them quite predictable as a group, but very much less so as an individual. You never can really foresee what an individual is going to become. In his inner self, he carries the seeds for many different, even opposite expressions. There often is no telling whether in the end the great unselfish leader or the petty thief will emerge.

- The fact that employees always did and always will compete with the other stakeholders: shareholders, customers and suppliers.
  By its charter, the enterprise *must* represent the interests of the latter, and protect them against excessive greed on the part of the employees. Totally surrendering to the wants of the employee community would be just as deadly wrong as a myopic focus on shareholder value.
- The fact that employees always have, and always will compete amongst each other for the things the enterprise can give them.
  The enterprise has a lot of goodies that the employees want: money, status and power being the more prominent ones. But there clearly is not enough for everybody, so employees will compete for all this, and they will often do so quite viciously. Competitiveness and spite amongst employees is very often deflected and blamed on the enterprise. Very few people take total responsibility for what they do or say. It is much more convenient to claim that the enterprise made them do or say it in some shape. Such an explanation is as readily received as it is given. It is indeed much easier to put the blame on the enterprise, after all a quite anonymous abstract structure, than on the living person in front of you. But the truth is that most of the perceived atrocities are committed by *other employees* for very selfish reasons and without benefit for the enterprise. This phenomenon is quite detrimental for the relationship between enterprise and employee. It puts an undeserved and a priori negative spin on everything the enterprise says or does. From there on it really is an uphill battle.
- The communication and group dynamics within the employee community.
  The employee community has no structure, no strong identity and no natural leadership. It has no proper means of internal communication. But like every human community, it constantly feels the need for all those things. In such a situation, all groups of people react alike. If they cannot get the real stuff, they will readily accept surrogates. Some surrogates are worse than others. The surrogate for communication is the rumor. It's a bad one!

Rumors have very little information value. If you kept a scorecard, you would find that they have about the same probability to be real as total fantasy. That makes them virtually useless. If you could at least count on them being always wrong, that would represent some form of information. But why then is something so absolutely worthless given and received so eagerly throughout the organization? Why is it that rumors are often passed on with a kind of sardonic pleasure, and other times with clear traces of masochism? The answer is obvious. Rumors are not about communication. They are the expression of the hidden fears and suspicions that live in the employee community. They are their way to share their concerns. That is why rumors are important and we should pay attention to them. They let us feel the pulse of the organization.

The damage done by rumors is in the departure from reality. The crystallization of surrealistic suspicions happens without management getting a trace of a chance to take a standpoint or give an explanation. That contributes to widening the gap between the "classes".

18.2 The Human Resources Department

The contemporary HR department is a truly problematic creature.

All enterprises have an organizational unit especially conceived for and with no other purpose than to deal with the employees: the HR department. It is meant to represent the enterprise towards the employees. The latter have, decreasingly so but still, their own representation: the trade union. I came to deeply suspect both of them, and even today, I could not possibly say which one I consider the most destructive.

If there were again our scout from Alpha Centauri, totally uninformed about the dealings of us earthlings, he would probably report home that there exists a gigantic worldwide conspiracy between HR departments and trade unions to run the system down the drain. We humans do of course know that this is nonsense, but only because we know the history of the phenomenon. If our view too were restricted to the same momentary snapshot, we might very well come to the same conclusion.

The reason is really simple. We have already elaborated on the contemporary problems with the phenomenon leadership. In today's context, it is very difficult to make a group of people *feel* real leadership as it was developed by evolution, even in a closely-knit operating environment. Just imagine what happens if part of the authority and power that normally comes with leadership is claimed, no, usurped by a remote, even alien organization that calls itself HR. The name is absolutely revealing, in spite of all good intentions that may have been present at the baptism. Human Resources means: we do not deal with individuals, not with persons but with resources that are no more than anonymous means to the goal. There is even more extended damage. By virtue of the rules and regulations that HR releases – must release – it contributes to the all too comfortable abdication of the burdens of real leadership by the local bosses, big and small!

I certainly believe that we need an "Employee Administration" department. We need an organization that assures that all the data we need about our people are available and correct. On the other hand, behavioral rules, does and don'ts need to come from line management as a natural part of the exercise of leadership. Sorry, folks, we cannot have surrogates or substitutes when it comes to leading people. If we were not so blind, we would have seen it by now.

18.3 The Trade Union

In the Belgium of the 1960s I had to work with pretty myopic leftist union representatives. They dealt with me rather prudently, because they knew that my people would have followed me against them if I ever requested that. I dealt with them prudently, because I believed that they were not really evil men, just terribly misguided, uninformed and indoctrinated. I also saw no long time benefit in driving a wedge between my people and the union. Further, I had a whole lot of healthy respect for what the unions had achieved in the past. So, we kept an uneasy, but fairly intensive dialog going. I remember saying to one of them: "You seem to believe that the enterprise is a kind of milk-cow. I have absolutely no issue with that. But have you ever considered that it would then be in everybody's interest to take good care of the cow, to feed it well and keep it healthy. If you force it to give milk beyond its capacity, it will get sick and stop performing. The owner, who rightfully expects some milk for himself too, might then very well decide to bring it to the butcher, and all you will ever see from the cow again is a really small steak!" But of course, they never thought about next year's milk. They wanted it now, no matter the cost. I observed that their approach showed an amazing similarity with the attitudes of top management. In reality, it's quite obvious why. A trade union is a big enterprise in its own right. It has a bureaucracy and a leadership. It has policies and shareholders. It has its own John Doe's. Its leadership is just as obsessed with making the next career step or keeping their job as any other management is. It's about getting appointed, confirmed or elected. It's about appearance and pleasing people. It's about now, not about tomorrow.

With time, I could convince them that polarization and ideology did not contribute much to anybody's agenda. I helped them understand the financial statements, and I saw their initial disbelief at the fact that the workers got much more of the company's revenue than the owners. That certainly was not an ideologically correct experience. This kind of communication worked really well. I fancy that the employees as well as the company benefited. But invariably the next election would come. Then there was nothing I could do to refrain them from becoming their disgusting old self again for some period of time. Demagogy and class struggle reemerged with a vengeance. All I could do was sit and wait until it was all over and we could go back to normal.

Through this experience, I observed that there was something entirely wrong with the process. The discussions between Trade Unions and HR were in reality negotiations between two very bureaucratic power structures, each of them equally focused on self-preservation. I felt that neither the enterprise nor the employees were represented properly. I found that conspiring with low level Union officials, we together could do a much better job. Nobody as much as blinked at the fact that I asked chemical plant operators to paint the equipment in their free time. On the other hand, I made certain that my people were properly paid, treated and continuously educated, without anybody having to twist my arm to that effect. I do not think that I ranked highly on the most liked list of neither Unions nor Management, but I ranked high on my people's favorite guy list, and I knew that I was serving the entitlements of our owners equally properly. There is after all no real conflict between those two objectives! Nothing else truly mattered.

American Unions were a quite different experience. Not so much ideology here, but more often than not a killer dose of greed and paranoia. The polarization between Unions and management is in a sense worse than in Europe, and often becomes downright hostile. The worst part is that Unions interfere in operations in a way that could be understood as a deliberate destruction of efficient processes. The most frequent justification that is put forward centers around safety. I don't think that anybody, even within the Union, buys that kind of bull. What they really do is hold the company in a kind of strangulating grip in order to keep more people employed than would otherwise be necessary, but also to have a bargaining chip in the next contract negotiations round. They claim to need that in order to be able to deal with management. Sadly enough, that might be at least halfway true!

The following story seems to support this pessimistic view. At one of our US production facilities, we had one of these absolutely outrageous contracts. The thing was about an inch thick, and everybody knows that something that voluminous can and will never work properly. One result in practical life was that something as trivial as replacing a mechanical seal on a pump took the involvement of seven different "trades", each of those surrounded by it's own "cordon sanitaire". If you ever wanted to paralyze a chemical plant: this is the way to go. The Union was particularly stubborn about this. We came to the point where we were ready and willing to close the site. We insisted on a drastic simplification of the contract. We were very serious, played hardball and ultimately got what we wanted *and needed*. The psychological climate in the aftermath was as sad as interesting.

The union thought it had lost big time. But what really happened was that the site had gotten a chance and in fact, a good shot at long term survival. The real winners were the employees *and* the company. Management felt that they had won. They had pushed the union further than they ever had in their boldest dreams. Immediately after the signing, we had a management meeting. I had prepared a little speech, emphasizing the importance of this moment, and the new beginning it marked. We needed to start working with the union in a rational, constructive and pragmatic fashion, without gloating too much. The whole thing was hard enough to swallow for them as such. But one of our senior managers beat me as the first one to speak. What he said will not go into the world's records of profound wisdom: "Now we finally have them by the balls..." The primitive stupidity of this struck me like a sledgehammer. It does indeed take two to tango, and it also takes two to have an irrational counterproductive fight. A more cynical person would probably have thought that American management deserves its unions and vice versa. This was way beyond the level where it is appropriate to ventilate anger. All that I could experience and express was an immense and exhausting sadness.

If I had to summarize my experience with this kind of situation, I would say the following:

- Class struggle is not a member of the set of solutions. We clearly need to place it on the list of problems in a quite prominent position.
- When class struggle starts, it will start like a war and proceed like a war. It will, like most wars, start due to
  - gross miscalculations of the factual situation,
  - lack of insight.
  - emotions and instincts (like greed, fear, mistrust) taking over from reasoning.
- Class struggle will also proceed like a war. It will not create value but damage, and although one or both antagonists will ultimately claim victory, in fact everybody will have lost.
- Class struggle is unnecessary. If the enterprise were indeed a zero sum game, if it were actually true that every dollar you want to give to the owners is a dollar you have to take from the other stakeholders, there might at least be a trace of rational explanation for it. But everything depends on your time horizon. If that's one microsecond – which seems to be the prevailing school of thought for a lot of MBA's – we are indeed dealing with a zero sum game. But if we take a longer time perspective it is very well possible to create *added* value and wealth that can be equitably shared by all stakeholders. This becomes even more possible if we can eliminate the non-productive friction from the system. Class struggle is a prime example of non-productive friction.

Unfortunately, management does as much to keep class struggle alive as the unions do. Like in many situations in life, also here polarization is the simplistic way to deal with the problem, not necessarily the intelligent or productive way.

The mere existence of unions and HR departments, facing each other in an antagonistic zero sum scenario constitutes an engraved invitation to polarization.

18.4 A Possible – But Unlikely – Solution

The only way out is for line management to offer *real* leadership. That means representing the enterprise towards all stakeholders in a fair and equitable way. People will react to real leadership with trust. Not immediately though, you have to be very patient.

Giving real leadership is a though, thankless and lonely job. The leader needs to deliberately and knowingly position himself *outside* of the "normal" framework. It takes a strong back to carry such a load. Nobody in the world is going to accept the kind of hardship that comes with this for the sake of money alone. Without a deep philosophical, humanistic or religious background it is almost impossible to endure this kind of stress.

The more our society moves away from true moral values towards an agnostic hedonistic hypocritical, even nihilistic culture, the more unlikely real leadership will become. It is not overly important what exactly we are selling our soul for. Whether it is for the almighty dollar or for the simple answers of fundamentalism doesn't really matter that much.

Our employees are our most important assets. It is true. It has been said and printed a thousand times, but I seriously wonder whether anybody really believes it.

We could, theoretically, overcome the sins of the past. We could recognize labor and capital as equally important production factors, but we won't, because we are human and thus weak. In doubt, we will rather gravitate towards polarization. Much easier to understand and explain. Much more conducive to maintain you as a member of the ruling class on either side.

Of course, employees want to make a living. But they want more than that. They want to be part of something that is truly humanely great. They want to have a reason to be proud of what they are doing. I happen to believe that this is not only their human right. I happen to think that it would be efficient and effective for all stakeholders to arrange such a situation. I also happen to believe that this would be nearly impossible in the existing climate.

19 Attention Span

Everybody can just keep track of so many things. But for a human being, there are a lot of areas of concern. Let's start with a person, having inherited $50 million, and thus independently wealthy. What is he worried about?

- How is my health?
- How is my relationship, my family evolving?
- How is my acceptance in society, club, church?
- Leisure, sports, hobbies, art.
- Dark, hidden desires. Nobody will admit to them, but they are there, and not only in the oval office.

Let's call these the personal problems.

But let's now suppose that he is not independently wealthy. Then a number of other concerns come on top of the above:

- Will I have an income?
- How will I finance retirement?
- How about that mortgage, and how about John's college tuition?
- How about health insurance?

Let's call this the financial problem circle.

Now let us assume that our subject is the employee of a large company. Then additional worries pop up:

- How secure is my job? Will they downsize?
- What if XYZ became a vice president with the next reorganization? He could never stand me!
- How will XYZ react when he discovers that our project is in trouble?
- They are going to put me in a cubicle for Christ's sake!
- They have established this ridiculous deadline. I will never be able to make it!
- The rumor mill says that they are going to move. That will add an hour to my commute.
- They are going to change the health plan, and not for the better.
- They are introducing this ridiculous dress code, and it's going to cost me a ton of money.
- God, they have discovered something in my expense report. XYZ is certainly going to exploit that in order to can me!

Let's call these "existential anxiety" problems.

Now just suppose that our individual has the honest desire and intention to actually *contribute*, that he is not just sitting there for his paycheck. Then a completely new set of thoughts starts spinning around his head:

- If we do this to customer XYZ we are going to lose him. That would be catastrophic. How can I prevent this from happening?
- That process is ridiculously ineffective. How can we change it?
- We could make much more out of product ABC, if we ...
- We are loosing money here, let's stop doing this.
- This project is going to be a low quality job. What can we do to prevent this?

These we will define as "productivity concerns".

It is very easy to see that only the last category of concerns benefits the enterprise. The problem is that they all compete for the resources of the same brain, the same person. One could see them represented by "agents", as Marvin Minsky described in his brilliant "Society of the Mind".

Neither is a person's attention span deliberately expandable, nor are the competing sub-goals infinitely compressible. The final distribution of attention has to be a compromise! There also is a clear hierarchy. Some can be compressed more readily than others. This is essentially nothing new. We had these "pyramidal" hierarchical models of human requirements around in all fashions and colors for quite some time. The closer the concern is to our existential level, the less compressible it becomes.

That, sadly enough, makes the productivity concerns, which are the most remote from our existential anxiety, also the first to give way in a "system overload" situation.

I could of course argue for 20 pages why productivity concerns are in reality the proper battlefield to counter existential threats, why the only way to secure an income is to have a healthy profitable company. That is unfortunately a very theoretical standpoint. The problem is that for the vast majority of people, the world does not work that way. The working classes understand that perfectly: it pays more to butter up XYZ than to do a super job. That is clearly not the way we *want* our enterprises to work, but that is "the way things are". Our enterprises are no cathedrals of reason, determination and common purpose, but much more Roman arenas with cohorts of gladiators defending their own skin in the lowest "catch as catch can" style.

The problem is not just that things are this way, but even worse: we constantly lie and cheat about that. We will say: "Our employees are our biggest asset." At the same time, we are ready to can them by the thousands in order to please a couple dozen Wall Street analysts. The latter are more enticed and convinced by immediate cost reduction (how ever expensive in the medium term) than by a bold plan to expand our revenues utilizing the hidden reserves in our loyal and well-trained workforce! The hypocrisy surrounding this whole mindset may in the end be even more destructive than the mind set on and by itself. But that hypocrisy as such is not just an expression of the villain nature that is supposed to engulf the leading classes. It is a kind of defense mechanism that kicks in to preserve their threatened self-respect. They would dearly want the world to be like they claim it is. Some of them almost certainly believe what they are saying, not because of the facts, but because of their eternal longing for a just and good world. That's not your typical villain!

Before we get too appalled about this, we should try to recognize what we see here. This is a very natural conflict between on one end the evolutionary absolutely logical selfish individual competition drive, and on the other end the fact that we are, within the enterprise, at the same time members of a higher entity that competes with others of its kind. While I do not believe that this rather fundamental conflict of interest can ever be totally reconciled, I still think that we could find a better balance between the two. To find, implement and maintain such a balance is the core mission of leadership. I fail to see what else could be more important for a real leader. So far, I believe we deserve an F. No miracle: the leader too is subject to the same schizophrenic shear stress! While he is fighting and plotting to save his own skin, it is very difficult to intensively worry about his subordinates.

One obvious result is the decline, close to annihilation, of altruism. The working people have determined that it doesn't pay. The leading classes do no longer believe that it exists, even if they see it!

We will come back to these mechanisms in another chapter, but for the time being, we must understand that things are not at their best.

20 Women

The Israeli armed forces, the first in modern history to accept female officers in combat units, made a very interesting experience.

- Over many years, units commanded by female officers got higher than average fitness marks. There is a clear statistical case for superior performance by female commanders.
- When the Israeli army occupied southern Lebanon, the female commanders did not perform as admirably as their peacetime records would have lead to expect. They generally took too much time to make decisions, with quite detrimental results.
- After that, the Israelis revised their policy: no more women commanding first line combat troops.
- But the female fighter pilots performed admirably under fire, so the Israelis kept those.

Not even the worst anti Semite is going to accuse the Israelis of stupidity, and fooling around with sexism in their situation would be plain vanilla stupidity, so what happened? Very simple: men and women are different. You might sneer at me: "What a surprise!" But in this "politically correct" but factually so often very incorrect world, even trivialities like this need to be pointed out. So the gist of it is:

- When it comes to putting their own life on the line, women are just as brave as men are.
- If this has to happen in a highly complex, inherently confusing environment, like a jet fighter, women have certain advantages over men.
- When the issue is to send other people, especially subordinates, which means practically family for any good officer, male or female, into grave physical danger, women are more hesitant than men.

Again, no real surprise. Women are more caring, more prudent protecting life. Their biological role dictates it. We should be happy about that. Without it, we might not have succeeded or even survived as a species.

I happen to know a lot of people that would love to draw some conclusions from the above, like: "We said it all the time, women are inferior to men in extreme competitive situations." That would be naïve. If this were a case in court, the only thing I would need to do is to call the – by the way exclusively male – competition, shot out of the air by the gallant Israeli airforce ladies to the witness stand. The only problem I would face doing so would be to find a big enough courtroom!

Women have been dramatically underestimated in their ability to contribute to our society and to our enterprises. The glass ceiling still exists. I vividly remember the situation in the 80's. I then was an executive in the research area of a very large European enterprise. As such, I was responsible for hiring a lot of Ph.D. chemists, physicists and mathematicians. At that time women just had started to invade those allegedly classical male domains. They did so with great success. I hired a statistically significant overdose of women. Why did I do this? Out of sympathy with the fashionable women's liberation movement? I suggest that you forget that right away. I hired them because they were the best! How could that be? Very simple: the education system produced an abundance of absolutely fine female scientists, and nobody wanted to hire them. I was quite content with that situation: it offered me the cream of the crop on a silver platter. But even so, my boss in those days, a gentleman in the real sense of the word, a man of absolutely unimpeachable moral quality used to say: "but, Mr. De Beuckelaer, not yet another woman please ..." With all his decency, with all the objectivity resulting from his training as a scientist, he could not take any other position after spending a lifetime in the highly prejudiced "old boys club". It was one of the biggest satisfactions of my career to hear him say, many years later, that he thought "my ladies" were giving a very good account of themselves. He still had to think about them in relationship to a male anchor, but we are going to forgive him that, aren't we? Of course, I had debated the issue with "my ladies", and told them very bluntly what kind of weight they had sitting on their shoulders. In the contemporary United States those statements would probably immediately be misconstrued as sexual harassment. But that's the other thing with women: they have such a sense for the moment where things get serious. Of course, they did not let themselves – or me for that matter – down. We were victorious, and the world (in that little part of Europe) will never be the same anymore. I remember a particularly vicious debate about one Ph.D. Chemist, where I wrote to my opponents: "You would probably forgive her for being pretty, because that is what you expect her to be. What you do not forgive her for is being brilliant, because you believe that this is your monopoly. The world after us will not condemn you for this. You probably could live with that. But it will utterly ridicule you, and I think that is more than you want to risk." She was hired, and she is now a vice president.

The ladies did not do just fine. I discovered that female commanders are exceptionally good in retreat battles. Let me explain this. Every idiot with a sufficient testosterone level can lead a cavalry charge. But when you are under constant pressure, under constant scrutiny, when you have to give ground, without giving substance, when you are under the constant threat to be destroyed, that is where other characteristics are brought to the table. I saw women do extraordinary well under such extremely difficult circumstances. I especially remember one Ph.D. mathematician, who held her ground under the most difficult circumstances possible. She never just loaded her stress off on her coworkers. She remained a competent, respected and caring leader through all this. I don't believe that I could have done so much for so long so well. My only pride is to have hired her. The fact that I sponsored and counseled her probably did very little beyond what she was capable of herself anyway.

I also had female colleagues that I am extremely proud to have known. I will always remember one Senior Vice President, a woman of towering wisdom, conscience and human dimension. Her confidence over the years honors me more than any prize or award ever could. In my relationship to these women, I still was the "strong" partner, but that is a relict of the past. I saw them, to my great satisfaction, sponsor and counsel quite a number of men. This means that, ever so slowly, a strange sense of "normality" is seeping into our society.

Now you will probably understand why I never subscribed to this "he or she" kind of theatre. That is far too little and too easy to make a difference. It is one of those gestures that cost nothing and do nothing either. It would simply offend the female allies I had – and have – in the battle for a better world. They don't need or want that kind of superficial deference. They want to be taken truly seriously, as allies or opponents. That is not achieved by a couple of words, and pretending the opposite would be detrimental to their – just – cause. The whole thing is for instance very conducive to all sorts of ridicule. Suppose that I am no longer allowed to say "mail*man*" but I have to use "mail-*person*" instead. Shouldn't I then also say "wo-*person*" instead of "wo*man*"?

Of course this whole subject grew so confusing by our rather dramatic – exquisitely male – mistreatment of it in the past. We managed for many centuries to treat women as an oppressed minority. We should not be astonished when they now react precisely like such a group would. Many contemporary men are – reluctantly – beginning to accept the facts. Any man who seriously studied the oppression of women in the last 1000 years will be so guilt ridden that he is willing to be pulled over board. But there is no way to right the wrong of the past. What are we going to do about this? Will we declare this to be a hereditary guilt and now prosecute the males for 2000 years as the Christians did with the Jews for their "hereditary" responsibility for the execution of Jesus Christ? There must be a way a better way, one that leads to a brighter future.

It constantly amazes me how people deal with this issue. One of the greatest farces occurred in the United States: declaring women to be a protected minority. Women of the world, how in heavens can you let this happen? Why don't you shout in their faces: "WE ARE THE MAJORITY, and if you want to file for minority protection, please stand in line." I see very little serious debate about these things. It is understandable. This *is* a very uneasy, touchy subject. Little to gain, much to loose, so apart from the little token gestures, we leave it alone. But we really can't, because it is one of the most important questions of our time. And no, it is not resolved. In many cases it just went underground, which makes it stealthier and more vicious.

There is an easy answer to the fundamental question in front of us and it happens to be my answer. We, men and women of the world, are all God's children, bound together in our responsibility towards His creation. That is our most important property. Therefore we are equal partners for all times to come. Our force as equal partners comes from our inequality. We should accept and exploit the latter. In all its apparent naïvety, this is the most convincing argument I can come up with.

But what if one does not buy the religious answer? And many of you won't! What if you make the point that religion has contributed so much to the existing derailed situation that it can hardly be seen as part of a potential remedy. Strangely enough, my compelling wish to accept your refute comes from my understanding of religion...

In our history (and I am now referring to the Western so called Christian civilization), we made a big point of the following principle:

"If you are different, you are inferior".

There are a lot of collateral statements to that:

- Even if you *appear* to be superior – which means different – you are in reality inferior.
- If you are different, and thus inferior, there is no place for you in my world.
- It is then not just my right, but even my duty to control you, oppress you or even remove you from this world.

This is neither the place nor the time to go through a comprehensive historical treatment of this mindset, but still we need to deal with a couple of remarks.

Do you really think that the "superiority of the German race" was an invention of the Nazis? The Nazis were far too void of fantasy to invent anything. Even this, rather core, principle of their doctrine was "borrowed" from Christian Europe, as was anti-Semitism, and then slightly modified to suit the occasion.

We (Christian Europe) destroyed invaluable works of art, even complete highly developed cultures for no better reason than the principle quoted above.

We also applied the same principle *within* our society. Women as a group were only *one* of the victims.

Men established themselves as the ruling sex. They did so on no better foundation than

- their greater physical strength
- the fact that they were not burdened with bearing children
- their more aggressive, less inclusive approach to most situations in life.

Such an argumentation would hardly withstand serious scrutiny, but it was enough to make the one all-important overwhelming point: women are different, and *thus* inferior.

This is the point where the quite futile and helpless gesture to pretend women to be a "minority" starts to make some sense. We suddenly see that all those vicious divisive forms of bigotry, whether it is racism, discrimination against women or deadly hatred towards the other class or the other religion all have the same terribly simple roots. All the more astonishing how victims of one form of oppression are all too willing to become perpetrators in another form of just the same old scheme. There were a lot of "good" Nazi women, and there certainly are a lot of female racists!

And let's not forget that also extreme forms of feminism are made from exactly the same stuff. Some of us might be able to see some justice in that. I can only see inefficiency, because I know to what this kind of "tit for tat" exchange leads. Look at Ireland, look at Yugoslavia! Are we going to wait that long for a reasonable solution?

It had to be expected that there would be a reaction, and it came in the form of the French revolution. I happen to believe this to be one of the great yet undigested turns of history. But again: this is not the place to clarify this issue. The French revolution coined the slogan: "liberté, fraternité, égalité". In its powerful simplicity, it is a wonderful slogan. I have no problem with the former two. But the latter, "equality", is kind of difficult.

I do not believe in equality. I believe in *equivalence*. Let's look at the origins of both definitions:

Equal:

[Middle English, from Latin aequâlis, from aequus, even, level.]

Equivalent:

[Middle English, from Late Latin aequivalêns, aequivalent-, present participle of aequivalêre, to have equal force : aequi-, equi- + valêre, to be strong.]

The demand for equality is absurd. No two people are equal, and that may be more than just coincidence. Inequality is more likely than not a powerful tool of evolution, carefully engineered into our species.

Equivalence is a much more difficult concept, because it extends beyond things that are crudely measurable. Equivalence cannot exist as an isolated idea. It derives its meaning from a goal. This makes it very elusive for the ontological mind set, and much more accessible for the functional worldview. Equivalence means: "contributing to a comparable extent towards a common goal." In order to be meaningful, equivalence *needs* inequality and the complementarity that creates synergy. Equivalence is hard to prove in a quantitative way. In order to do so, we would need a common metric for very different properties. But if you see a process, with a lot of partners each needing to do their share in order for the whole to work in a proper way, assuming equivalence between their efforts and contribution *is at least* a prudent position. Indeed, it would be just as difficult to prove the absence of equivalence and if we tried, we would still be stuck with the fact that taking away one of the partners will stop the process. So equivalence is still the safer bet, especially if we deal with something as complex as evolution, and we do!

Equivalence together with inequality means that there are going to be areas where one of the partners clearly does better than the other. Further, the importance of such differences may very well vary through history. Let's examine physical strength. Being quite different between men and women, it almost certainly was a powerful contributor to male domination. But what if the importance of physical strength suddenly diminishes? This is quite obviously the case in the modern world. We now have machines and other contraptions for the brute force side of life. That makes physical strength less and less important, and further weakens the case for male dominance. But there are infinitely more subtle changes in the broad cultural framework. The ontological worldview with its stubborn focus on single objects was a quintessential male worldview. As we know, it is now being succeeded by the functional view as the principal framework for understanding the world. The functional view, with its inclusion of goals and means in the understanding of an object is much more accessible to the female mind. We may be seeing one of these strange recursion loops again. Without any doubt, the emergence of the functional worldview was facilitated by an increasing contribution of women in all areas of science, philosophy, literature and arts in general. But it also created an environment where it would be easier, more natural for women to contribute.

I can clearly see areas in the world where women will have to assume leadership for serious progress to happen. I was quite extensively exposed to Latin America, and I am convinced: if this quintessential macho continent is ever going to make it, the women will have to take charge. In Peru a period of indescribable suffering due to guerilla activity virtually came to an end when Mr. Fujimori, in a truly untypical gesture for someone whom the western media love to taint as a dictator, actually *armed* the campesinos. Significantly, the militias the "Shining Path" found to be more than their equal were mainly formed by women. They had seen enough suffering, and they were going to *do* something about it. Well they did! It were again the women who bravely kept accusing some Latin American governments of very real atrocities that the rest of the world would just have loved to forget.

If you should derive from all this that I must be the honorary president of the "Women's defense counsel", you better forget it. I believe to see women the way they are: they are after all just ... people. One very unfavorable characteristic I saw was that they are pathologically critical about other women. I vividly remember our discussions about so called "potential candidates", people that were about to be earmarked to rise through the ranks. The one female executive we had in our meetings had a quite fatal and predictable tendency to vote down every woman that showed up on the list. Was this malignity? I don't think so. It was just a critical attitude towards another person she could understand so much better than the men that were being presented. But it would have had consequences, if I had not constantly opposed her, which she will of course think I did because ... she is a woman! These things are often more complicated than one would say at first glance. As the previous example shows, they often come in layers, and not everybody is able or willing to explore all of those!

Today's society and today's enterprise do not quite wish to exploit the properties that women bring to the table. We are only halfway willing to accept them if they shed their last trace of femininity, and appear as super-men. That is sad for society, because it inhibits better solutions for difficult problems, but catastrophic for the enterprise, because the female approach is the correct prescription for many of our contemporary woes.

If I would claim to totally understand the female approach to problems that would be quite preposterous. But I do know a couple of things nevertheless that seem to support the idea that our modern enterprise *needs* women in the executive ranks:

- The female approach is *different*. I think that we can all easily agree on that. Difference as such should suffice to indicate an evolutionary advantage, if it were applied more regularly. Different viewpoints just show more of the object under study, no matter what! Only different viewpoints can lead to a "stereoscopic" picture that also shows depth!
- If we trust evolution somewhat, it has to be meaningful that it bestowed the responsibility for one of its most fundamental processes, namely procreation, upon mixed teams of one woman and one man. That at least supports the suspicion that male and female characteristics *need* to differ, and will be complementary far beyond simple biology.
- The *average* female approach to leadership is much less divisive, much more inclusive than the *average* male approach.
- Women will apply feelings to a much larger extend, also to very practical situations.

I see a lot of things go wrong with modern enterprise, and we will come back to that later, but maybe the most important problem is the total loss of feelings. You may think whatever you wish about the paternalism of the past, but it was centered on feelings of responsibility and concern for the employees. Today's enterprise is steering with a vengeance towards becoming a totally impersonal, even inanimate, money making machine. It is rapidly shedding everything that stood in the way of this goal: morality, compassion, loyalty are seen as nothing more than inefficient relicts of the past. But that can't be the future. We cannot simply ban humanism from such an important part of our lives! Women are of course riding with the rest of us on history's roller coaster. But they still seem, on average, less willing to throw the humane values over board. We need women at the helm, and we need them now, badly!

What we need, however, is not necessarily what we want, and our wants don't govern our actions all that clearly either.

One very elegant way to deny women their proper place in the enterprise is our eternal and deep concern for "family values". This needs some closer examination. Let's not get a misunderstanding here. I absolutely understand the paramount importance of the family in the framework of evolution. I happen to believe that we have two important tasks in our lives:

- Prepare the world for the next generation.
- Prepare the next generation for the future world.

I don't think that our contemporary society would get an "A" for either of them. Maybe one could give a C- (maximum) for the first one and a B for the second. The fact that the latter is still dealt with somewhat better may be because it constitutes clearly the core mission for the family. Therefore, very little in this world can be as precious as the family and the values that hold it together. The question is just: what do you understand under family values?

Let me tell you first what I understand under these ominous "family values":

- Life long, unconditional love and support for each other.

One could of course also see something different:

- Mother stays home, neatly boxed in between children, church and kitchen. She takes care of the numerous offspring all by herself, while daddy goes off into the world trading horses, selling real estate or doing whatever he pleases.

We will have no argument about the fact that the latter definition truly describes the paradigm of the past. While there will be very few people left that *fully* subscribe to it, this concept still casts its long shadow over our contemporary understanding of the family. If one thinks this through, there are a couple of consequences:

- Women need very little education. They should be able to read, write and do simple arithmetic. That's it!
- Girls and boys need to be educated in a segregated way, because they need to be prepared for a very different life. As a beneficial side effect, this separate education would also accommodate our puritan desire to suppress a natural development of their sexuality.

And that was very much the way things were. But in the past, there were at least some opportunities to put a positive spin on the whole thing.

I had an opportunity to observe this while growing up in Flanders about half a century ago. I saw a lot of families running small businesses as a true partnership between the spouses, each of them contributing what they did best. In such cases where the men were in some kind of craft – carpenters, plumbers etc. – the women often took care of administration and accounting. When they were smart, they arranged things in such a way that the fathers spent quite some time with the children. I still remember that this was the kind of people you wanted to deal with. They simply had and were more fun than the others.

Farming was a completely different question. That was where women, not just the spouses but the daughters as well, were nothing more than cheap unskilled labor. The women took care of the cows, the pigs, the chickens, the vegetable garden, the orchard and the house. On top of that they had to do all the normal household chores like washing, cooking and cleaning. They did all this without modern household appliances, surrounded by a bunch of kids and while pregnant most of the time! The farmers had a saying that told it all: "A horse's teeth and a woman's hands must never rest!" Their wives repeated it joyously to their daughters. Providing young women with any shape or form of education was considered a total waste of time and money in such a setting. Of course – and fortunately – there were exceptions. The more enlightened the people in question were the more likely a better, more respectful treatment of their women used to be. But we are dealing with averages here.

The supreme authority presiding over all this was an all-male counsel:

- the village priest
- the schoolteacher (only the boys' school headmaster of course, his female colleagues that taught the girls under supervision of the nuns were still fired if they had the audacity to do something as outrageous as marry!)
- the doctor (if there was one)
- the notary (if there was one).

I did not mention the mayor, because that position would most likely be occupied by one of the latter three! These people were the intellectual muscle of the village. They would meet once a week to play cards. On that occasion all matters of public importance were discussed and decided. That clearly included moral issues. Their authority was unchallenged. They executed their power in the most conservative possible way. Life was good, and things should never change. They knew about change, and they feared it. Change was like water seeping through the dike, a phenomenon they were intimately familiar with. They understood that, if you allowed a little bit of it to happen, it could easily get out of control and drown you! They were no villains. I am certain that they by and large tried to do "the right thing". But in spite of their higher education, they were just a little bit fast to accept the traditional century old model as "the right thing"… forever. It would be easy, too easy, to condemn these people in the aftermath.

Now, half a century later, things are quite dramatically different.

- The social structures I described above have all but disappeared.
- Farming and small business are no longer the main sources of employment.
- Families have become smaller. That's not a consequence of decaying family values, but of paramount social common sense.
- Women have joined the workforce in high numbers, albeit still in lower valued, lower paid jobs.
- Female education has improved by leaps and bounds. With the gender parity we see in most universities today, it can only be a matter of some 20 more years, before the female education handicap finally belongs to the past.
- Modern communication technologies are helping to eradicate the perceived incompatibility between working and raising a family.

These changes are so profound that even *if* the old paradigm ever made any practical sense, it surely doesn't do so anymore!

I probably have an obligation to explain how I see a solution.

First, there are a couple of rather hard boundary conditions.

- No matter what, the mother's importance in and obligation to the life of an infant is greater than anybody else's, and that includes the father. You may not like this statement. You may find it reactionary, even sexist. All that would not impress me in the least; biology is a tough opponent and it's on my side!
- This even remains the case if the parents are an "ideal" team, ferociously committed to share everything. That would certainly ease the burden on the mother and reward the couple and their children in many other ways, but it would not do anything to remove the fundamental inequality as engineered by biology/evolution.

You may find this situation unfair. Please be reminded that objects like biology and evolution totally elude moral qualities. The term simply does not apply here.

But I still refuse to feel sorry for the women. Probably for totally different reasons, evolution has arranged things so women live on the average 5–6 years longer than men. That's at least a more or less decent compensation.

If a nation has the desire and the vision to exist in the future, its government needs to create an environment supportive and conducive to procreation.

Every sign we can see today points to a world where we can do with less labor.

If you look at all these boundary conditions, the ideal romantic solution seems simple:

- Educate women (and men) as far as their intellect and desire will let them go.
- Don't worry about overproduction of qualification. Qualification reserves are good for society in many ways. I fail to see why a baker with a master's degree would be a problem!
- When for instance a Ph.D. in physics marries and becomes a mother, put her in a financial situation to stay at home and take care of her family.
- There definitely is nothing wrong with smart mothers!

There unfortunately is a lot wrong with this concept:

- Without the day to day rub with reality, without intensive, percolating communication with peers, knowledge decays pretty fast. That would be the fate of our Ph.D. mom, and I don't think she is going to like it.
- Women would be condemned to ponder forever "what would have been". Some would take that better than others, but I see a lot of unfulfilled, frustrated mom's around the corner.
- Would that be so excellent for the kids? If you could choose, wouldn't you rather have a part time mother that feels socially recognized and proud about her professional achievements and at ease with herself?

But there is one KO argument that would be sufficient to discard this option even if there were no other problems.

- It would deny to our enterprises the benefit of the female view and approach.

It would do so at a moment in history where this female view and approach seem to be needed more urgently than ever in the past.

So that won't fly, but the romantic do-good approach really never does. This calls for a more radical approach. How about this:

- We will accept women as our equals, but then they will have to behave equally.
- We can't have part time executives.
- They will have to make a choice, a hard choice: either to pursue a career or a family.
- This may seem harsh, but isn't business all about tough choices?

To that proposal, I only have the following answer:
My dear young friend – you must indeed be very young and inexperienced to make such a proposal – you are committing one of the few cardinal sins: you try to tamper with evolution. Oh, you didn't think about that? Well I believe you of course, because I assume you are not even remotely interested in these things. But probably to your great astonishment: they do exist, you know!

Suppose your proposal were generally adopted. What would be the result?

- Roughly 50% of the population is female.
- So roughly 50% of the gene pool, which happens to be our future, is too!
- You just proposed to introduce a negative selection principle. In your scheme the brightest, the most ambitious among 50% of our population would not have offspring.

There are many more things wrong with this approach, but as it stands, I really believe that we would take a quite insane risk following your proposal.

We should have known it: radical approaches normally show as little promises as romantic ones.

So how about a pragmatic approach? We will borrow a couple of elements from previous approaches:

- Educate women (and men) as far as their intellect and desire will let them go.
- Don't worry about overproduction of qualification. Qualification reserves are good for society in many ways. I fail to see why a baker with a master's degree would be a problem!
- When for instance a Ph.D. in physics marries and becomes a mother, put her in a situation to continue to work and take care of her infant at the same time.
  How can such a thing be done? Well we are soon going to live in the 21st century!
  Give her a less stressful job for a certain time. Of course that would take *real* personnel planning and we have visited this issue before. But in order to survive the next century's troubled waters we need such a thing anyway.
  Would that not be unfair to her male colleagues? No, because you should do exactly the same thing for them! How can that be – they don't get pregnant? Well, as a former *male* executive, I know "burn out" intimately. I met it to the brink of physical destruction. This is a very negative selection criterion, because only the ones that are truly detached, and thus to a large degree indifferent, are not threatened by it. We could get to a much better quality in the leadership if we provided occasional regeneration periods. That does not necessarily have to come in the form of a sabbatical leave, strolling around a university campus. Why not let people in upper management do for some time what they really enjoy? The ones that only enjoy wielding ever more power are not the ones we need anyway. But again, that would require a working personnel planning system.
- Let her telecommute for some time. Modern technology allows that, and it does not diminish someone's effectiveness. I did a lot of my best work at home, undisturbed by the environment of the big corporation.

I am quite certain that this would work, because I practiced it with excellent results!

But no reasoning in the world will help if we truly don't *want* to do it. Reasoning is particularly impractical against hidden fears and longings. That is when things become somewhat surreal, and they are!

A typical example is the ominous glass ceiling. There is something quite remarkable about this one.

- It does exist.

I do not believe that I will get too much debate about this statement. Just look at the statistics. No law is going to demolish it. The morally laudable attempts at that will prove ineffective to the limits of ridicule. The only thing in the world that can break the glass ceiling is a very thick and strong female skull! Of course that skull will need momentum, but that is increasingly available. The rest is only a matter of time. The problem is that we don't have all that much time.

- It is *not* the result of a conscious male conspiracy.

Wouldn't it be nice if the world were that simple? On one hand the villains, on the other side the righteous that, after a heroic struggle, will always be victorious in the end. The world isn't that simple, and it might even be better this way.

Do you remember our excursion into the "selection machine"? A lady who wants to penetrate the glass ceiling has to pass through that machine, just like her male peers. There would be nothing wrong with that, if the machine were not built to exclusively accommodate males. That is quite understandable, because in the past the job to be done was to select males from a male population. Change to the selection machine comes slowly. We are not going to see a lady's bathroom there for quite some time.

You may remember that the first "sieve" is formal education. Women are doing exceptionally well there, and increasingly so. You may also remember that this sieve is becoming increasingly dysfunctional. I have no trace of a suspicion that this would be engineered to rob women of an advantage they are building. I much rather believe that this is just one more expression of our contemporary culture (or the lack thereof!)

The next hurdle is the hiring interview. I hear that some interviewers, at least in Europe, ask female Ph.D.'s whether they intend to have children! What a ludicrous question! What do you expect the poor woman to answer? Shall she simply lie, diminish her opportunities, or maybe rightfully respond that she has not resolved that question yet? And what should you think if she answered downright "no"? What would you think of a man giving the same answer to the same question? But of course, men are never asked. What a way to start an important relationship! And all this for the sake of a couple of months of maternity leave, that should not matter anyway, because we – statistically proven – pay women so much less than men in comparable jobs that this will more than compensate the mere *possibility*. And don't you think that our enterprise culture could vastly benefit from the wisdom motherhood seems to encompass?

As they progress through the sieves women are exposed to increasingly abusive behavior. There are several reasons for this. First of all, the participants in the game get older, and thus more remote from modern developments in society. But further, with increasing status, the probability of a lawsuit, especially a successful one decreases. Thus it can happen to a female Senior Vice President that her boss tells her: "We can do all kinds of things together, but you can't go to the bathroom with us." That is not the pointlessly rude statement it appears to be. It is rude OK, but by no means pointless. It sends a very powerful message: " You are different. You will remain different. You can never truly belong to the club!" I am telling her: "Throw the towel! You are wealthy enough. Go teach, write books. You don't need to deal with these jerks!" And then she looks at me in some kind of desperation and asks: "But what about my people?" She is worried about all the good men and women that she has been developing, grooming for years, and she is not quite done with them yet. I start to mutter something in the sense of "Well, one day they will have to fend for themselves anyway." But I know that I have no good answer. I have spent my life being a patriarch. One of my coworkers once made a quite amusing caricature of me as a bishop in front of his cathedral. But I came to learn that the attachment of a matriarch to her flock is something completely different yet. That is what we desperately need. It is also what we absolutely do not want.

Will the women arrive at the front in time to save the day? Certainly not if it depends on us men! But the battle goes on, and who knows?

21 The Problem with Reality

"For a successful technology, reality must take precedence over public relations, for nature cannot be fooled."
Richard Feynman[1]
to President Reagan's Challenger Accident Investigatory Commission

Reality as we can observe it is infinitely and confusingly complex. First of all, what is reality? Quite obviously it is the world around us, as we can observe and perceive it. But it also is the world *within* me, the perceiving and exploring subject. And by extrapolation, it must also be the world within our fellow men. When you start to think about this, you rather soon bump into quite bizarre observations.

- Is this rock reality?

Rather likely it is. But what is the more important aspect of this reality "rock"?

- Is it the material?
- Is it the shape?
- Is it John's opinion about this rock?
- Is it the harmonious contribution to a romantic landscape?
- Is it what Maria feels when she observes the rock at sunset?
- Is it the sum of all this?

In that sense, reality can become rather surrealistic. I somewhere read the following:

"I had a dream that I was a butterfly. I woke up, and from now on I will never know whether I am a man that dreamt to be a butterfly, or a butterfly dreaming to be a man."

This may be great inspiration for all kinds of artists: poets, novelists and painters, but if you have to deal with the world in a practical sense, it often gets slightly in the way. There obviously is a need for a kind of classification if we want to approach reality in a rational way.

Like almost everything else, reality seems to come in layers. Further, we can observe a very clear hierarchy. Deciding about the classification order in a hierarchical stack is not as difficult as one might think. A very simple trick will help a lot. Just ask yourself: "If I took this layer away, what happens to the other ones?" Clearly, the layer that can be taken away without affecting any of the

---

1 Nobel Prize for Physics in 1965

others is the upper one. If the removal of one layer encompasses the collapse of everything, that obviously must have been the lower layer, the basis on which all the others rest. Taking this further, one can come to a fairly convincing hierarchy. The following model (as described in fig. 21.1) seems quite reasonable.

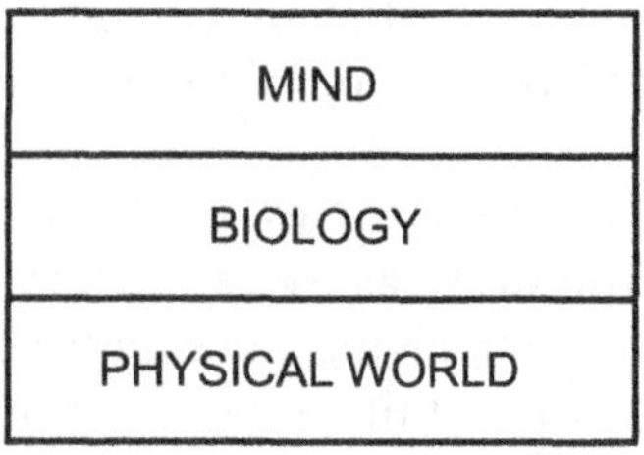

Figure 21.1

The most basic, fundamental layer is the purely physical layer. Space, time, matter and energy seem to constitute the foundation of everything we observe and – more or less – understand. This clearly must be the lower layer. It is quite obvious that if it were taken away, everything else would fall apart.

Building on the physical world, we see life emerge in all its glorious diversity.

Supported by life, something very strange that we call "mind" appears. This seems to be the contemporary top of the stack.

Apart from being convincing on the level of "what supports what?" there is quite overwhelming evidence that this stack also represents the sequence creation follows. In his "Phenomenon of Man" (1955)[18], Pierre Teilhard de Chardin describes in a quite awesome way how Biogenesis happened in the physical world, adding a layer of living creatures to the system. Afterwards the biological world in its turn supports Noogenesis, an equally dramatic discontinuity leading to consciousness. But Teilhard de Chardin goes even further. He postulates that the borders between the layers are not as absolute and impermeable as one might think. He sees traces of consciousness over the whole biological sphere, and albeit more diluted and less obvious also associated with matter. This complicates things. The idea that there are spiritual components in the animal world is something I can easily accept. Assuming rudiments of consciousness in the physical world is a totally different matter. But on the other hand, how could the physical world in the end produce minds, if it did not contain first principles of spirituality to begin with? I find it very difficult to understand and internalize this, but it is certainly not less believable than homeopathic medicine. The only reason I brought these complications up is to avoid the impression that I believe my rather simplistic classification to be the ultimate answer to everything.

Anyway, something should be clear by now. There is a strict order of precedence. Nothing can happen on the biology layer that would contradict the rules governing the physical world. For the same token, nothing can happen on the level of the mind that would disobey the rules of biology. There is however a snag. Our mind allows us to *believe* or *pretend* that such violations are possible, and our beliefs are clearly a part of reality. Not *what* we believe of course, but the fact that we *have* this conviction. At this point things start to fall apart and our relationship with reality becomes incurably complicated.

The transition from an ontological to a functional worldview, as positive as it is in most respects, is not very helpful here. With less emphasis on naked isolated facts and more attention for relationships, functional thinking seduces to be less observant of the cold strict order we explained above. And so it can actually happen that "political reality" collides with physical reality, without the protagonists that are proclaiming the former understanding that this is in the end a hopeless conflict. Propaganda (or "public relations" as Richard Feynman so sensitively called it) can cover up conflicts like this for a long time. The tragedy is that usually, the longer it takes for the bomb to go off, the more violent the explosion.

The question is now: how does modern enterprise deal with reality?

Let's look at what kind of questions we are confronted with when we deliberate the health and future of our company:

- How *are* our products contributing to our customer's success?
- How solid and reliable *is* our production technology?
- How solid and reliable *is* our information technology?
- How solid and reliable *are* our supply chains?
- How good *is* our innovative potential?
- How solid *are* our finances?
- How well *are* we complying with the law?
- What long-term return *are* we producing for our shareholders?

There are many more questions like these, but they all have one thing in common: they deal with reproducible measurable *facts*. We could call this "objective reality". It deals with things that *are* in the physical world.

There is however another class of questions that is of no lesser importance:

- How do our customers *perceive* our products and services?
- Are we *perceived* as a reliable supplier?
- How are we *perceived* by the market place?
- What is our *standing* in the financial community?
- How are our employees *perceiving* us?
- What *opinion* does the government have about us?
- How do our shareholders *perceive* our potential?

And again, there would be many more questions like these, but they all have one thing in common: they deal with *perceptions* and *opinions*. We could call this "subjective reality". In deals with things that happen in our mind.

We are obviously confronted with two quite different views on reality, but they are interconnected. In the end, perception will always follow the facts, and in some cases, strong opinions will lead to actual changes in the physical world. The problem is that the feedback mechanisms between the two worlds are convoluted and often show rather large time constants. You can easily verify this for yourself. Ask somebody whether spinach contains considerably more iron than other green vegetables. In over 90% of the cases, the answer will be an unequivocal "yes". The reason is that many (50?) years ago, somebody made a decimal point error. He tried to correct it, but it was too late. Then Popeye the Sailor took over, and from there on spinach will forever be almost pure iron. Physical reality, the fact that spinach shows about the same iron concentration as other green vegetables, seems to matter very little in situations like this. In the business world, things are not any different. If your product is the answer to all your customer's needs, but he does not believe it, you are not going to sell. If, on the other hand, you have absolutely nothing, but your customer thinks differently, you make the deal. One might believe that "looking good", without being good would be a short-lived pleasure. In reality, a positive corporate image often survives actual poor performance by years. Conversely, if you were once tainted by a perception problem, it can take a long period of good solid delivery before anybody notices.

No wonder that image is such an important topic for every enterprise. No miracle that corporate leaders often let perception concerns guide their decisions with an apparent disregard for physical reality. In the occasional collision between form and substance, form will always win the first round. We spend billions every year for something called "advertisement" that is in the end nothing but the manipulation of our appearance. If it's that expensive, it *must* be valuable.

When talking about the truth, we have to carefully distinguish between the official truth, and the true truth. Many people don't even bother with the latter. The next step is that we start to believe our own propaganda (or "public relations" as Richard Feynman very sensitively called it). If this takes place in a high tech environment, something terrible, like the Challenger accident, is about to happen. Nature cannot only "not be fooled", as Richard Feynman put it so gently. Nature is a rather vain revengeful monster. It does not really like to be ignored and strikes back with awesome brutality. We then go into a state of collective shock. We mourn the victims with a sorrowful vibrato in our voices. We call a commission, make a couple of cosmetic changes, and the whole circus starts all over again.

There is nothing crazy about all this. Enterprises just react to the world they are living in. That world is like a smoky backroom, full of partly inebriated mediocre little crooks playing poker with marked cards. It's all about smoke and mirrors. All that matters is that I get the money and thus unfortunately you don't. We can think about this whatever we want, but there is very little we can do about it. Changing this means changing humanity and that might be more than even genetic engineering can accomplish.

So far we have explained the situation as if the enterprise were an organism that needs to come to terms with reality. But what happens *within* the enterprise? One might believe that we should have a different set of rules and behavioral patterns here. Of course, both views on reality will still play a role. But one would think that the appearance issues would be more aimed at the outside world, where it is indeed important to project a positive image. *Within* the organization one would expect more focus on improving physical reality, of course also – but not exclusively – from the viewpoint of its supportive role for the perception we offer to our customer base. The contrary is true and increasingly so. Vicious competition, mainly based on appearance and perception issues, is getting as violent within the enterprise as between companies. Think of our executive, on his way to the top through the selection machine. What are the questions that circumscribe his concerns?

Of course, he needs to pay attention to the sets of questions that we mentioned previously as relevant for the enterprise. But he also has a number of questions of his own:

- Are my projects on time and on budget?
- Will I make the projected net cash flow?
- Can something be done to improve the yield of plant X?
- How can the 10% reduction in force target be met?
- What can I do to make our price increase hold?
- Who can solve customer Y's problem?
- What lessons are to be learned from the failure of project Z?

This class of questions again addresses the facts or objective reality. It more or less seamlessly flows together with the similar class of questions on the enterprise level.

Nobody will be surprised that also on an individual level, there are a number of questions regarding subjective reality:

- How do my boss, my peers, and our Executive Committee *perceive* me?
- Did my presentation make a good *impression* on Mr. X?
- How can I *endear* myself to Mr. X?
- How can I make Y, my main contender for promotion, *look* bad?
- Should I work on improving my *relationship* with colleague Z?
- How can I put a positive *spin* on the terrible difficulties we have with project A?
- How can I make the fact that our price increase did not stick *look* like a victory?

At the first glance, we might believe that we see no more than just the mirroring of the corporate situation on the individual level. That is not the case! There are important differences. On the enterprise level, serious preoccupation with both classes of questions will contribute to the success and wellbeing of the company. It would be harmful to blindly focus on one side neglecting the other. A balanced approach is what is needed most.

In the case of the individual and his dealings *within* the enterprise, only the energy flowing into the resolution of the questions in the realm of objective reality create value for the company. Whatever is thought, said or done about the subjective reality component is a total loss from the company viewpoint. Unfortunately, our individual, as a resident of the selection machine, has learned that the way he deals with the subjective reality questions is more decisive for his career than anything else. Passing the sieves is, as we saw, all a matter of pleasing people, making a good impression, projecting the right image. The career artist will sacrifice the last shred of objective reality for that purpose. What we see here is a deadly trap. We have things organized in such a way that the good of the company and the individual's benefit demand opposite courses of action. One could do such a thing with some degree of confidence to a bunch of saints, but not with real people. The ones that focus on creating value for the company will automatically have a detrimental handicap in the career race. It is quite clear what that is going to mean for the output of our selection machine. That things do not yet completely fall apart yet is due to a couple of factors. First of all, there still is a certain amount of residual altruism alive in the ranks. It is frustrated by its environment on a daily basis, and it is visibly dwindling but for the time being it is still enough to fend of catastrophe. And further there is the blessed influence of coincidence that every once in a while produces a truly competent leader. His influence will be very restricted in scope and in time, but he often can generate enough of a recovery to endure the next blow.

At this point in time, more and more energy is funneled into dealing with subjective reality. Physical reality is generally being neglected. Intensive preoccupation with it is considered to be a waste of time. It is not unlike the stock market. The whole thing is so heated up, so out of whack that we all know that it is going to collapse. We just don't know when! But there is no end in sight. As more and more attention is paid to subjective reality, the people that are good at dealing with that aspect get more influential. As they get more influential they will, like all people, claim that the tiny little part of the world that they happen to understand well is also the most important part of the world. Hence even more attention on soft skills. We clearly see a control mechanism with positive feedback. It is bound to bounce out of control.

The defiance towards physical reality is taking grotesque proportions. It often reminds me of a conversation Hitler had with one of his more capable ministers, Albert Speer. Speer warned that if the prosecution of the Jews continued, very soon the whole German Physical Society would be either in exile or in camps. Speer was very worried that this might mean a setback for Germany that would take a century to recover from. Hitler's response was very logical ... for Hitler: "In that case Germany will have to do without physics for a century or so!" One may think: how silly! But many of our contemporary business leaders operate on exactly the same level. Unfortunately, the comparison does not stop here. With dwindling respect for the physical reality, also morality gets pushed back into insignificance. The relationship is easy to see. We ignore physical reality because our compulsive desire not to be restrained by its limitations is stronger than our reason. We want to be free and unrestrained, no matter the cost. We believe that we can become whatever we think, and do whatever we want. If we see physical reality as one kind of handcuffs, we will see moral constraints as just another. The ancient Greeks would have called this "hybris". They would have – correctly – smelled the material for a great tragedy.

I understand that the above must sound like one of these very detached descriptions of a horrible problem. You may believe that I have made my piece with the world, that I have matured to accept even its most dismal expressions. That is not so. I am outraged and terrified at the same time by the situation I described above. This is not the innocent, borderline ridiculous soap opera that it may seem. It maims and kills much more people than you would believe.

Industry, especially chemical industry, is always a potentially dangerous operation. The reason is that one is manipulating huge amounts of energy. There is nothing in our evolution as a species that could have prepared us for this kind of activity. Consequently, in this environment we totally lack the kind of hardwired behavioral patterns that serve us so well in other circumstances. We have to do it all through reasoning, meticulously and correctly. Neglecting even one seemingly unimportant detail can be fatal. Things will become worse when this has to happen, as it often does, under a lot of time pressure and stress. As long as I was a leader of men in this environment, my worst nightmare was always that one of my people could be killed on my watch. Under whatever circumstances such a thing happened, I knew that it would always be in a sense my fault, because I was the boss, and there would always be things that I *could* have done. This puts a weight on your back that is hard to imagine for people who never experienced it. I am grateful until this day that I was spared from such an ordeal. It will certainly have helped that I was extremely careful and took no chances. But we all know that it could have happened nevertheless, had the Lord shown just a little less mercy with poor me. I had fatalities. People got killed in traffic to and from work. It was heartbreaking enough to drive to their homes and tell their wives that "your husband is not coming back." Just imagine doing the same thing with in your stomach this nagging feeling "... and it could be my fault."

In the old days, the position of plant manager came with unchallenged power, which of course entailed total and indisputable accountability, as it very well should. This makes a powerful impression on your life. I remember clearly that I suppressed my emotions, especially fear, almost to non-existence. The reason was simple: I felt that I could not afford emotions. I had to live in absolute harmony with physical reality. That is a cold, rational and intimidating environment. Only flawless reasoning will help you survive.

There are of course different ways to deal with this kind of responsibility. Let's look at a simple example.

Top management, in one of its seasonal cost saving sprees, decides a 10% cut in maintenance expenses across the board. As most phenomena in life, this is an ambiguous thing. On one hand, you know that there is a lot of fat in the maintenance budget. You have seen some people waste money in ridiculous ways. So somehow, the demand seems justified. The problem is that you have been running a tight ship. In your case, there are no 10% fat to be shaved off. A cut would be a cut into the substance. Apart from putting the shareholder's equity in unjustifiable jeopardy, it would also increase our exposure to accidents. Of course, you do not have a neat mathematical model that lets you argue the case quantitatively, but you simply know from your experience that the previous statement is true. What shall you do now? There are options:

- You simply comply, after putting your concerns in writing in a carefully guarded way so that you do not appear obnoxious, but clear enough to get you off the hook in case something happens. This is going to endear you with top management. You support their program. The fact that you found it necessary to cover your backside is not held against you. This is something they deeply understand. They would probably have done the same thing themselves. If an accident does happen and instead of "I told you so" you show total solidarity with them, that will further help your career. They will have the feeling to be in this together with you. Nothing is more conducive to your entry into the brotherhood than a sentiment of shared guilt. If you can then find ways to also get out of the ensuing mess together and in one piece, there is no longer any doubt about your next promotion. This really seems the way to go doesn't it? There is only one small problem. What you really have done is abdicate your moral responsibility for the life and wellbeing of your men to people that often, and increasingly so, do not understand the difference between a chemical reactor and a vacuum cleaner. Exaggerated? "I'm a financial guy. I prefer to look at the numbers." End of quote. The source: an Executive VP responsible for very dangerous chemical production plants, deliberating a cut in the maintenance budget. But then, if you are one of these career artists, you probably have ways to deal with your conscience. More likely than not, you learned how to suppress it many years ago, just like I learned to suppress my emotions. It does not matter too much that you make your next promotion quite literally over dead bodies.

But there is of course another way:

- You take an "over *my* dead body" posture. You go to see your boss. If that does not help, you go to his boss and so on. You first try to reason your way through this gently, but if that does not help, you ultimately have to come to the "Their blood will be on your head" approach. This works astonishingly well. Many of the power mongers are, when their pompous cover is taken away, in reality little cowards. They flee accountability as if it were the plague. On the other hand, their enormous egos do not allow them to be exposed evading their responsibility. They absolutely hate to be placed in an "either – or" situation they cannot weasel out of. Now that is precisely what you did to them. Needless to say, this is not going to increase your popularity with the top brass. You may have done the honorable thing but you also stacked overwhelming odds against your further career. They will talk about you. The least they will say is that you are a "difficult" person.

I was very fortunate. In the most dangerous phase of my career, I had a boss who totally understood and accepted the technical aspects as well as the moral obligations of what I was doing. After carefully thinking through what I told him, he would say: "Do not worry about this any more, it's my fight from here on." He was a towering personality. He knew exactly what he was doing, what the consequences for his own career would be, but he did it nevertheless. The problem is: what are the odds for such an individual to pass through the selection machine? 10% would have been a wildly euphoric figure 30 years ago. That number must have substantially decreased in the mean time! On the other hand, the memory of this man has inspired my life. If confronted with a difficult decision I still deliberate: "How would Heinrich Laib have approached this?" As positive as this experience has been, it also resulted in a lifelong obligation. I simply could not deal with my subordinates in any other way and still look into the mirror. I cannot do anything that would not pass Heinrich Laib's standards. Only if I can see him nod and grin from Heaven, I know that I did the proper thing.

I do realize that most people did not have such an undeserved amount of luck. They just got "standard issue" bosses, fresh from the selection machine. This often leads to situations that are so cruelly absurd that they seem to have escaped from a Kafka novel. I simply have to describe to you one experience that truly got under my skin. It happened in 1991. Through an exceptional combination of greed, world class stupidity and political correctness we had created the possibility for one of our plants to blow up. The problem is that plants seldom miss such an opportunity. Two people lost their lives. Fortunately at that time I was not yet working for this company so that I did not have to deal with the terrible question whether I could have done something to prevent this. Most of us knew how it had happened, but it would not have been wise to discuss the issue openly. Top management tried to deal with this very hush-hush. And of course, there were lawsuits pending – this was happening in the USA. The company leadership had been quite shocked by this experience. They must have felt a need for healing and closure, because they called a meeting to rehash the whole thing. It was a beautifully choreographed affair in a large luxurious conference room. Our whole US top management was present. One after the other the people that had played a role in the incident reported about their experiences. The summit was a man from the emergency response team. I immediately noticed all the attributes of contemporary leadership. He was tall, slim and good looking. He had a nice tan and wore the appropriate dark suit for the earnest occasion. He could easily have doubled for a dummy in an expensive tailor's showcase. He spoke well, with a pleasant voice. He was absolutely not abrasive and clearly not plagued by and embarrassingly high IQ. This was obvious management material. He recollected how he went through the neighborhood, visiting the people whose homes had been damaged and offering help. Without knowing it, he came at the house of one of the victims. The devastated widow let him in. He reported how "they talked for some time, and then they fell into each other's arms and cried silently together." He did not forget to mention that "this was a very emotional moment." The audience was visibly moved.

At the end a couple of things were clearly established:

- This accident had been a terrible case of bad luck that hit poor innocent us.
- Nevertheless, we had handled the crisis very well.
- Due to our extraordinary skillful dealings with the insurance policies, the financial loss remained painful but quite bearable.
- Our interaction with the victims had been compassionate and generous. It had been recognized as such.
- We had come out of this stronger, wiser and with a better image.

There was an overwhelming, almost compulsive collective desire to believe this story. Consequently, there could not be any doubt that things happened exactly as reported. We now could all feel better about ourselves and about our company. Mission accomplished.

I was observing this whole spectacle with increasing bewilderment. They seemed to be living in a different world from the one I knew. On the level of objective reality things looked quite different:

- We had failed to take the necessary steps to prevent this from happening.
- We had done so for a lot of poor reasons, one of them clumsy cost cutting.
- Many people knew that this was wrong, but they were effectively silenced.

- Whatever money we saved this way was later lost 1000 times over as a consequence of the accident.
- We had killed two people.
- We damaged scores of houses in a poor neighborhood, some of them beyond repair.
- We disrupted the lives of dozens of people.

In my opinion, that looked like total and abject failure. And even in this tasteless mopping up operation:

- No word about the root cause.
- No word about the dangers of group dynamics in a technical environment.
- No word about how ridiculously substandard management allowed this to develop.
- No word about what we were going to do in order to assure that such a terrible thing could never happen again.
- No word of emphasis on our social responsibility.

It crossed my mind that even *politicians* would resign if their department had made such a blatant error in judgement with such catastrophic consequences. But we were sitting there, feeling all warm and balmy! That's how we deal with reality! If it does not treat us kindly enough, we just create another one. If we can collectively and strongly believe in this, it becomes our primary reality, successfully replacing the less gentle older one. It does not often happen that there is a Richard Feynman available to call us back to our senses.

One more question may remain on your mind: why didn't I say anything? I was relatively new in the group, and I wanted to observe them somewhat longer before starting any battles. There was in fact very little to gain. The victims would not have been less irreversibly dead. I would never have achieved anything against the strong collective will to accept this nicer reality. There was no way I could have won, so I didn't fight.

We do not just observe these things happen. We also witness the construction of a gigantic infrastructure aimed at nothing but enabling such operations:

- abundant literature
- countless seminars
- workshops
- The creation of quite powerful "Communications Departments", the modern euphemism for "Ministry of Propaganda";

all point in this direction.

We saw 1984 pass and Orwell's horror vision [12] did not materialize. But it is not over yet. I believe that the main danger does not come from the authorities, but rather from within our enterprises.

In Chapter 8, "The Enterprise and the World", we looked at the cultural context in which enterprises thrive. We saw that always then when one facet of our limited view on reality takes over the whole picture, we meet a destructive aberration. The same is true here.

22 The Moral Side of It All

André Gide, 1869–1951, wrote "The Immoralist" [3]. An interesting character Gide describes here! He makes it his business to defy morality. He fights the constraints society puts in front of him. Modern executives are not like that. They do not deliberately sin against morality. They rather ignore it.

In the business world, you will hear a lot of talk about ethics, and almost none about morality. There is a reason for that. The two concepts are quite different.

Let's look into the "American Heritage Dictionary of the English Language".

Morality:
"The quality of being in accord with standards of right or good conduct."

Ethics:
"The rules or standards governing the conduct of a person or the members of a profession."

Morality requires judgement about right or wrong, good or bad. That is, as we all know a horrible chore.

Ethics is a much simpler proposition. It asks for the degree of *conformity* with a set of rules applicable to a *profession* (there we have the dreaded word again). That set of rules is defined by *consensus* within the given profession. Now we are jiving! We find all the warm fuzzy words again.

So now, in corporate America, we do have "rules of ethical conduct", which means: "rules to abide by the rules". In an abstract logical sense, a quite curious construction! But we never wrestle with morality. That would be too complicated anyway, and we have this strange feeling that it is none of our business.

This situation leads to interesting effects. I once asked a coworker how project X was going. Project X was quite difficult, and technically demanding. It also was quite important for the future wellbeing of the company. The answer I got astonished me: "Very well. Mr. Y (one of our notorious grumbling grave diggers) is feeling all warm and balmy about this." It never occurred to the poor man that his answer was deeply amoral. It ignored the objective stakes, to fully concentrate on consensus and conformity with a man who did not care a rat's backside about the wellbeing of the company anyway. You may call this pragmatism. Mr. Y is indeed a powerful man. His frequently and skillfully exercised obstruction could not make anything happen, but it could surely break you!

The proper equilibrium between moral principle and pragmatism as drivers of our actions is a question as old as our reflections about morality. Like many other questions surrounding morality, this has never been resolved to any degree of satisfaction.

The concept of morality resulted from the reflection of man about himself. It became evolutionary necessary when we started to become our only enemy ourselves. We needed something to prevent us from thoughtlessly exterminating each other and thus ourselves. Following Marvin Minsky's ideas as expressed in his "Society of the Mind" [11], we already introduced the notion of different agents constantly struggling for control over the human mind. We already met the "competitor" and the "cooperator". Those live in a quite difficult and controversial relationship. If we also had a very powerful "moralist" present, the latter could act as a kind of Supreme Court, preventing the competitor from jumping out of control. But there is a need for yet another agent. In depth deliberations about something that cannot practically be done anyway are quite futile. So we need a "pragmatist" to keep us aware of what will and will not work.

The pragmatist has no easy job. He needs to be aware of countless facts about the countless entities in the world surrounding us. The physical world would already be daunting enough to discourage the bravest, but human society with its complex network of interaction and feed back is arguably even more complicated. Nevertheless, there are limited domains where the pragmatist can achieve quasi certainty.

The moralist is in an even more difficult situation. Physicists use the so called "actuality principle". This means that certain physical laws are assumed to hold everywhere and always, even if we have not been able to prove this by experiments. If we just had the corresponding "absolute morality", a strong, provable and invariant set of rules to decide between good and bad, valid everywhere and for all times, things would be much simpler. For instance there would not be any of those annoying conflicts between morality and pragmatism. One problem is that we never had such a thing. A worse problem is that some of us, in our eternal longing for absolute truths, deny that fact. Morality *is* variable, because it has to do with choices that are made in reference to our value system. It *did* change quite dramatically in the past and will keep doing so in the future. Look at the value we attach to very basic things like human life or freedom, and you will see that it underwent rather substantial changes even over the last couple of centuries. How else can you explain that at least some of the founding fathers of the United States, people who are universally believed to be the carriers of high moral standards, endorsed slavery quite intuitively? We can go back about 4000 years in history and rather clearly see how people felt about the value of human life. Not only do we observe vast differences between cultures that coexist at the same time, we also see a lot of controversy and debate *within* almost any one individual culture about this important topic at any given moment in time. But only when we introduce the dimension time, things become really relevant. There is a wild up and down. We cannot even claim that there is clean evidence towards what we would so dearly *want* to see: a consistent upward trend.

Some of us will try to weasel out of this dilemma by claiming: "These were the sins of a barbarian past, but now we have figured it all out." How incredibly naïve and arrogant at the same time! Don't you think that also the Romans already believed this for their own understanding of morality?

To make things worse, our most recent thinking patterns, shaped by our ontological worldview were rather inadequate to deal with morality. Morality cannot be isolated. It is in a very strange way at the same time the source and the result of our larger cultural context. The feedback loops are complex and mysterious. There is this one statement that the hemline of skirts goes up with the stock market. And there are these countless tales about decaying morality inevitably leading to the destruction of society, beginning with the story of Sodom and Gomorrah. When we are confronted with these things in practical life, we show reactions that are ludicrous at best. In 1203, the bunch of barbarians pretending to execute the fourth crusade under the constant malevolent influence of a greedy Venetian Doge arrived at the walls of Constantinople. The people of that city could not see that it came this far because of their own eternal intriguing and bickering that later would give birth to the concept "Byzantine", and utterly paralyzed their government. They did not understand that the eradication of altruism from their set of values had made their military powerless. They were unable to observe all this, because their morality had shifted so to accommodate the previously mentioned behavior as "normal". Still wrestling for an explanation, they chose to believe that the upcoming ransack was divine punishment for having welcomed the statues of the Greek gods within their walls. They repented, and literally burnt the irreplaceable work of Phidias in their lime kilns, the Zeus of Olympia, one of the Seven Wonders of the World, among them! Had they done this a year earlier, and used the lime to reinforce their fortifications, there might have been *some* very limited sense in the whole exercise. But as it really happened, it just was a totally futile gesture with a monumental price tag!

We never see the writing on the wall, because we cannot recognize the deviations of our moral compass. It can shift as much as pointing true south, and we won't notice a thing! We would only be able to do so if there were an absolute morality we could calibrate against, but, as we said it before, there is no such thing. One may argue here that religion provides such a stable framework. We just don't want to accept it any longer: our problem! I would suggest a more thoughtful approach here. Let's take the example of the Catholic Church. One of the major bones of contention was the dogma that the pope is infallible, when speaking "ex cathedra" about moral issues. Have you ever contemplated *why* the Catholic Church needed to introduce such a controversial concept? If the scripture could have provided the moral framework for all times, there would not have been a need for such a divisive move. It was the painful awareness that morality changes, and needs to be constantly redefined that drove the Church to this ominous move. The Catholic hierarchy, with its priceless access to the information generated in the confessionals was probably more aware of the tectonic movements within morality than anybody else. The fathers taking confessions were the predecessors of today's psychoanalysts. The darkest secrets of humanity came to the surface in their presence.

So now, in all this confusion, we have our foursome: cooperator, competitor, moralist and pragmatist trying to decide what to do next. Now let's assume that capitalism, without being a religion or a philosophy, has some bearing on morality, by declaring that the norm of all things is dear old me, here and now, and absolutely nothing else. Even if you have not been monitoring the "Zeitgeist" very attentively, you will have noticed some push into that direction. Let's further assume that the moralist buys this story. What is the consequence? The moralist is out of the game. He just abdicated and became the competitor's humble servant. From now on, the still existing conflicts between competitor and cooperator will be arbitrated by the pragmatist.

This is very much what we see happening today in the executive suite. The people that live there are simultaneously much more and much less than what they pretend to be. After all, they are just children of their time. They cannot possibly escape the Zeitgeist. They are utterly and abjectly amoral. They have no desire or intention to do evil, but they have no urge to do good either. They are just making money. *First and foremost* for themselves and if that appears as a necessity to reach the prime goal, they will also try to make some money for their enterprise. Morality was chased out of the executive suite as if it were a bad odor. It was totally substituted by the sterile fumes of ethics that could of course never really replace it.

The extreme feeling poverty of modern enterprise is only one of the consequences. All the things that used to stir passions in humans like good, bad, ugly and beautiful are irrelevant. The enterprise became a cold inanimate moneymaking machine. That means that a large part of society became so. This cannot possibly be the final word. I do not believe that we can evolve that fast. This is a development that clearly overshot. There will be a reaction and the pendulum will swing back.

23 Equilibrium and Symmetry

If we want to understand at least something about the mysterious world surrounding us, equilibrium is a very important concept. Our environment is in constant turmoil, but sometimes, opposing processes can come to a kind of stalemate, practically canceling each other out. That is the essence of the phenomenon equilibrium. It presents us with the illusion of an island of stability in a turbulent universe. For the benefit of those of us that are not familiar with the concept, let's look at the following examples.

Suppose we have two vessels, A and B. They are connected by pipes X and Y. Further there are two pumps P_x and P_y. Those pumps are not equal: P_x is a lot more powerful. At the start of our experiment, both pumps are shut off. Quite obviously, the liquid levels in both vessels will be the same. We know this from grade school: communicating vessels. We could call that a *static* equilibrium. It is depicted in Fig. 23.1.

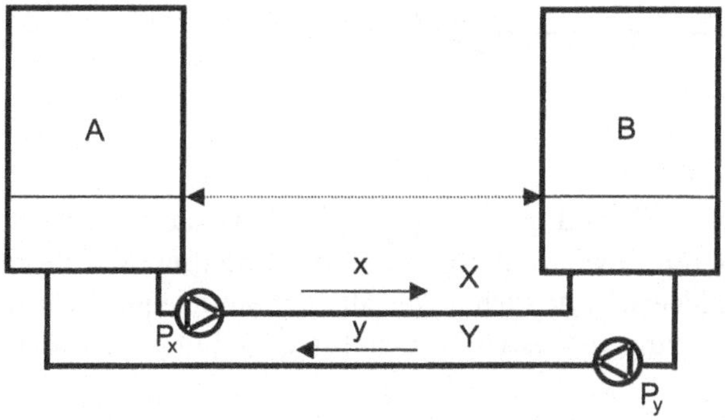

Figure 23.1

Now we start our pumps. Remember: they are not equal. In the beginning the flow x from A to B will be larger than the flow y from B to A, and thus the levels in the two vessels will start to change. After some time, the situation will look like Fig. 23.2.

But now, P_x is facing a decreasing suction head helping it, and an increasing pressure to work against. Therefore flow x will decrease. P_y on the other end benefits from an increasing suction head, and faces less pressure to work against. So flow y will increase. At a certain moment, $x = y$. Now we get to what Fig. 23.3 represents.

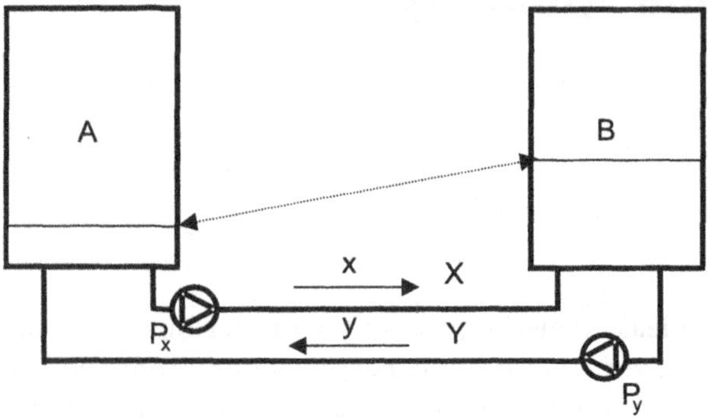

Figure 23.2

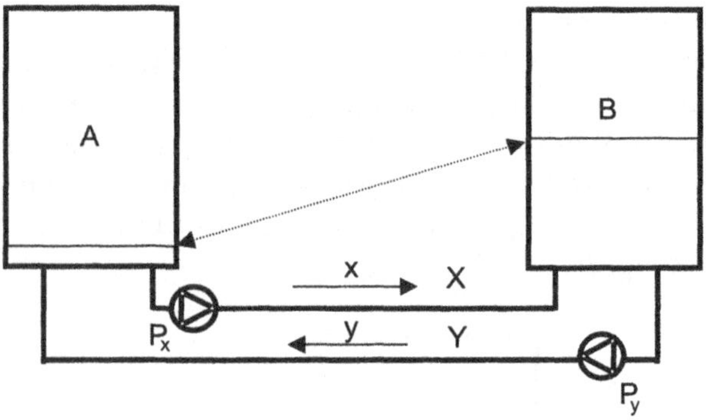

Figure 23.3

The system seems to have stopped changing. The levels remain constant. There is still a lot going on, but flow x remains equal to y, and therefore there is no further change in the levels. That's what we call a dynamic equilibrium. There are powerful forces trying to destroy the status quo, but they cancel each other out.

There is a fundamental difference between static and dynamic equilibrium. If a static system is left alone, it will remain stable. It would in fact take energy input from outside the system to change the status quo. Such a situation appears to be quite robust. A dynamic equilibrium is different. Think about our example again. Suppose one of the pumps broke down. Then the equilibrium would be obviously destroyed, and the system would start to change again ... until a new equilibrium is reached. A dynamic equilibrium is much more fragile than a static one. This is a ubiquitous phenomenon in nature. We observe it in all kinds of shapes and forms. By now, you will have seen how this basically works.

- For anything to happen there needs to be a potential driving change.
- Change then starts to take place with a given intensity.
- There is always resistance to change, and it often increases with the intensity.
- As change takes place, the potential driving the change will decrease.

Obvious examples can be found in electric circuits.

For instance Ohm's law. You can observe this in Fig. 23.4.

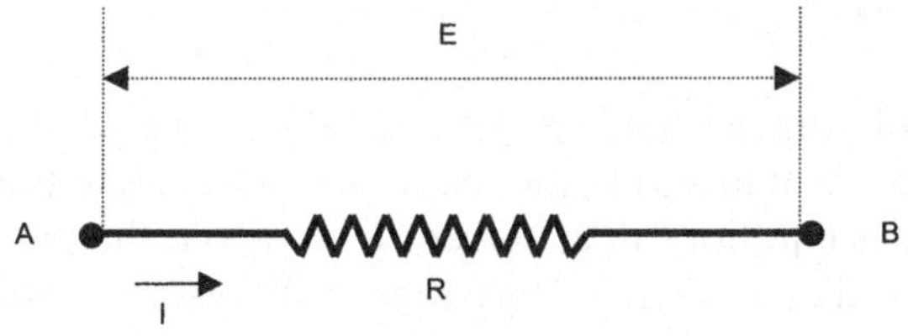

Figure 23.4

It states that the electric current I (in Ampere) going through a circuit is directly proportional to the potential E (in Volt) applied to the circuit, and inversely proportional with the resistance R (in Ohm):

$I = E/R$

Now let's say that the potential E is delivered by a battery. Of course, Ohm's law will go to work, and if we know E and R, it's easy enough to calculate I. That represents a dynamic equilibrium as seen in Fig. 23.5.

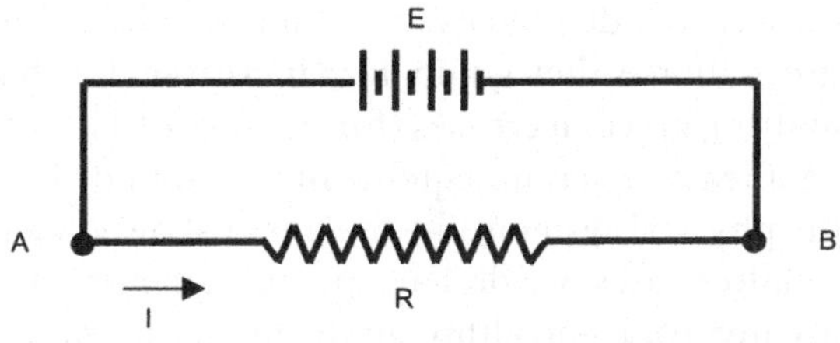

Figure 23.5

But we all know that, while delivering current, the battery will deplete! In the end E will become zero, and a static equilibrium will be reached.

Now let's go one step further, and replace the resistor by a lamp as in Fig. 23.6.

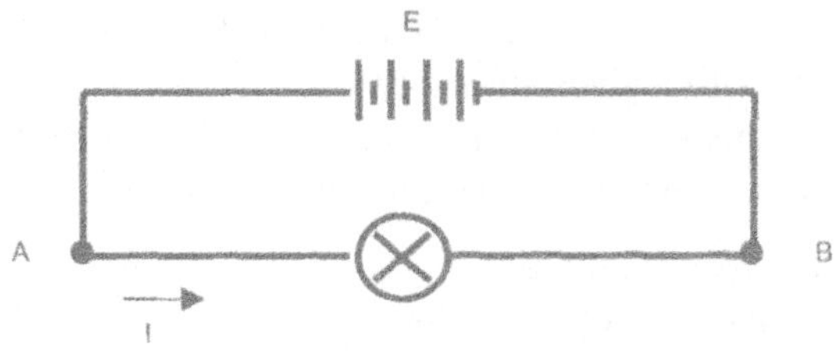

Figure 23.6

Now yet another kind of regulating mechanism kicks in. When it is cold, the lamp has a very small resistance. As it heats up, the resistance increases to the value R. Then the system reaches equilibrium at current I. However, the previously explained phenomenon still takes place. The battery still wears out. So, "I" decreases slowly, until it gets to zero again and steady state is reached.

The world is full of such "self-regulating" mechanisms. In many cases, the resistance does not just increase with the intensity, but with the square, or even higher powers of it.

Let's take a car. Air friction increases with something between the square and the third power of speed. If your engine is in its highest gear, the only way it can deliver even more power is by increasing rpm's. But the torque your engine delivers starts, from a certain point on, to decrease with increasing rpm's. The interaction of those two effects very much determines the maximum speed of your car, which again represents a dynamic equilibrium, this time between engine power and air friction.

Social systems are not very different. They show the same basic mechanisms. Stock prices for instance are clearly defined by an equilibrium between fear and greed. They go up by greed, but as they go up, fear increases (for the sake of an augmented loss possibility), greed decreases (for the sake of a lower profit potential), and a kind of uneasy dynamic equilibrium is found. But there is a huge difference with the physical systems like the ones I showed you in the previous examples. In the latter cases, we do have precise quantitative descriptions of the effects that are involved, and although the math can sometimes become a bit cumbersome, we are able to make absolutely reliable, accurate predictions, also about a quite complex circuit that we have never seen before. Further, our prognostic ability is not limited to just the equilibrium, but also includes the dynamic behavior while moving to it.

For systems involving the reactions of human beings, we have no such certainty. We often don't even know the shape of the equations that are involved, but we do know that those will frequently show large differences from one individual to the next. In spite of Herculean efforts by economists and sociologists, we are barely past qualitative reasoning about these things, but even that, however primitive and inconclusive, still helps to understand the world.

We use the following model a number of times in this book. It represents the enterprise as a kind of countercurrent machine, processing money against material, labor and information. It is sitting there like a gigantic switch enabling, controlling and regulating the interaction between the various stakeholders. Let's have a look at Fig. 23.7.

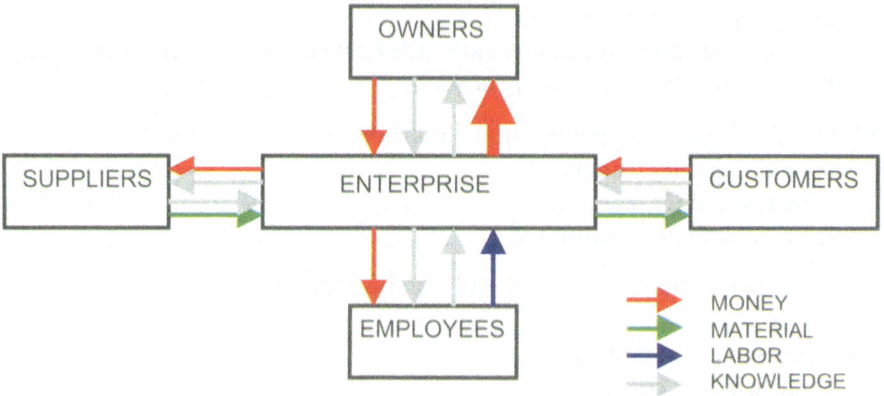

Figure 23.7

One does not need anything more than common sense to see that, with all the various flows through the system, each with its own drivers and rules, any form of equilibrium will at best be a rather fragile dynamic one. There is something else that immediately becomes obvious: if only one of the stakeholders disappeared, the enterprise would cease to exist.

For our reasoning about the system, we will assume it to operate in a completely free market, with multiple suppliers and multiple consumers for everything.

Let us look at the enterprise–customer relationship first:

Equilibrium in this case would mean a solid relationship. But what would we call a solid relationship? Let's try ourselves at a definition.

A constantly growing, or at least stable flow of materials, money and information between the partners.

How could such a situation be sustained? Quite obviously only if *both partners feel* that they benefit from it. Here, like everywhere, equilibrium is not quite possible without symmetry. If one of the partners *believes* that he does not receive sufficient added value from this relationship, he is going to shop around for a different one.

Let us assume that such equilibrium exists between Manufacturing Corp. and Clientes SA. Let us further try to understand the potential forces that could disrupt it and the resistances that such disruption would need to overcome. We will also see that the all-important boundary conditions can differ quite a bit.

- First of all, a lot will depend on the nature of the product:
  - On one side of the spectrum it could be a commodity, deliberately interchangeable without effort on the part of the customer.
  - On the other end it could be a specialty system, technically so complex that the product is not readily interchangeable with a competitor's.
  - Substitution would entail considerable retooling or changes in the customer's production process.
  - With the product comes intricate technical service, deeply entrenched in the customer's production process.
- Then, the supplier's position in the market place will matter:
  - Is he the quality leader?
  - Is he the service leader?
  - Is he the low price supplier?
- The culture in both companies will also be a factor:
  What is important to them?
  - Aggressive cost cutting?
  - Quality at any cost?
  - Service?
  - Continuity?

We may understand this better if we first of all try to isolate the stabilizing factors, reinforcing the equilibrium. We will however see that those are a great deal more complicated than the ones that governed the relatively simple electrical examples that we used.

First of all the supplier wants to keep his customers for many reasons:

- Continuity or the fear of change:
  - An existing and loyal customer gives us planning security.
  - We simply know that he pays on time.
  - We want to build a new plant next year, and we really need his 20,000 tons to assure a decent capacity utilization.
- Resource and cost issues:
  Acquiring a new customer can be a quite elaborate and expensive affair:
  - We would have to submit quotes.
  - We would have to deliver samples.
  - Our technicians will need to learn about their production process.
  - We need to take their people out golfing – or God knows what – for quite some time before we penetrate to the decision-maker.
  - In the beginning there may be problems resulting in expensive complaints.
  - We may need to undercut the – quite advantageous – price they get from our competitor.

- I just hate to think that I will have to deal with their legal department.
- Our people don't know each other. There will be misunderstandings, and we are of course going to pay for those.

Keeping an existing customer seems a lot simpler:

- Over the years, we built all these personal relationships, collected all that know how. Let's not throw it away.

Indeed, every customer represents a kind of investment. That investment will of course be larger the more technically intricate our product is, but there always will be some. Unfortunately, you will never find this in the balance sheet as an asset. It has been sunk in cost and that's that. Thus our awareness of the investment we have here does not do justice to the factual situation.

The customer too has all kinds of reasons to keep the relationship stable:

- Continuity or the fear of change:
  - An existing and loyal supplier gives us planning security.
  - We simply know that he delivers on time.
  - We want to build a new plant next year, and we really can't afford any hassle in the supply situation.
- Resource and cost issues:
  Dealing with a new supplier can be a quite elaborate and expensive affair:
  - We would have to study quotes.
  - We would have to test sample material.
  - Their technicians will need to learn about our production process (the Manufacturing Corp. ones know it by heart).
  - In the beginning there may be problems resulting in expensive production outages.
  - I just hate to think that I will have to study and sign another contract.
  - Our people don't know each other. There will be misunderstandings. We can probably make the supplier pay, but we will still have the trouble.

So far, there is a remarkable degree of symmetry between the two parties' motives. But there is more:

- History:
  - I recall clearly that day when our production process went haywire. At first we suspected that it was the raw material, so we complained with Manufacturing Corp. Their technician came, found the problem - it had nothing to do with their product - and fixed it.
  - We stupidly enough got into a liquidity problem once. They just extended our credit line.

- Convenience:
  - If there is a problem, I can call John of Manufacturing Corp. after midnight at home. He will immediately take action to help us.
- And then, there are the little selfish motives. They are as despicable as they are widespread. We are all just human, and Manufacturing Corp. has a competent sales force; they are fully aware of the facts:
  - Manufacturing Corp. always invites my wife and me to the US Open. Brenda just loves it!
  - Their golf tournament is so much fun!

  We will stop the allegations here, but we all know that this is not the end of it. I do not believe that in today's Western world, downright bribery plays an important role. The reason is certainly not to be found in a superior morality of our powerbrokers. They are just more sophisticated and prudent. We all have heard about the "donations" to political parties that often accompany weapons sales in Europe. But certainly it is only governments that are corrupt? The variations are endless, but here comes something that I saw myself. You try to sell to Pirates AG and you get nowhere, until you find out that in order to do business with them you have to go via a consultant: Baksheesh Ltd., a one-man show in London. The consultant takes a commission of three percent. In order to earn that commission he does nothing more than establish the contact. Does anyone need further explanations?

If Manufacturing Corp. has managed to create a relationship like this, all of the above combined forms a formidable resistance to change. But it is very easy to see how this resistance can be decreased. Technical problems with the product or delivery, especially if repeated, are only one of the possibilities.

Where is the potential that threatens the equilibrium? What forces drive change?

- Resource and cost issues:
  - If there is an alternative competent supplier with a cost advantage, willing to expand and therefore willing to accept a considerably and consistently lower price, the relationship is highly threatened.
  - If Clientes SA introduces a new product that is more demanding on the raw material, and Manufacturing Corp. cannot consistently meet the new requirements, there will be a strong incentive to shop around for another supplier.
  - Suppose Clientes SA wants to go to full blown electronic commerce. They want electronic orders, automatically generated by their transaction system. They do not want to deal with invoices. They will go to two way matching and pay for what they received, based on the data from our order confirmation. If our systems do not allow us to accommodate their

plan, we are in trouble. If on the other hand, we can play along, that will further cement our relationship.

But as always, there are also less objective motives and as so often, they can be the decisive ones:

- Mr. X is the new purchasing director for Clientes SA. Mr. X is the prototype of our young, aggressive hard driving manager. His intelligence, morality and dedication to the company are rather mediocre, but his ambition is limitless and so is his talent for public relations. He wants to go up in the hierarchy and he wants it fast. He needs to make a big splash, to be noticed. A change of supplier might fit the bill. He can present a convincing case to the executive committee and upon their approval rather easily carry the thing out. He is not certain himself that this will in the end benefit his company. There may be considerable hidden costs. But that's the operative word: "*hidden*". We, at Manufacturing Corp. are quite powerless against this turn of events. Nothing will help. Not even a large price discount will keep us in business. Mr. X wants change for the sake of change. When you start to think of this, it's really the corporate equivalent of cancer. But the top executives love Mr. X. He is *so* charming.

There is an almost symmetric possibility within Manufacturing Corp. Over the years, the price Clientes SA pays for our product has degraded. It should never have happened, but it did. There would of course be cautious ways to correct this, but we too have our Mr. X. He is our new marketing director, and he recently discovered activity based costing. I am not going to repeat the remarks about the other Mr. X. All X's are equal!

Let's pause a moment and sum up what we have seen so far:

- The basic mechanisms are not different from the examples pertaining to electricity.
- The complexity of the total structure and the near total absence of quantitative information lead to a situation where the understanding that this is after all just about potential and resistance becomes useless for practical purposes. Even the most dauntingly complex electronic circuit is fairly simple compared to this.
- The relationship between the enterprise and its supplier is almost the mere mirror image of our dealings with our customers. The "almost" comes from the fact that we do something to the products we buy: we add value. Therefore, what we sell will probably be somewhat less of a commodity than what we buy. But nevertheless, a considerable degree of symmetry remains. It would enormously help if we better understood this.

Let's do one of our fantasy experiments again:

I am a rather mediocre chess player. Nevertheless, I claim that I could play simultaneously against the two most powerful chess players in the world and guaranteed achieve a draw. The conditions are just that one of them has to play white, the other black, and my white opponent makes the first move. The rest is quite simple. Once I see Mr. A's opening move, I repeat it against Mr. B. On that board I have white, so I open. I now need to wait for Mr. B to counter my move. That's what I play against A. I keep doing this throughout the game. I cannot lose. In fact, I have A playing against B. I am just an innocent bystander. Even the clock will not get me in trouble. The only way my magnificent scheme might be crossed is if one of them gives up. Then I would have to face the other one on my own, and we know how that will end. But wait a minute. If A gives up, I have a point. When I then quite predictably lose against B, it will still be a draw.

There are of course zillions of arguments for not applying this to the customer supplier game. The markets are different etc. I still believe that we could do a lot more in that direction, especially in those cases where we have partners that are customers *and* suppliers at the same time. But of course, for this to happen purchasing and sales have to talk to each other, and that would be a revolutionary novelty.

Symmetry on this level is impossible to detect from a cubicle, and the perspective from the executive suite is not much better. That is one of the fundamental problems of the contemporary enterprise. We are all so much involved with the little part that is important for "dear old #1" in the immediate future, that we have lost our view on the whole.

Let us now look at the relationship between the enterprise and its owners: the shareholders. Their situation is somewhat unique in the following respect: they are the only ones that give money to the company *and* receive some as well. Please do not get irritated by the thick red arrow I drew in Fig. 23.7 from the enterprise to the shareholders. It is only meant to symbolize that, over time, they expect and need to get more out of the enterprise than they put in. Any other arrangement would be inherently and dangerously unstable.

We dealt with the idiosyncrasies of the stock market in a separate chapter, but for now, we should try to define what constitutes a stable relationship between shareholder and enterprise. A loyal shareholder reinvests. What we are looking at is a set of cash flows over time. Investment money goes to the company, dividends to the shareholder. The only objective benchmark for such a situation is the DCF (discounted cash flow) rate. The latter should be consistently and considerably above the return one could get from bonds, CD's or similar low risk investment opportunities. In the latter case, the owner will reinvest his profits and we have a stable relationship. There are a number of obvious incentives to preserve this equilibrium. The owner sees a long-term reliable source of income. The company has a vital interest to keep owners that are interested in the company's future and that are going to stay for the long haul. It may strike you as remarkable how similar such an arrangement is with the family owned business from the past. When both parties in a deal have so much of common interest, one could be tempted to assume a very robust, almost intrinsically stable equilibrium. Unfortunately, there are parties that, although having a lot less stake in the enterprise, will be tempted to pursue a quite different agenda. They are also influential far beyond their degree of commitment to the enterprise. Top management in their quite detrimental interaction with public opinion and an increasingly noncommittal stock market is a prime suspect when it comes to the destruction of the equilibrium. Wait a minute! Why am I picking on top management again? The simple truth is: I am not picking on anybody! But knowing that top management is just a subset of humanity, not very different from the statistical universe they live in, I am merely taking the same approach that a criminologist would use if he had to identify suspects. The main question is: who has a motive? Top management does. They are presented with so many enticing incentives to do the wrong thing for the enterprise that they must be suspects. After all, they are just human, like you and me, and there is only so much temptation we can deal with.

A return of 2% or less is not going to present an enticing reinvestment opportunity. Quite the contrary, it might even convince our long-term, loyal shareholders to sell. Such a situation is not completely management's fault. One could argue that the stock market does it to itself. Nevertheless, management is all too often a quite willing accomplice in the process.

Our last group of stakeholders is the employee community.

In this case, the stability of the relationship is measured in terms of average employee retention time. We invest in our employees, just like the shareholders invest in the enterprise. We do it very much for the same reason. We hope that in the long haul, we will get a decent return. For that to happen, our employees need to stay.

It is quite easy to see an astonishing amount of symmetry between the last two stakeholder groups. Both groups are rather fragmented. Individually they have very little leverage with the enterprise. They both found a way out of this: representation! The employees were traditionally represented by trade unions.

The shareholder's equivalent of that is the Mutual Fund. There always were big shot shareholders as well as big shot employees that could do without representation. Today the trade union's influence is on the decline. But that is just one more sign of the total focus on shareholder value.

The equilibrium's worst enemy is the excess. The age-old knowledge about this has been preserved in our traditions and sayings:

- Moderation in everything!
- It's never the substance that kills, it's always the dose.

We know indeed from biology that certain substances that are, at a given intake, essential for life will nevertheless kill if administered in a much higher dose. This again seems one of these universal principles that one encounters everywhere in some shape or form. We will understand this best if we ask ourselves where the focus, the center of gravity of attention and concern is to be found in our dealings with the phenomenon enterprise. We all know where we would *want* the center of gravity to be: right in the middle, equally reaching out to all stakeholders, like in Fig. 23.8.

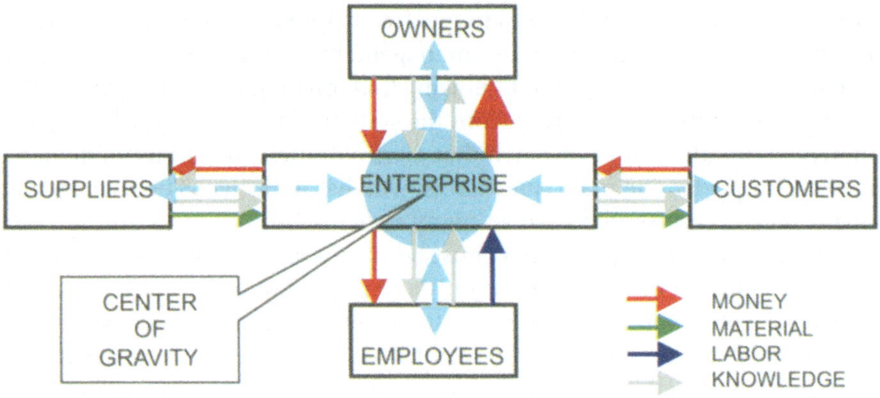

Figure 23.8

That would be much too nice to ever happen in real life. The latter is, more realistically, represented by the following diagram. That includes the contemporary position of the center of gravity clearly in the realm of the owner, as shown in Fig. 23.9.

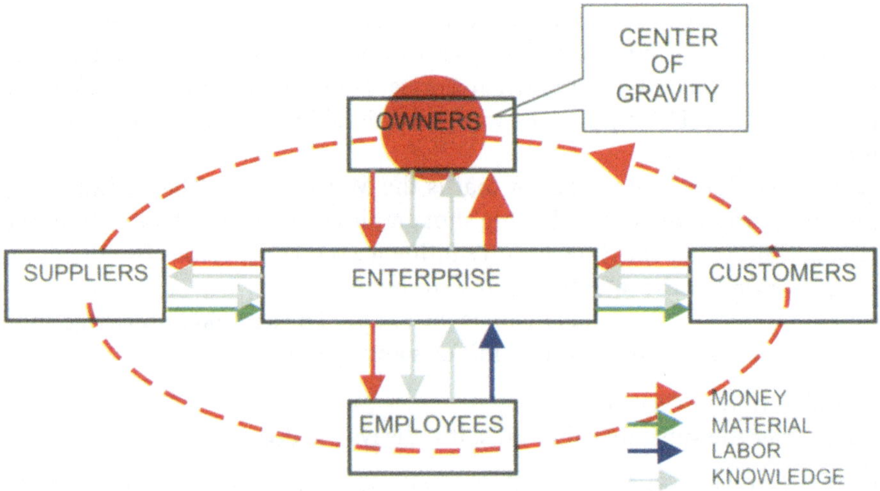

Figure 23.9

The center of gravity is moving around all the time. That makes the enterprise behave like a kind of oscillator. But wait a minute! The enterprise was never intended to be an oscillator. It was meant to be an amplifier, a value amplifier more precisely. Sure! Do you know Murphy's law of electrical engineering?

- If you try to build an oscillator, nothing in the world is going to persuade it to swing.
- If you try to build an amplifier, *that* one will oscillate right away.

Imagine for a moment that the enterprise, as we depict it here, were a space station. That's not such a crazy comparison. All the stakeholders live in it, sharing the same crucial life support systems. Further, suppose that by some magic the center of gravity would move along a trajectory as shown in the drawing. What would happen?

- Our space station would uncontrollably wobble.
- It would not be a very pleasant place to live.
- It would also be a fairly dangerous place, because the oscillation would create continuous and considerable stress in all the connections that hold the different modules together. Such a situation is known to lead to fatigue failures.
- If we ever really were in such a situation, we would not take long to come to the realization that we cannot afford to have one of the modules break loose. That would also be the case if you were an ultra-left Marxist employee that does not grant the owners as much as a glass of water. Even such a person would be horrified by the thought of the owner module being separated from the space station enterprise.

Unfortunately, we never experience the direct physical threat that would be associated with the previous scenario and thus we can *pretend,* with *temporary* impunity, that reality is different. We can act as if this were in fact just another competitive situation where the mission basically is to outsmart the other stakeholders and to take advantage of them.

But there is another question. The equilibrium as depicted in the first diagram is so obviously and so much better that one could wonder how and why we afford ourselves this crazy rotation. Who determines the center of gravity anyway? Certainly top management again! Of course, lets round up the usual suspects. That is only true in a very limited sense. It is the Zeitgeist that determines where attention is focused. The Zeitgeist is something that lives in society. And there, our top managers are, like all of us, at the same time perpetrators and victims. They are often driven by the Zeitgeist like an autumn leaf by the wind. They are at the same time tragic and comic: tragic in their helplessness and comic in their compulsive refusal to admit it. Nevertheless, they play a crucial role. They cannot change the Zeitgeist, but within limits they have the ability to decide how enthusiastically they are going to follow it.

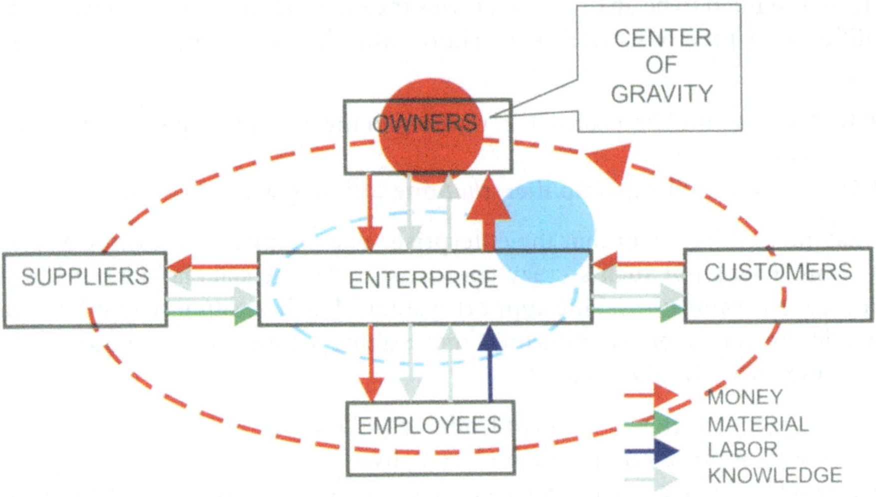

Figure 23.10

Just imagine an enlightened top management, able to keep the center of gravity on the green trajectory (as shown in Fig. 23.10) instead of the red one. Would that not considerably reduce the stresses in the system? Would that not free up energy, otherwise wasted on internal friction, for the benefit of the whole? That might very well be the ultimate challenge to management: to *resist* the Zeitgeist to a certain extent – one cannot get away with too much resistance – and to *preserve* the equilibrium for the future, rather than trying to erect a flamboyant monument for oneself. However, that's not just everybody's chore, and we should not be astonished that only a few honestly try to do this. Even fewer succeed.

24 The Problem with Change

24.1 The Merits of Small Steps

What can be done better? The moment we use the verb "to do", we know that we are talking about interacting with the world. That always means change. The word change seems to exercise a strange kind of fascination. And as always with things human, fascination and fear are not far apart. If I take the functional viewpoint, my life cannot be truly valued in an isolated fashion. It has very little value per se. It can only be understood and appreciated in terms of its interaction with the world. So in a strange way, the doing becomes part of the meaning. But doing means change!

If we want to achieve anything in the world, I believe it is highly advisable to study the phenomenon "change" first.

By now we will all understand a couple of things:

- We are dealing with processes in the framework of evolution.
- Due to the nature of evolution, we are not just undergoing its effects, but also shaping its course.
- Our observations indicate that evolution behaves chaotically. This means that apparently very small causes can have very substantial effects.

That leaves us humans hanging in limbo. On one hand there is our relative insignificance as individuals. On the other hand, one can never be quite sure what action will help to tip what scale in what direction in the future. We all know the story of Manlius Capitolinus and the geese. What it really tells is that even the behavior of animals can change history!

Our lives are like a stone thrown into the pond. We all do make waves, albeit small ones. As time progresses, the waves get weaker and weaker, reflect on the banks of the pond, and interfere with other waves either attenuating or reinforcing them. But the waves really never completely die.

So on one hand, it is highly unlikely that I will achieve something really magnificent in my lifetime and the possibility that I will do something abysmally evil is equally remote. On the other hand, I am somehow contributing to every future victory and every defeat of mankind. Due to the chaotic nature of the process, however minute my contribution is, it just might be the decisive one!

So while we cannot ride high and proud, because we are indeed not all that important, we cannot abdicate our responsibility either. That's probably the true essence of human life. It happens between "on one hand" and "on the other hand". It happens between the infinitely large and the infinitely small, between important and futile … somewhere in between. Already Pascal [13] had noticed this striking ambiguity in human nature: "L'Homme est un roseau, mais un roseau pensant."

And here we are, pondering what we are going to do about some quite important aspects of evolution, that mysterious bigger than life engine of creation itself! If it were not so dramatic, it could be funny.

If we are serious about this – and we better be – our first order of business must be to take a closer look at the mechanisms of evolution. What we find is that it is all about change. Even with our very limited understanding, we can still see that evolutionary pressure does at least show some similarities with optimization processes. There is however no simple objective function and we are probably dealing with optimization in a multi dimensional space. One rather useful way of looking at these things are the so-called "hill climbing" and "deluge" models [10]. Imagine a three dimensional representation of an objective function. It looks like a landscape with valleys, hills and mountaintops. Each summit represents a local optimum. In the "valleys", you put a number of objects, each representing a strain in evolution. Now you switch on the factor time. In every discrete time period, the water level will go up a bit, inundating more of the landscape. Each of the objects can take a step of variable length in any direction. Length – up to a limit – and direction of every step needs to be determined by some algorithm that is part of the object's properties. There is however one paramount rule: don't go into the water! As time progresses, we see our creatures climb the hills. This is another way to say that they become better and better in the sense of the objective function we are looking at. Some have sought refuge on mountains that were too low and they drown. Let's try to project this kind of model upon evolution as it happens in reality.

- We are now at it for millions of years.
- The water level is quite high.
- Our creatures are all relatively close to the summits of the respective mountains they have been climbing.

As a consequence, they take smaller and smaller steps, because *any* big step is highly likely to lead downward or even end in the water. So, for the natural species I believe that we have a convincing case against big moves.

How about our species "enterprise"? It is of course much younger, and had less time to adapt to its environment. On the other hand it is much simpler in structure and scope than even the simplest bacterium. One could believe that the enterprise is far from its optimum, if one contemplates what it theoretically could do. But so are all natural creatures if you look at them in the same way. Of course, I also see that our enterprises are far from perfect. Otherwise, there would not have been a reason to write this book. But I still believe that the enterprise achieved a quite remarkable adaptation to its habitat. This only becomes clearer if you look at what modern enterprises are able to achieve compared to their predecessors of only a couple of centuries ago. I happen to believe that also the enterprise is in the mean time much closer to the summit than to the valley. If that were true, a course of action involving big leaps would be bad business. In gambling terms: a low probability of hitting the jackpot and a high likelihood of substantial damage. But "big leaps" is what all the fashionable fads nowadays prescribe. "Change" is the buzzword of the day. This is insane. I don't want change. Nobody in his right mind can want change. I want *improvement* but that's something entirely different. It is change *with a direction*. It is no longer fashionable to say such a thing. Improvement was the buzzword of a previous era ("continuous improvement", do you remember?). People grew impatient with that. Now they want *CHANGE*. Let's think a moment about this. The cry for unspecified change really means: "We don't really know what we want or need, but one thing is perfectly clear: we don't want what we used to have any longer." This is an astonishingly frequently observed popular sentiment. Nations have elected parliaments and governments that they truly didn't want via this mechanism. The process is very clearly represented in Fig. 24.1.

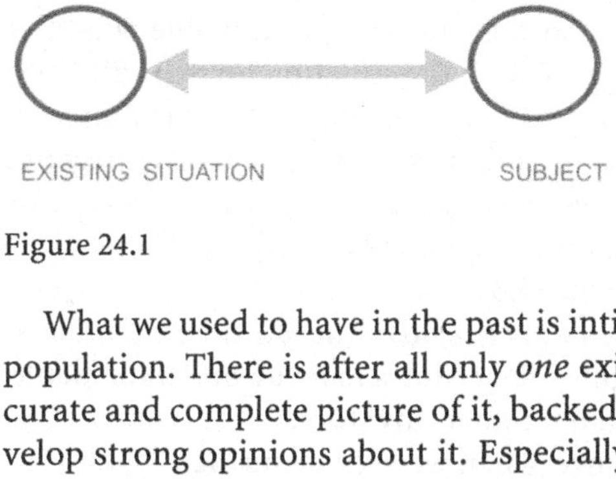

Figure 24.1

What we used to have in the past is intimately known to broad layers of the population. There is after all only *one* existing situation. We have a fairly accurate and complete picture of it, backed by experience, so we are able to develop strong opinions about it. Especially masses have a very clear tendency to let their perception drift to the negative side of reality. We will almost always perceive the existing situation worse than it objectively is. Communication and the media certainly play a role in this, but also the inherent unbalance in our weighing of the known against the unknown contributes. We know exactly what we have, but we have only a very vague cursory idea of what *could* have been instead.

When it comes to visions for the future, the situation is much less clear. We can approach this through Fig. 24.2.

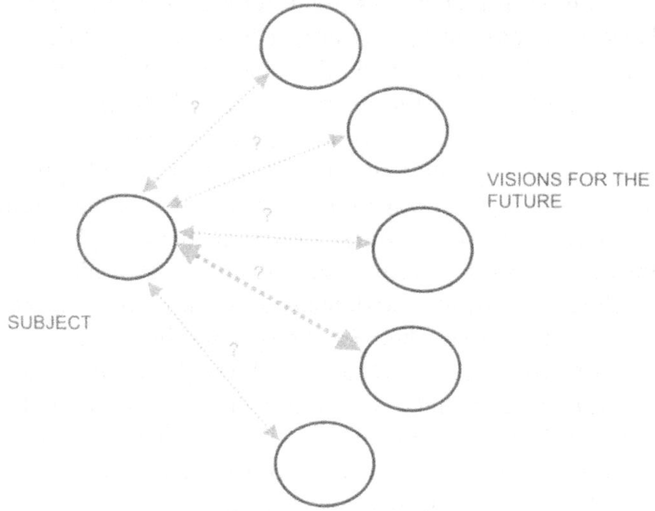

Figure 24.2

First of all, there is almost always more than one such vision under consideration. The alternatives compete with, and partly contradict each other. Although we have a tendency to deal with the future much more graciously than with the past – meaning that we will have a more positive bias here – we will still remain suspicious and uncertain. Because of all this, we can never have, even with our preferred future scenario the same unquestionable cognitive bond that we have with the known past. That is the situation for an individual. For society, there are additional aspects. We all together have many alternative futures but only one common past and existing situation. The negative spin on the past will be concentrated on one object. Any negative expectation, however vague, towards any of the future scenarios will be "diluted" due to the number of alternatives. Just look at Fig. 24.3.

Suddenly, the idea to uncompromisingly get rid of the left side, without exactly knowing where to go on the right side becomes halfway understandable. All we know is that we don't want what we have anymore.

We will get rid of it, with a vengeance. Then we will see further.

Our desire to get away from the past as far as possible invites to a big leap that will probably end in the water. But you still see that something that started out looking like fairly childish moodiness has in reality a sound mechanistic background. Not that this matters when it comes to the end result!

Change is dangerous stuff. It is like explosives. It should be handled with great care, and only by experts who know what they are doing, in which case it can be extremely helpful. But the general population hardly qualifies as an expert. As soon as they start to play with change, mostly hyped up by ruthless demagogues, you better take cover!

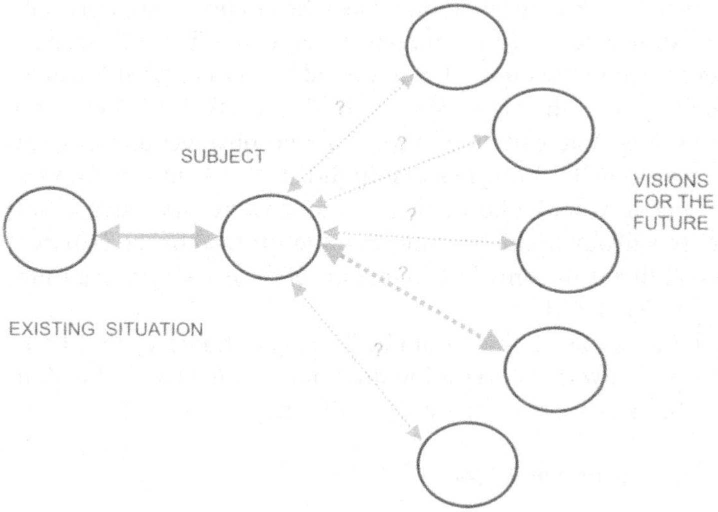

Figure 24.3

Change is a term with an infinite scope. It can mean change of almost anything. That means that there is change and change. Of course replacing a pencil by a ballpoint pen is change but it is benign change. Replacing tools by more effective ones is not always easy, but it does not create the controversy and the tension that arise when we touch the fabric of society: the relationships among people, and the interaction between people and the enterprise.

24.2 Lessons from the Past

Let's look at how different organizations fared with different approaches to change in the past.

24.2.1 The Catholic Church

When it comes to the "longest living organism award", the Catholic Church will of course face some competition: the sequoia tree for instance, or more seriously Judaism. I do not consider Judaism an organization; I believe it to be a tribal affair. I have checked with my Jewish friends and they happen to agree with me. But I know far too little about it anyway to deal with it in a way that would do justice to its breathtaking history.

The Catholic Church has by now survived 2000 years. Even without a closer look at the circumstances, that is a most remarkable achievement. I do not know of any other human organization even remotely showing a similar accomplishment. It is however only when one takes the circumstances into account that the true dimensions of this miracle become tangible. The leadership committed every sin in the book! If you wanted to analyze what it would take to ruin a powerful organization, you would find it all right here. 2000 years is a very long time. You can do a lot of different outrageous things in such a period. At times the Catholic leadership did stuff that makes Clinton *and* his zealous persecutors look like a bunch of immaculate altar boys, if not saints. I often – only halfway jokingly – said that the survival of the Catholic Church in spite of all this is the only irrefutable proof for divine intervention on earth. But they still survived.

I am far from claiming that all this would be the result of the way they handle change, and we all know that correlation does not yet mean causality, but let's take a look at this aspect nevertheless. How did they do it?

24.2.1.1 Extreme Conservatism in Doctrine

The Catholic Church is excruciatingly slow in adapting to new discoveries and developments, even if those happen in the scientific arena. They traditionally lag behind several generations. That drives some of their followers completely nuts, me being one of those. This is all the more astonishing because the Church counts so many fine scientists in her ranks. When the old cardinal Ottaviani was interviewed (must have been in the early 70's) and was asked what his biggest disappointment had been, he mentioned the fact that "Evolution theory was still taught by some catholic universities". Now this was the prefect of the congregation for the conservation of the faith, a prince of the Church, and absolutely no dummy. He had helped to steer the Church through very troubled waters before, during and after the Second World War. He was old and blind, and must have felt his end near. The physical evidence at that point was absolutely overwhelming. Pierre Teilhard de Chardin, a French Jesuit and paleontologist had written his "Phénomène Humain"[18], a loving and deeply religious reconciliation between faith and facts. For Ottaviani all this did not matter. The *only* concern was conservation of the doctrine.

We all remember the clash between Galileo and the Church. He weaseled out of the problem. I don't blame him. A healthy portion of cowardice is often a life-preserving asset. The Church was deadly serious. They would have tortured and killed him over a question that was in the end just about ... practicality! This may amaze you, but look at the following. That the earth revolves around the sun (the "new truth") is, in an absolute cognitive sense, not a bit "more true" than the opposite (the "old truth"). But the modern model of the solar system makes it a whole lot easier to describe and predict nearly all celestial phenomena (pertaining to the solar system) that we are interested in. Therefore, it would be highly impractical to assume that the earth is the center of the planetary system, and thus we don't. Please mind the selection of words:

"impractical", not "wrong", unless of course you define "impractical" or "lack of elegance" as implicitly "wrong". But the church was not so much concerned with the simplicity of calculations, as with the simplicity of maintaining its teachings and doctrine. If you claim to own the eternal truth, you need to present a monolithic picture, including past, present and future, without the slightest contradiction. You cannot just say that yesterday's absolute, universal and eternal truth became untrue this morning! Looking at things that way, maintaining that the earth is the center of the universe, beginning with the planetary system, seemed a quite practical standpoint. To hell with the astronomers, let them work somewhat harder; what do they contribute anyway? Is it amazing that people could fight with such a passion over issues that, in the end, were merely about practicality? Could the church have maintained that the earth in a philosophical sense still was the center of the universe – and that would have been a quite outrageous statement as such – while for the sake of the ease of calculations we could have used the heliocentric model? Could Galileo himself have proposed such a compromise? Of course not: none of the players understood the limitations of his "truth". Their "truths" were as absolute as they were opposed.

There shall not be any undue amusement among the Protestants! Luther and Melanchton condemned the heliocentric model as violently as the Catholic Church did. They were only "saved" by their lack of worldly power to follow through.

Up to this day, there have been similar "clashes" over things like contraception, and "liberation theology". The thought patterns have not truly changed, neither have the discussion methods, but torturing and killing have been out of fashion for quite some time now. But once again, one of the perpetual miracles that seem to escort the Church on its journey through the centuries strikes. When you hear today a man like Karl Lehmann, the speaker of the indecently rich German Catholic Church, give his view on the errors of the past, you experience the kind of intelligent and compassionate love that made and makes the Christian faith irresistible.

Nevertheless, the church has clearly recognized the need for some controlled, organized change. To that effect the dogma of the pope's infallibility was introduced. This controversial authority that is, in a philosophical sense, the equivalent of a thermonuclear weapon is used very seldom and with extreme restraint.

24.2.1.2 Dealing with Dissidents

Dissidents are difficult people. They come from within the organization. They have seen the light and accordingly demand a lot of change in a short time. Dissidents do not fool around with peripheral or pragmatic questions. They go right to the heart of the matter. There are of course, also within the Catholic

Church, such disputes regarding more core questions, like theology itself. It is quite remarkable how that is dealt with. The church may be slow to accept new ideas, but it is often equally slow to condemn them. In many cases, the time gained before taking irreversible positions is used wisely for attempts to reconcile, even absorb the adverse standpoints. In some cases this worked excellently, Saint Francis of Assisi being a prime example for the very successful absorption of a potentially dangerous dissidence. In other cases it didn't work out, and Martin Luther might be the prototype for that. There are, depending on the mood of the time, also cases where the decision is lightning swift, but that remains the exception. However once the church has determined its position and condemned the "heresy" it will bring down all its – at times considerable – worldly might and influence on the poor dissident. That is done with a determination and cruelty defying the defense systems of any worldly organization in terms of amorality.

24.2.1.3 Centralization – Decentralization

These things are quite rigorously regulated. The doctrine is centrally controlled, but there is a lot of leeway for decentralized interpretation and expression. That does not just refer to geographical diversity. Also the different religious orders have a – centrally sanctioned – particular way of living the religion. This once in a while leads to tensions between the papal bureaucracy and some religious orders, especially the more progressive ones, but all this seems to be digested quite well.

As the Catholic Church is entering the 21st century, a shortsighted analysis may find enormous problems. In all industrialized countries, the membership dwindles. There are big unresolved questions like contraception and the role of women in the church. If one takes a somewhat longer view, and for an organization of this longevity that would be no less than appropriate, things look different. The Church is standing stronger today than in most periods of its past. It has addressed a number of truly scandalous hot potatoes like its relationship to Judaism and the inquisition. It is exercising a strange attraction especially on young people. Its moral authority is unbroken, even recovering. There is a huge following in the third world. The Catholic Church will be around for some more time.

24.2.2 Ancient Rome

Just the question how long Rome lived and ruled is controversial and depending on the eye of the beholder, but let's settle for a rather modest and defendable period of 1000 years. Even now, about 1500 years later, Rome fascinates us. Its language and judicial concepts survive. From our perspective Rome was at the same time astonishingly modern in some of its concepts, while other aspects would be classified as "utmost barbarian brutality." The Romans were no great scientists. I can hear a loud protest from the lawyers here, but I am going to survive that. I happen to think that lawyers aren't, and never were scientists. They are highly structured wheelers and dealers, making, arguing, interpreting and applying the rules of human society. They never bake bread but they will readily interfere in the argument about the distribution of a loaf that was made by someone else. The Romans were considerable engineers, they invented the arch, but I keep wondering how far they would have been able to go without the Greek slaves they kept for minor tasks like intellectual work and teaching their children.

How did they do it?

24.2.2.1 Extreme Conservatism in Doctrine

The Romans did not have a very elaborate doctrine. I believe that they were to a large extent pragmatic no-nonsense people. Their core doctrine was quite simple in terms of scope:

- Rome rules, and you are going to respect our laws.
- The Roman Gods will be worshipped.

There was very little apart from that. They even lacked a constitution that regulated the succession of their rulers.

However, the small core doctrine was upheld with a vengeance. The Romans seemed quite open and receptive for foreign culture. They accepted temples of foreign gods, even in Rome itself. But they insisted that *also* the Roman gods be worshiped in the most remote corner of their provinces, no compromises. That explains the exceptional problems they had with the Jews, because the latter could never agree with such an arrangement. That must have baffled the Romans, because all other conquered provinces had settled for their deal without much ado. The Romans were not particularly narrow-minded when it came to the application of force and brutality. The Jews paid a horrible price for their loyalty to their – *and our* – one and only God. They were driven into the Diaspora with all its terrible consequences. I have always had this eerie feeling that the Jewish problems were not unwelcome as a manageable demonstration of Roman power and ruthlessness, for all other nations to observe and learn from. As strange as the Jews were, worshiping an invisible God without being able to show as much as a statue, it must have been the Christians that really flabbergasted the Roman policy makers. Those people were *atheists*. They had no gods at all. They were willing to die for this Jesus: a Jew executed on the cross! The Romans immediately sensed that they saw an aberration so abominable that it needed to be eradicated with all due brutality, and so they acted.

Another less visible but possibly even more important aspect was the unwavering commitment of Roman citizens to their state, passed from generation to generation and jealously guarded against any form of change.

Rome went from a kingdom to a republic and from a republic to an empire. There were horrible civil wars, intrigues, murders, revolts and much more. Several times, total defeat loomed over the horizon. But as long as Rome stubbornly stuck to its core values, it survived.

24.2.2.2 Dealing with Dissidents

Rome had a senate, where the ruling class could express itself, also controversially. Rome was in reality being run by a limited number of families. They eternally disagreed, but in most cases the conflict could be kept civil. If you were a Roman aristocrat, you had as a dissident a good chance to be co-opted. But if you were a slave, and you disagreed with slavery, your prospects in life were not all that good. In order to suppress the Spartacus revolt, Rome had to call back three legions from the provinces. That was as extraordinary as using the US Army within the United States to suppress a coal miners strike. Such a thing was unheard of. The brutality of the punishment was accordingly.

24.2.2.3 Centralization – Decentralization

The Romans dealt with this notoriously difficult question in an extraordinary skillful way. They allowed the provinces quite some autonomy. They could keep their own gods, as long as they were willing to *also* worship the Roman ones. Their leadership could participate in government, as long as it would not take issue with Roman core doctrine. During the conquering of foreign lands, the legions did of course take booty, but afterwards there were no asphyxiating taxes, and if you could advance to the status of "Roman colony", even none at all. All that the Romans would do was levy troops, and the soldiers were – for the time – treated really decently. They even had a kind of pension plan!

When they changed their state religion to Christianity, that was probably too big a step. It replaced the one pillar of their core doctrine that never before had moved an inch. Other parts of the core beliefs that cemented the Roman State had been in slow decay for some period of time already. But this was a very dramatic move, too much too fast. The size of the struggle shows through the fact that they went back to the previous religion, and then back to Christianity again. It was more than the Empire could digest. One could, with terrible simplification, claim that Rome died of an overdose of change.

24.2.3 The Soviet Union

Russia in 1917 was not exactly an appealing take over object, but the communists could not pass up the opportunity. There were a host of foreseeable problems. Socialism was designed for the proletariat of the industrialized nations, preferably Germany. Russia, still completely focused on agriculture and partly immersed in an almost medieval feudal structure, was a very unlikely candidate. But it was all the communists could get, so they took it. They had great plans. Russia was going to become the workers' paradise. From that base the idea would spread to soon encompass the world. But in order to achieve all this, the fabric of the "old" society needed to be destroyed. Communism demands "the new man". There was no other way than starting with *a lot of change.* Age-old habits, institutions and rights had to disappear, among them:

- private property
- religion
- the previous social order and ruling class.

Very soon, it showed that these changes were too much for the people, in which name all this was done, to digest. The new leaders had to react by – inconspicuously of course – distancing themselves from Marx and Engels, and embracing Bolshevism, a very radical and brutally violent interpretation of socialism, leading to the dictatorship of the proletariat. That of course meant dictatorship of the leading clique. The Soviet Union was officially created in 1922 and peacefully passed away in 1991.

24.2.3.1 Extreme Inflexibility in Doctrine

We have argued before that communism in reality was a religion. It probably had the most rigid dogmatic structure of any religion I have seen. After exposing the popular masses to an excruciating amount of change affecting every aspect of their lives, the soviet leadership declared change dead. From now on things were going to stay the way they were. This gave birth to rather interesting thinking patterns.

One of the most hilarious examples was the Brezhnev doctrine. The reasoning goes as follows. Dialectical materialism shows us how society has evolved and will evolve in the future:

- hunters and collectors
- agricultural society
- urban artisan society
- industrial society
- impoverishment of the industry proletariat due to capitalism
- revolution leading to socialism
- socialism evolving into communism.

Not only did they know that the process was always and everywhere going to follow these steps. They also knew that it would be impossible to reverse the direction! It could never happen that a socialist state would slide back into capitalism. They had proof for that. It went as follows:

Should any socialist state ever be threatened by a reversal of its historic development, the Soviet Union would interfere, also with military force, to prevent this from happening!

And therefore it couldn't happen! That's what I call sound reasoning. But it was the whole content of the Brezhnev doctrine, seriously! All the grandmasters of logic, including Aristotle, had missed this one: the proof by military violence! It took a genius like Leonid Brezhnev to introduce it.

Communist doctrine penetrated all aspects of everybody's life. In a total misunderstanding of dialectic reasoning, they created two classes of everything: bourgeois and socialist. There were for instance bourgeois and socialist art and bourgeois and socialist science. There were also committees that distinguished between the two. You could go to jail – or worse – for bourgeois poetry and if you wrote a book about mathematics, you better started it with a long laudation on the party.

There shall be no undue amusement among the Catholics here! May I recall that a Renaissance pope saw it fitting to hire a painter for covering some areas of strategic importance in Michelangelo's Sistine Chapel frescos under veils. I am so taken with the poor man who had from then on to go through life as "the veil painter", that I will not mention his name.

During the "great patriotic war", with Russia on the brink of destruction, concessions were made, even on the very touchy subject of religion, but after the victory, everything was taken back.

24.2.3.2 Dealing with Dissidents

There were no dissidents in the Soviet Union. How could there be any dissension about the eternal truth? There were however class enemies, bourgeois, revisionists and reactionaries. There were millions of those, real ones, proven ones, suspected ones and potential ones. That did not matter so much. The KGB tortured a lot of them. A great many were shot and even more were starved. But most of them got a second chance. They were allowed to redeem themselves by making a contribution to socialism in the slave camps of the Gulag. The majority of them died there.

There were eternal "discussions" with the leadership of the socialist brother nations. Some of those were misled or just weak. Soviet tanks had to roll into Eastern Germany, Hungary, Czechoslovakia, Poland and Afghanistan. There were bitter feuds over the correct interpretation of communism with the Chinese. The only possible reason *not* to use military force in these disputes was the unpromising perspective of an armed conflict in some of the cases.

In general deviating opinions were crushed with all possible brutality, and that included brutal torture and assassination of those that had managed to escape the country.

24.2.3.3 Centralization – Decentralization

Everything was centralized. Nothing went without the blessings of the deeply stacked hierarchy of committees in Moscow. It all had to be planned, because nothing worked by itself. There was no market, that elusive creature that does all the planning for us without employing a single person. Thus somebody would have to figure out how many shoestrings Armenia was going to need next year, and somebody else would add this up for all the republics. Then yet somebody else would plan the production capacity, and so on. It never worked. It cannot work. It was just too rigid. In mechanical terms, one could say that the number of degrees of freedom the mechanism had was negative. It was solidly frozen!

The more enlightened leaders recognized this, but they drew the wrong conclusion. They believed that the plan did not work, because it was not truly embraced by everybody. So the remedy was even more centralization.

I have three questions here:

- How could this happen?
- Why was it doomed to fail?
- How could it last that long?

It could happen because it happened in a vacuum where anything could have happened.

It was doomed to fail, because it exposed human beings to too much very fundamental change. The Russian muzhik was – and is – a deeply religious person. Religion has helped him to endure immeasurable hardship for centuries. And now suddenly religion is opium for the people? Further not all the feudal masters were brutal oppressors. Many serfs had a very cordial relationship with their lord. And now suddenly our good Lord Count Alexei, who sent his doctor when our son was so ill, and who gave our daughter a dowry would be a criminal? Then the abolition of property robbed people from their association with the land. It took their last hope – however illusionary – of an independent existence. The intelligentsia was chased away or into hiding by the cultural policies. All this resulted in a lukewarm support from a small part of the population. It was not enough to face the competition of the modern world.

It could last so long because there never had been a tradition of freedom in Russia. The replacement of one retarded oppressive regime by another is not all that obvious to the popular masses. And some idealists hoped and believed.

Extreme brutality in dealing with any opposition or even mild criticism, and the absolute rigidity of the doctrine helped cement the system.

But if the Germans had treated the Russian villagers that met them offering bread and salt with dignity and respect, if Hitler had not been Hitler but a wise humane leader the Soviet Union would not have survived 1941. It was simply internally too weak to deal with outside pressure. Only the criminal behavior of the Germans in Russia provided sufficient fuel to go on for another half century. Then the inevitable happened.

24.2.4 The Third Reich

Some people have claimed a similarity between the third Reich and the Soviet Union. Although Stalin and Hitler killed about the same amount of their own people, I still find this comparison far fetched. In spite of the immeasurable suffering that the Soviet Union created, it started with a noble goal. The elevation of the oppressed working classes and world solidarity were part of its vision from the very beginning. It was not the core communist beliefs, but the means deployed while *not* achieving them that made the Soviet Union a negative force in the world. The third Reich was a completely different animal.

The 1000-year Reich achieved 1.2% of its longevity goal. The fact that it could exist 12 years – which was about 11.9 years too long – is due to the undeniable ingenuity and endurance of the German people. Let's see how they dealt with change.

24.2.4.1 An Extremely Rigid Doctrine but Big Change

The philosophical basis for the Nazi doctrine as recorded in "Mein Kampf" and "Mythos des 20. Jahrhunderts" appeared to me, when I read them, not just pathologically confused but also boring to the extreme. Accordingly, I doubt whether many people finished these books, if they started them at all. I honestly believe that the world could have been better off if a couple more people (and I do not just think of Chamberlain and Daladier, although that certainly would have been helpful) had indeed read them at the time when they appeared. Even today, I still strongly recommend the reading of these books. Unfortunately, this world is condemned to either, remember and learn or repeat! If we refuse to deal with the insanity of the past, for however understandable reasons, we just open our gates for the insanity of the future.

The Nazis did a thorough job. They tore up the whole network of moral values that had kept the world more or less together for centuries and simply threw it away. They replaced all this by a set of values that was completely centered on the superiority of the German race. Questions about morality for instance would be decided by measuring them against "Gesundes Volksempfinden", the "healthy popular sentiment" that more often than not proved to be quite unhealthy! Trivial things like property or religion did not distract the Nazis. They went right to the core of the matter. They tampered with the understanding of humanity about itself. Very basic terms like "human" and "humanity" were redefined. Everything was re-oriented in the framework of the "German super race". Things that would previously have been greed, spite, barbarian cruelty and treason suddenly became duties and virtues.

This was such a radical change from the past that neither the German population nor the world could really cope with it. Human imagination was unable to encompass the things the Nazis were planning and doing, although they had described them astonishingly explicitly in their writings.

One of the reasons for the fact that only relatively few Jews escaped while that was still possible is that they could simply not believe what they were seeing. This was an amount of change that totally defied their imagination. The Jewish Germans were absolutely committed and loyal to Germany. The number of Jewish officers decorated for gallantry during the first world war by far exceeded the army average. Try to imagine this 60-year-old Jewish dentist in 1933. His nephew has read "Mein Kampf", and now tries to convince him to immigrate to the USA. Look at the answer: "This is absolutely ridiculous. I fought four years in the war. In the end, I commanded an infantry battalion. His majesty the Emperor himself pinned the Pour le Mérite on my tunic. And now you think that any German is going to be willing to do anything bad to me? All that they are going to do is salute me and say: 'Zu Befehl, Herr Oberst!'"

It was not just the Jews. People in general needed a lot of time to believe that there were death camps, not because the evidence was lacking, but because it was just "too horrible to be true".

The new doctrine was a radical, even cataclysmic departure from the old values, but once in place it was enforced and maintained with rigidity that the world had never seen.

24.2.4.2 Dealing with Dissidents

There was zero tolerance for as much as expressing doubt about the doctrine. Punishment was draconian. You could get your head chopped off for outrageous crimes like distributing leaflets or listening to the BBC. Very few people know that the Germans executed 40,000 of their own soldiers. That adds up to four divisions, annihilated by the Germans themselves without any help from their enemies! They died for crimes like defeatism. Punishment was often more than just cruel. It was barbaric on a deep inhumane level. It is one thing to kill your opponents by shooting them, or neglecting them in labor camps, but still quite something else to garotte people, using piano strings, make a movie of their long agony and then watch it with great delight. The latter is what the top-Nazis did with some of the people that were implicated in the coup against Hitler.

24.2.4.3 Centralization – Decentralization

The regime was extremely centralized, and it had to be. Trust was an even scarcer commodity than gasoline. Everything had to go via Berlin. The Nazi top got involved into incredibly detailed decisions.

One might have three questions here:

- How could this happen?
- Why was it doomed to fail?
- Why did it last so long?

Quite amazed myself I believe that the answer to all these three questions is the same: an overdose of change.

- It was the overdose of change that, in spite of all the relevant information just laying out in the open, made it impossible for people to imagine what this was truly going to be like. Therefore the resistance within and outside Germany formed too slowly to prevent the catastrophe.
- It was the overdose of change that mobilized the world against this, quite late, after the substantial time that was needed to acquire an awareness of the real nature of the beast, but then decisively.
- It was the overdose of change that allowed it to last full 12 years. The bulk of the Germans could not change their values as fast as the Nazis. They were stuck with their old perception of morality. They believed in decency and expected it from their government so strongly that they postulated it to exist. The officers in the armed forces felt compelled by their oath until it was way too late. When they finally overcame that, they still were no match for the Nazis in areas like brutality and deceit.

24.2.5 What Can Be Learned?

- An overdose of change kills, especially if the change touches the core of human nature or very old traditions.
- Rigidity in the core doctrine helps.
- Rigidity in everything is deadly.
- A formal mechanism to guide and control moderate change helps.
- Persecution of dissidents is a losing proposition. Absorbing and integrating them is much more promising. The latter requires careful change management.
- Flexibility in peripheral issues is good. It also can be used as a proving ground for essential change.
- Distributed decision making in non-core issues is beneficial.

24.3 Different Strategies

The only purpose of the previous excursion was to create awareness for the pitfalls of change. I believe that we have a strong case for caution here. Any form of change puts a strain on the fabric of society. If the stress becomes too high, the fabric tears. Too much change is clearly going to shorten the life expectation of an organism. The problem is that too little change is going to do exactly the same thing. Please remember our deluge model. The organism in the valley that decides not to take any steps at all will be the first to drown when the water level rises.

Change is not a miracle drug, whatever the vocal change addicts say or write. An overdose will kill you, but so will total abstinence. Like with most other things in the world it is moderation, the proper dosage that does the trick. So change needs to be carefully planned, and we will address that question now.

Let's use our deluge model again, and try to relate it to corporate behavior.

Here we are sitting in the valley, and we know that the water is coming (see Fig. 24.4).

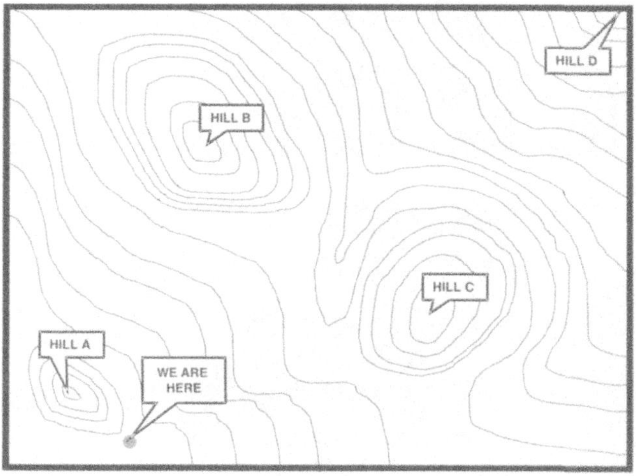

Figure 24.4

Let's look how the deluge will progress (Fig. 24.5). And please do realize that this kind of insight is an advantage you will very seldom have in real life.

What shall we do now? First of all, there are a couple of things we do not want to do.

Just sit still.

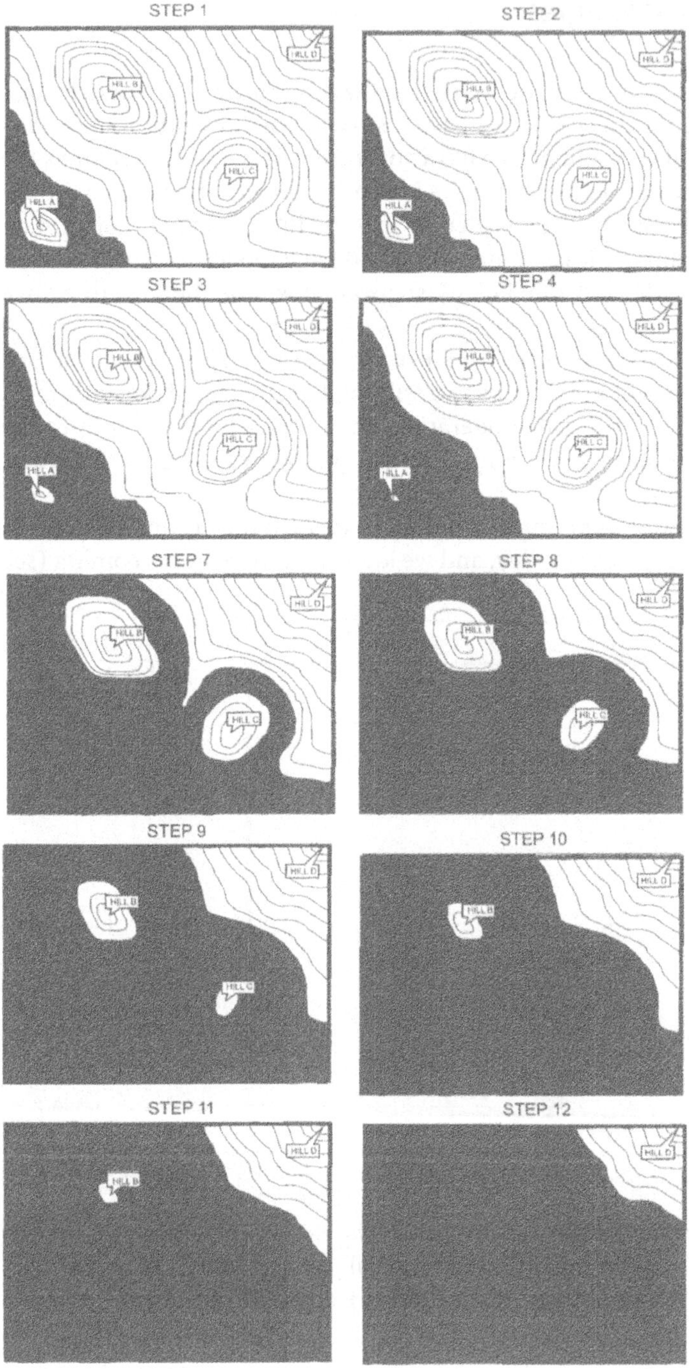
STEP 1
HILL D
HILL B
HILL C
HILL A
STEP 2
STEP 3
STEP 4
STEP 7
STEP 8
STEP 9
STEP 10
STEP 11
STEP 12

Figure 24.5

The corporate equivalent of this would be:

- I just don't believe that the deluge is coming. Otherwise, there would have been an article in the New York Times.
- You just made this up in order to justify a bigger budget.
- We have been doing well for the last twenty years, why should we suddenly move?
- We can always wait until we actually *see* the water coming.

This obviously will lead to swift destruction. We know that we *have* to move, *have* to change. So:

We go up the nearest hill (Fig. 24.6).

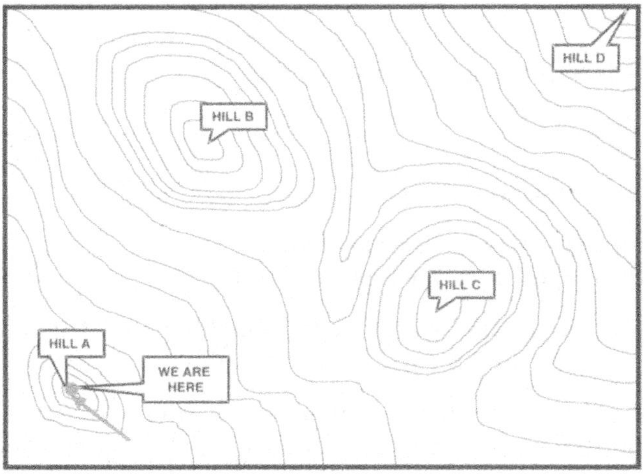

Figure 24.6

The corporate equivalent of this would be:

- I want action, and I want it now. No analysis–paralysis here!

The nearest hill (HILL A) is for sure a local optimum, but not near to a global optimum. Highly likely it will be low enough to get us killed.

The water rises and already in "Step 1" we are trapped (see Fig. 24.7). We can't get off our hill anymore.

You see: as early as Step 5 (Fig. 24.8) we are history. That was not a good plan.

Now here is a more radical idea:

Find the global optimum and walk to it.

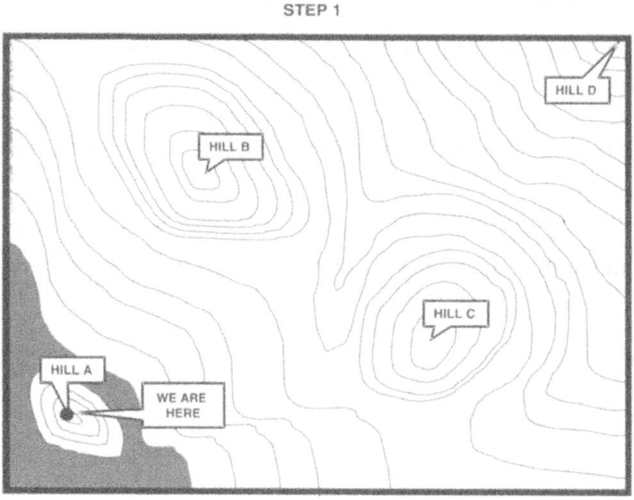

Figure 24.7

The corporate equivalent of this would be:

- We should not settle for anything but the very best.
- Just good is not good enough for us. We want excellence.

Although theoretically attractive, this will prove to be highly impractical for the following reasons:

- I don't know where the global optimum is. I cannot see the whole landscape, especially from the bottom of the valley. For instance, in the beginning of the game my view on HILL D is blocked by HILL C.

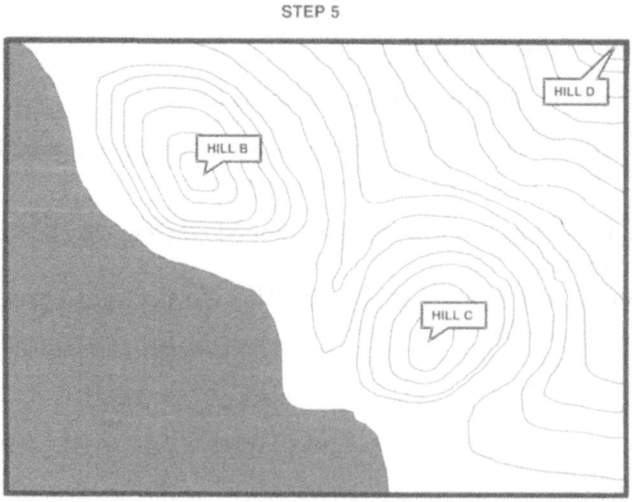

Figure 24.8

- Even if I saw the global optimum, it might be unattainable. The road leading to it might require crossing valleys that will be filled with water before I arrive there.

This is starting to look more and more like real life. The things we can do are undesirable and those that look promising are impossible. There is no real *good* solution. In such a situation, we have a tendency to exhaust ourselves by stubbornly insisting on finding the ideal solution that simply does not exist. It proves much more productive to ask: "what cannot be completely wrong?" We are looking for a strategy to guide our steps. Let's look at a couple of those:

Go up as steep as possible.

The corporate equivalent of this would be:

- Let's face the challenge.
- Let's hit this hard and fast.
- Make your assets *sweat.*

Unfortunately it is easy to see that this amounts going up HILL A, and we already know that's bad.

Go up the highest hill we can see from where we are.

The corporate equivalent of this would be:

- Let's soar with the eagles.
- Let's strive for the best.

So there we go up HILL B (as in Fig. 24.9).

Let's see to what this leads.

Within six periods we proudly reside on hill B (as you see in Fig. 24.10). We are also surrounded by water. We can only hope and pray, probably in vain that the water will not rise to our level. We also have a magnificent view on HILL D, which extends beyond our previous horizon and is much higher than HILL B. Too bad that we are here and not there. Figure 24.11 tells it all.

This was really not much better than going up HILL A! Let's try something more sophisticated – a two-rule strategy:

1. *Go up perpendicular to the contour lines.*
2. *Do not cross closed contour lines.*

This means:
Go up as steep as possible, but without climbing any single hill. Or in other words: avoid mountaintops! The corporate equivalent of this would create a quite interesting debate in the executive committee.

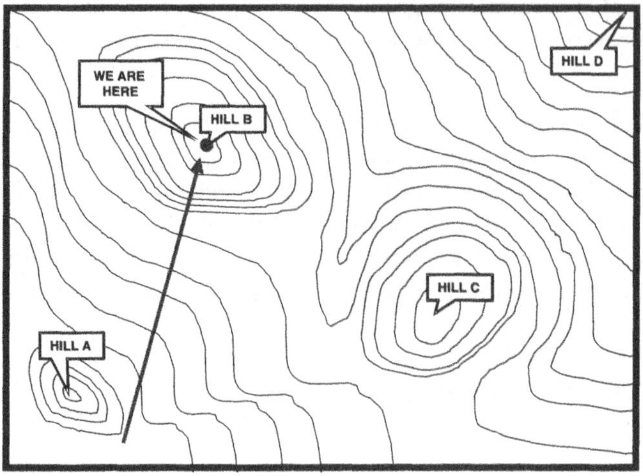

Figure 24.9

STEP 6

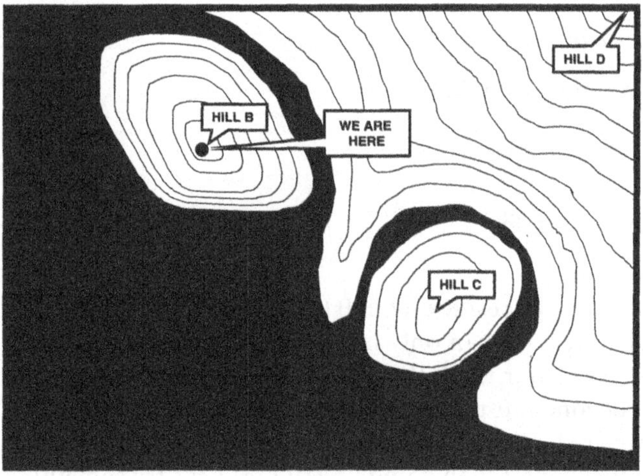

Figure 24.10

Mr. X:
Gentlemen, the strategy I just explained to you may be a little bit difficult to understand intuitively, but please bear with me. We are faced with destruction. There is no provable ideal solution. We must try to do the best we can while we keep our options open, so that we can exploit further possibilities if we discover them on the road. My recommendation achieves just that.

STEP 12

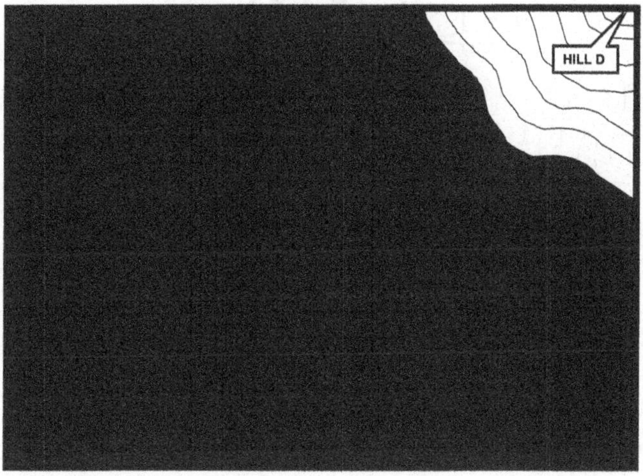

Figure 24.11

Mr. A:
Fleeing for rising water by refusing to go up hills seems a very strange concept to me. I cannot understand it, and I suspect neither will my people nor my customers!

Mr. B:
Why should we forego the safety of HILL B? Who says that the water is ever going to rise that high?

Mr. C:
You are proposing a hesitant course of action, without a clearly visible final goal. We can never communicate that to our people.

Mr. D:
Don't you have a better larger and more complete map?

Mr. X:
No, Sir.

Mr. D:
I am really getting irritated. You come here with ridiculously incomplete information. Nevertheless, you demand that we make a very important decision on that basis and as usual, it can't wait! I believe that you only recommend this convoluted strategy in order to be able to acquire the information that you should in fact have presented to us today. I think you are wasting our time.

And so on.

In spite of the stupid debate, this *is* the more promising course of action. Just look what happens if we did this, as described in Fig. 24.12.

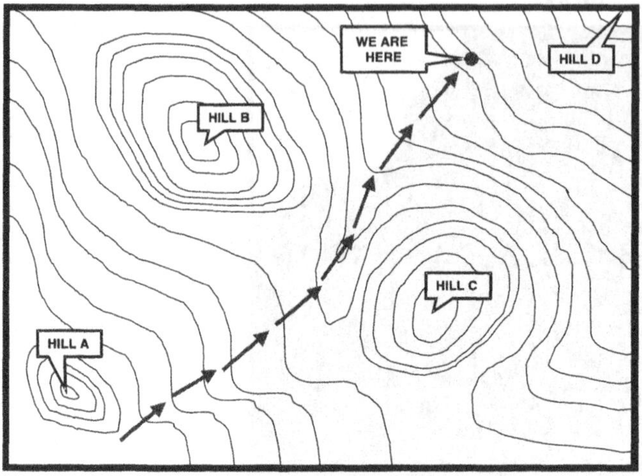

Figure 24.12

By Step 12, we reach the situation that can be seen in Fig. 24.13:

- We are now higher than HILL B, which is already flooded.
- We are not surrounded by water.
- We have an excellent view on HILL D, and it is higher than we expected.
- We also see the landscape behind HILL D and we notice even higher mountains there.
- So we do not go up HILL D either.

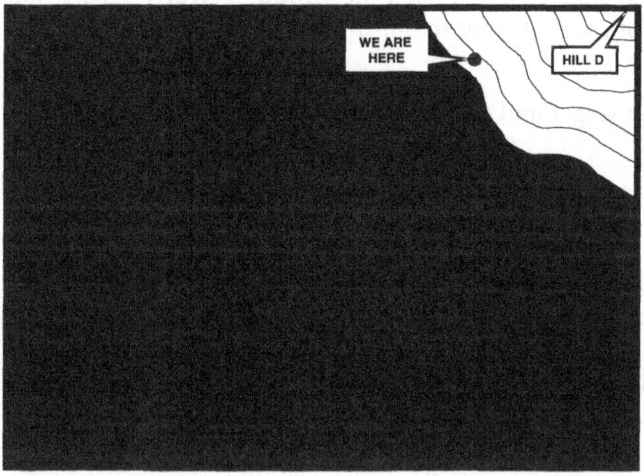

Figure 24.13

24.4 The Merits and Pitfalls of Planning

The purpose of this whole story was to show that the problems surrounding "change" and "choices" are not as simple as our slick shallow showcase manager of the 21st century tries to pretend. While immobility is certainly not an option, change is dangerous, disruptive and expensive. Further we should consider that although there is no improvement without change, we certainly see a lot of change without improvement. The latter means: all the risk, all the cost and disruption for nothing.

All this points to a really careful approach. That should begin with meticulous and rigorous planning. We all know that planning is one of these very casually used big words with a lot of content. Let us look at this a bit more precisely.

Planning encompasses:

- Knowing where you want to go.
- Knowing why you want to go there.
- Knowing what road to take.
- Knowing what resources are needed when and where.
- Knowing where to get those resources.
- Knowing how to explain this to a large number of people.
- Knowing how to deal with surprises on the way.

One could of course also say: "It's really simple, we only have to go from here to there," as illustrated in Fig. 24.14.

Figure 24.14

There are however a couple of questions like:

- Where is "here"?
- How did we get here?
- Where is "there"?
- Why do we want to go there?

One of the problems is that we tend to believe that these questions are trivial and that we have all the answers. Unfortunately they are not and we don't.

Where is "here"?
How are we going to know what situation we are exactly in? There seems to be a simple answer. Let's look at our balance sheet and our profit and loss statement. The problem is that, contrary to popular belief, these documents deliver only a very sketchy and fragmentary picture of our real situation. There are very important line items missing:

- Our staff
  - Competency
  - Innovative potential
  - Efficiency
  - Loyalty and motivation
- Our customers
  - Loyalty to our products/services
  - Survivability in their market
- Our suppliers
  - Competency
  - Commitment to the solution of our problems
  - Innovative potential
  - Efficiency
  - Survivability in their market
- Our owners/shareholders
  - Loyalty
  - Long term vision

All these things are extremely important. Their proper assessment will contribute more to a realistic determination of our actual position than many of the explicitly stated line items in a balance sheet. However, conventional accounting simply ignores these aspects and so does the better part of our management. You hear these hair-raising statements: "I am a financial guy, I rely on the numbers!" Whatever you bring outside the conventional number framework will be considered highly suspicious at least, even potentially fraudulent. This is of course not an easy question. In order to allow for proper consideration of all the above-mentioned aspects in the determination of our position, we would need a common metric. The common metric of accounting is money. As a consequence, all aspects that can readily be expressed in terms of dollars are included in our conventional accounting structure. The items that are left out are expressly treated that way because we have not yet found an unambiguous straightforward procedure to assign a money value to them. We therefore consider them "qualitative" or "soft". There are promising attempts towards a more quantitative treatment, for instance in "The Loyalty Effect"[15], by Frederick H. Reichheld. But even if my prediction that Mr. Reichheld will once be celebrated as one of the great innovators of economic sciences were to prove correct, we know that it will take quite some time for such an evaluation of "soft" factors to become standard practice. Our experience with society and its learning behavior simply forbids us to believe that anything that fundamental could happen in less than 10 years.

Every sailor knows that uncertainty in the determination of our current position will gravely jeopardize further navigation. That would also be the case if we knew exactly where we are going. A lack of confidence in our present position would always force us to make big detours in order to avoid charted cliffs and shallows. There is of course something much worse than not knowing your position. It is not to know that you don't know, and therefore assuming you do. That's how *really big accidents* happen, and it is unfortunately not uncommon.

For all these reasons, our first order of business must be to find a way to assign a value to the above-mentioned "soft" items. We cannot fall back on generally accepted standard practices and procedures. There is not such a thing yet. We will have to develop our own methodology. Even if we used nothing better than just gut feeling, the accuracy of our position determination would improve dramatically. It would of course be much better to devise a kind of standard evaluation methodology within our enterprise. Although there would be no guarantee for the accuracy, it would at least be more reproducible.

How did we get here?

Do we have to bother with this question at all? We might believe that we have this behind us, and therefore it cannot be all that important. I think differently for a lot of reasons. History is only futile for those of us who don't study it, don't understand it or don't learn from it. That does of course account for a substantial part of humanity and thus also of top management. History definitely contains important and very practical lessons. Here are a couple of questions that, if answered honestly, could be really helpful.

- Was our present position our past goal, or did we arrive here by accident?
- How did we evaluate our past position?
- How did we evaluate our present position in terms of target?
- How did we plan the journey?
- What important aspects did we miss and what were the consequences?

There are additional reasons to be bothered with the past. Most of our modern large enterprises have the inertia and maneuverability of your average supertanker. One can of course sweep this undesirable fact under the carpet and deny its existence. That amounts to denial towards gravity but it is not uncommon. Today a solid respect for reality is often confused with a lack of vision.

Champagne dreams are much more popular than the beer reality. But seriously folks, would you like the pilot that is driving your jet to operate in that kind of a mind set? And if it isn't OK for him, why would it be appropriate for you? Inertia is one of the most common phenomena we observe in the physical world. We even have a formula for it:

$$E_{kin} = \frac{m \cdot v^2}{2}$$

This expression describes the kinetic energy E_{kin} of an object in function of its mass m and velocity v. Especially if m is big, whatever change we make in v, magnitude, direction or both will result in major amounts of energy. If we make such changes in a short time, that will result in large forces working on the system. If the engine and the rudder of our supertanker would allow us to make the sharp turn we are wishing for, that might very well break our ship in half!

Where is "there"?
Apart from the fact that positioning our elected destination will be just as difficult as the description of our current situation due to the all important "soft" factors, we have a couple of additional elements complicating the situation. If this is to be a meaningful goal – and it better be one – we will need some time to reach it. In our fast paced world, the environment will change quite a bit during that period. That might change the evaluation of our goal considerably.

Why do we want to go there?
There is a whole host of questions here. What alternatives did we consider? How did we compare them? Why did we pick this one? These questions only *seem* trivial. We may deliberately *not* have picked the objectively "best" solution. We may have been rather guided by a compound view on desirability and feasibility.

Anyway, we will need a rather convincing and defendable story, because without that it will be very difficult to rally the necessary *real* support of the popular masses behind this.

Let us, for the sake of simplification, assume that we have resolved all the above questions satisfactorily. We will still be confronted with the question "how to get there from here?" The naïve answer to this will be: "in one big leap of course!" We see this in Fig 24.15.

But in the meantime we know that big leaps amount to an engraved invitation to Mr. Murphy, who usually appears at the party anyway. The dilemma is simple. If it can be done in one leap, the goal is not ambitious enough. If the goal is sufficiently meaningful, it cannot be done in one leap. We will have to find a better way.

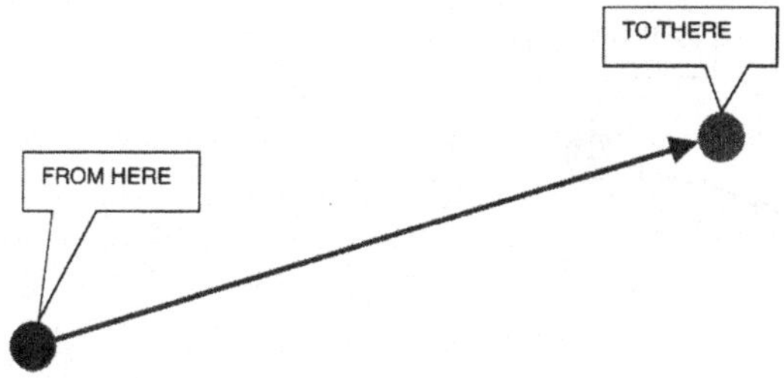

Figure 24.15

How about the following? We define a really ambitious medium term goal. We do this very carefully so that we are certain that we are aiming at significant *improvement*. Of course, we cannot get there in one leap, which is why we define a set of milestones. The properties of a good milestone are the following:

- The jump to our next milestone must lead into the general direction of our target.
- Standing on one milestone, the next one must be clearly visible, even in dense fog, and obviously attainable.
- Each milestone must, even isolated, offer visible improvement. In other words: the jump to the next milestone must be worth while as such.

Look at the following graph (Fig. 24.16). One might describe this as the Moses maneuver, hiking through the desert for decades in a row. As ridiculous as this may look, it is still by far preferable over the heroic – but doomed – one-jump attempts.

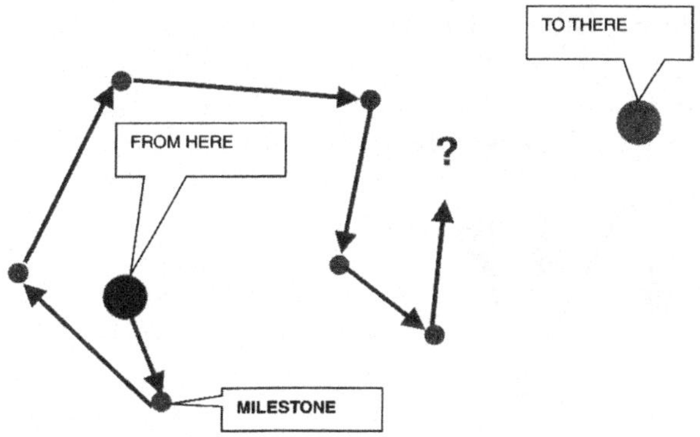

Figure 24.16

If we could have things our way, we would of course select something like the path represented in Fig. 24.17.

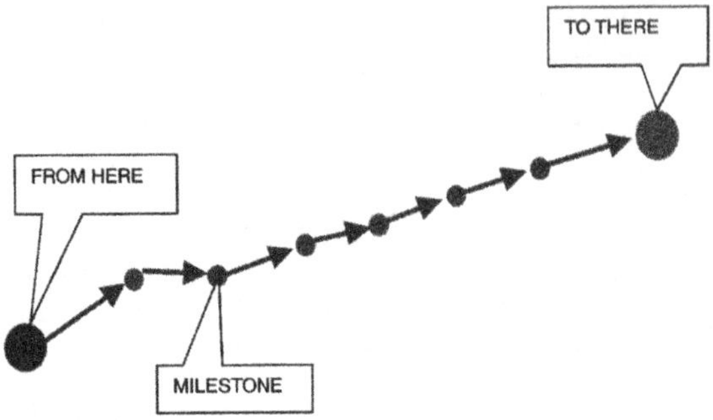

Figure 24.17

Let's be realistic though: the course of action represented by Fig. 24.18 can still make a lot of sense.

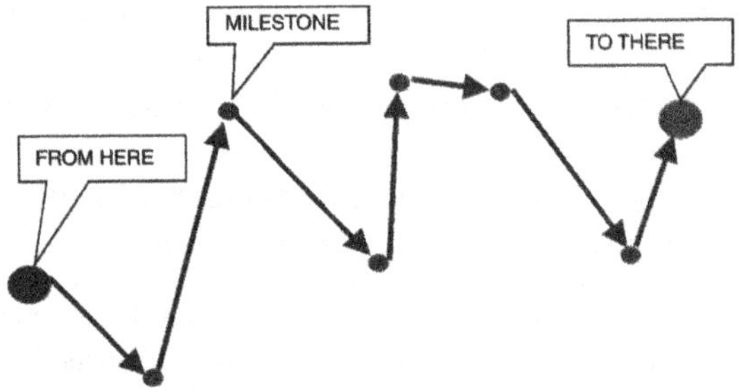

Figure 24.18

That would especially be the case if, as usual, there were a number of obstacles blocking the direct route, as visible in Fig. 24.19.

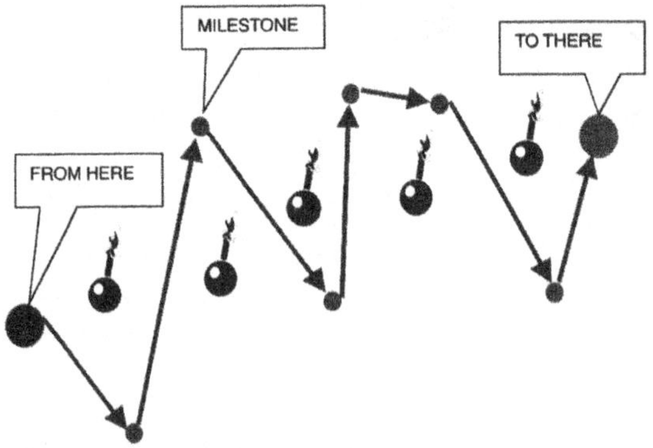

Figure 24.19

The milestone approach has an additional advantage. As we are on our way, the world around us changes. This may even compel us to alter our medium term target. Every time we arrive at a milestone we should survey the landscape and review and adapt the plan.

Let us suppose that by now we have clearly determined our current position. We also have picked our goal very carefully and we have devised a convincing route towards it. We are by no means done! We still have to enlist the active support of our partners, employees, owners, customers and suppliers. We can only really get them on board if we can show that what we have in mind is in the end going to be beneficial for all of them. We need to communicate the plan clearly and honestly. This is where things most frequently start to fall apart. We often develop sub-standard plans. If the plan fails to realistically promise significant gains, it will not offer a benefit to everybody. We are then back in the so destructive zero sum game. We are only redistributing wealth and there are going to be winners and losers. It is becoming more and more common in these cases to "put a positive spin" on reality, so that it does not immediately become obvious to the potential losing party. If not by outright lying, this is frequently achieved by holding back selective parts of the truth. That obviously amounts to just a more sophisticated form of lying. Such a course of action must rely on speed. These are typical surprise attacks that need to be completed before the general population sees the whole picture. The most likely victims of such a raid are the employees, because it is erroneously believed that they have the least opportunity to retaliate. This situation calls for the "big leap" approach. I don't understand why people do this over and over again. Experience shows that there are the following possible outcomes:

- The operation succeeds against all odds. In this case, there will be a horrible price to pay in terms of lost trust and loyalty. This "cost" is not going to appear in any accounting report. No Wall Street analyst will notice a thing, but it is all the more real. If this had been factored in, the objective of the whole action would have been exposed as not worth while from the very beginning.
- We fall flat on our face. This is the most likely outcome of a big leap anyway. We now have enormous damage and no gain.
- The whole thing deteriorates into a "Moses maneuver". This is the best conceivable outcome.

And it's not over here. There will be attempts to have the whole dismal outcome pasted over by propaganda efforts. We will try to talk this into a big victory. That will result in even more loss of trust and respect. Worst of all, it will expose the leadership to the most destructive of all contemptuous reactions: ridicule. The most amazing aspect of this might be that the people responsible for this nonsensical waste believe to be "clever" while they do it!

But let's assume that we have a really good plan that will benefit all the stakeholders. We have communicated it to everybody involved, clearly and completely, and it is totally understood and endorsed. Are we done now? No! I once heard leadership defined as: "showing people the way." This is preposterous. I would rather say: "showing people the way *and then walking it together with them, marching at the head of the group, sharing the hardships as well as the glory.*" Being there to encourage and inspire is of paramount importance.

If the maneuver is well executed every achieved milestone will increase the faith that people have in the plan. As they see all the pieces come together, they will identify themselves with the idea. There was a superb example of this during the Napoleonic war on the Iberian Peninsula. Wellington's army went through rough times, retreating from the French for months in a row. Morale was low. Then near the end of 1810 they arrived in Lisbon where they found to their amazement fully prepared defenses. There were supplies and deep entrenchments. They saw that this had to have been prepared over a long period of time, maybe as much as a year in advance. And suddenly they saw that it was all part of the plan, their difficult retreat as well as these impenetrable fortifications. It all made sense now. The leadership – in this case personified by Wellington – *did* know what it was doing. Morale skyrocketed. The tide reversed. General Massena hesitated. The French lost the war.

There are a number of pitfalls, in fact too many to deal with all of them here. One of the worst is the so-called "heroic approach". It starts with the definition of unrealistic goals. This can happen for different reasons. It could for instance happen that somebody in management, for totally egotistic reasons, wants to create a profile as a "hard driving hard hitting" boss. In today's world, such an image is indeed often conducive to a career.

But often it is just a matter of homework that was done too superficially or a lack of experience. Underestimating the necessary efforts is a routine error in our corporate world. Mistakes essentially do not need to have catastrophic consequences. We could after all, theoretically, recognize them, admit them, correct them and learn something from them. The problem is that people are not lazy. When they miss the mark on the technical aspects of the job, that is not because of negligence or indifference. It is because they did not have the time for thorough analysis. They were too busy designing and launching their propaganda campaign. That absorbed their full attention. With the propaganda campaign fully succeeding, and the technical side collapsing, there is no way back. The only way to escape is to charge forward. We know what comes next. "We worked long hours and weekends. In the final phase, we installed cots in the office so that people could take an occasional nap. But we got the job done on time!" We now all indulge in the shared glory of our heroic victory. We feel good and proud about this. We shouldn't. What I just described is a project that is totally out of control. Planning and management were substandard, and the final product will probably be seriously flawed as well. It is important to understand that these calamities happen *because* of the way corporate culture works, and *because* of the nature of the selection mechanisms. If we want to avoid this, we will need to change corporate culture.

As we can easily see, doing this right is going to be a very labor-intensive, even stressful task. But the reward is equally enormous. The prize is the ultimate positive form of change, namely improvement, and that is the basic ingredient of longevity for every enterprise.

25 Fixing the Enterprise

25.1 The Problems with Repairs

There are a couple of questions that one should carefully explore before touching anything. It does not matter whether our intention is to "repair" a camera, a complicated piece of electronic equipment, a personal relationship or a business process. Skipping the following checklist means accepting a high risk for things to get worse instead of better:

- Is there a pressing need to touch the thing?
- Do we understand enough about this?

Let us look at those questions in connection with our intent to "fix" the enterprise.

25.1.1 Is There a Pressing Need to Touch the Thing?

From all the previous criticism, one could have got the impression that things are so badly out of whack that some form of action appears mandatory. But let's stay with the facts here. While certainly our enterprises are far from the theoretical optimal environment that we could wish for ourselves, we have to admit that they largely do their job. Modern enterprise has, at least in the industrial world, provided us with an unprecedented standard of living.

On the other hand, we see obvious deficits. Enormous amounts of energy are wasted on activities that add no value. I honestly believe that about 80% of everything we say, write and do in our huge corporate headquarters are a pure waste. That may be less of a problem than it seems to be. Those 80% also are the field of opportunity. That is where a competitive advantage can be found and gained. That is the fuel that can be used to drive the engine of capitalism: competition.

Evolution is generally not very frugal in its unstoppable progress. It seems to carry out countless apparently senseless experiments in order to find that one small improvement. For not being very efficient, evolution is extremely effective. This is partly achieved by the fact that everything it delivers has some kind of superbly engineered, fully integrated self-healing mechanism built in. The latter will more often than not be able to repair the consequences of the expected occasional mishap. Social mechanisms that spun out of control are repaired in ways that show a striking resemblance with the healing of a cut finger. In these days, and in the corporate environment, those self-healing mechanisms are losing their potency quite rapidly. That is a serious reason for concern. The danger is that, should the latter progress unchecked, we certainly would get into considerable trouble in the intermediate future.

More and more people seem to despair at the difficulties we meet when trying to bite into the mentioned 80%. We see our fantasy as well as our creativity dry up. We see our arsenal of tools dwindle. Very soon, there will be only one recognized method left to combat corporate overhead: ever-bigger mergers. Of course, at the same time modern technology spawns a lot of startups, by definition small. This is purely a question of kinetics. How fast do the big fish swallow the startups? What fraction of our economic activity takes place in what size enterprise? I am convinced that the center of gravity is shifting towards ever-bigger corporations. We even have a word to describe the phenomenon: globalization! Please also keep in mind that whatever negative aspects of enterprises we have described in other parts of this book will grow exponentially with their size. Precisely this is one of the reasons for our limited success in mining the 80% inefficiency that seems to sit there for us to grab. For the same reason, the mergers very seldom deliver what they promise. Apparently, the benefit of scale allows for savings. We can see and identify those. We will never forget to claim them when we formulate and sell the project. The increased inefficiency of the larger organization is much harder to see and quantify, and almost impossible to publicly admit. In the aftermath we will, more often than not, discover that the synergies we used to justify the project do not materialize. But our pipe dreams about the next merger are so much more attractive, so much more interesting and powerful than sterile analysis of the past that we never really get the point. It's also much more fun to plan our future victories than to analyze our past defeats. And thus, with the eerie determination of a sleepwalker, we march towards the next merger.

The accelerating concentration of economic power in the hands of less and less people is, among all other concerns, also a serious challenge for democracy. We should never forget that we only had our relatively positive experience with capitalism in combination with democracy. What the former would do without the checks and balances offered by the latter is everybody's guess, but I am not optimistic.

So while there certainly is no basis for radical measures, there is a lot of incentive to try cautious gradual but continuous improvement.

25.1.2 Do We Understand Enough About This?

The amount of understanding needed largely depends on the scope of the corrective action we plan to undertake.

If we had the audacity to postulate that whatever evolution constructed so far is worthless, needs to be scrapped and totally replaced, we would not know one thousandth of what it really takes to embark on such an endeavor. That in a way would be walking with open eyes into what I call the "communism trap". It is a terrible and costly trap. Communism failed, because it was obviously not possible to have the cooperator control the competitor. All it did in the end was create a corrupt leadership exploiting subdued and impoverished popular masses, exactly what it had promised to abolish. I recently was a guest in one of the late Mr. Nicolae Ceauşescu's former "hunting lodges". I was trying to help the – quite competent – Romanian chemical industry, and they will have thought to do me a favor. It was eerie enough for a NATO reserve officer to be guarded by a squad of soviet style soldiers sporting Kalashnikovs, but in a way the unimaginable luxury of the place was even harder to swallow, especially against the background of wide-spread and obvious poverty. The reason why this could happen is simple: the communists too had a "selection machine", and it was not any better aligned with their doctrine than ours is with the declared goals of our enterprises.

But what *if* we had found a way to make communism work? Chances are that the long-term consequences might have been even more catastrophic. We should deal very prudently with evolution. It's not TNT. It has all the characteristics of Nitroglycerin. You do not shake or hit it with impunity.

If the objective would be cautious gradual improvement, we might live in the blissful illusion to have sufficient understanding to plan and execute such a thing. I would say that *any* interference with structures that were formed by evolution must always be an extremely risky venture. On the other hand, human interference is an integral part of evolution, and *not* interfering is as risky as involvement. We thus probably could justify such a course of action, but extreme caution would still be highly recommended.

Let us agree on the latter course. What will this mean?

After all the topics we discussed so far, it will be painstakingly clear that there simply is no single magic move, no isolated dramatic effort that will do what we want to be done. We must work with a basket of numerous relatively unobtrusive actions.

Also, there are very crucial things that can only be done within society. As previously discussed, society does not only shape the boundary conditions within which the enterprise has to live, but also is our supplier of all personnel, including future leadership. If we want to tamper with society, it is very clear that the steps have to be small and even then, they have to be taken slowly.

25.2 It All Happens Within Society

It is obvious that great enterprises will preferably thrive in a great society. Social changes in a democracy are mainly guided, albeit in a limited fashion, through the political process, but who wants to be a politician? Unfortunately, we have no choice. As defunct as the selection machines in our enterprises may seem, the political selection machine is a lot worse. One of the main reasons for this is that, contrary to the enterprise, society does not feed a representative sample of society into the political selection process. The problem sits in the question "Who wants to be a politician?" If the intellectual and moral elite distances itself systematically from politics, we must not be astonished about the apparent intellectual and moral inferiority of our politicians. Our decision *not* to get involved in politics immediately creates a share of the responsibility for the miserable state of affairs resulting from the perceived negative selection process. We take this too lightly. Our flirtation with the "no politics for me" posture is childish and irresponsible.

The influence of the political process on the all-important Zeitgeist is often underestimated. Many of the things we see happen on the political stage at least intensify the cynical and nihilistic ground swell that we see developing at this time. The situation in Europe is not much different from the United States. Scandals and waste everywhere!

Just in case that you would want to accept the challenge, here is a draft agenda for you.

1. We need fewer and simpler laws that are rigidly enforced. How about the following course of action:
   - A new law can only be enacted if two old ones are scrapped. If we did this for a couple of legislature periods, we would see some real progress.
   - Tax laws must be totally rewritten and drastically simplified. Nothing but a greatly simplified income tax (no bells and whistles, no breaks) and a reasonable added value tax.
   - A bill can only have *one* subject. No pork!
   - Laws must be written in such a way that everybody who can read is able to understand them.

The lawyers are not going to like that. The insane complexity and ambiguity of the existing legal system forms the basis of their quite comfortable living and unbelievable proliferation. The lawyers do not share your reluctance to involve yourself in politics. They have been *trained* to look at a complex situation that they do not truly understand, and nevertheless argue about it against the background of a formal framework. They further see no problem in *getting* right without *having* it. Their education contains interesting philosophical constructs to that effect. They are infinitely more adapted to the Zeitgeist than you and me. That it why they provide the majority of the leading politicians and we don't! We will further see that the medical profession creates its own market, but the lawyers do so in a much more destructive way. The mere fact that the lawyers will be against this is a powerful reason to do it!

2. We need a high-quality public education system. Academic standards must be rigidly enforced. We need a full spectrum of possible education levels. From a broad and profound general education to very basic trade schools. Non performing students must be removed and directed toward a lower level school. Zero tolerance for violence and drugs.
   This is another standpoint that is inviting strong opposition from powerful groups.
   - The left side will not like it because it contradicts the supreme law of "equality". Enforcement of discipline might further violate the perpetrator's civil rights.
   - The teacher's unions will not like it because they are now supposed to start performing seriously for their salary.
   - The right will not like it because it means deflecting considerable means for the betterment of the under-privileged.
   - The center will not like it because it sounds too extreme, too difficult to sell.
   - The Christian fundamentalists will not like it because the problem has already been solved by the decision of the US congress to post the Ten Commandments in every classroom.

But if you think this through rationally, would the sum of all these objections not be a very powerful reason to give it a try?

You know me by now: I just have to especially pick on the last bullet, but you will see that there is a sound reason. I never saw such an expression of almost hilarious helplessness. The Ten Commandments are a powerful set of rules that, if seriously accepted as a beacon by only a small percentage of the population would indeed make a huge difference for the better. But just *posting* them in your schools! Have you looked at your student's reading skills lately? And even if all students could *read* the posted Ten Commandments, that would not make that much of a difference. Seeing them practiced would of course be a completely different matter.

But how should that happen in a society where a man who has earned his fortune with pornography can offer a substantial amount of money to any woman that can prove to have had an adulterous affair with one of the self-proclaimed righteous? How can that happen in a society where then the leader of the so-called righteous has to make a fast retreat? How can that happen in a society where the performance of the righteous during the trial of their president flowed out of the TV set with a stench of hypocrisy so putrefying that one almost wanted to forgive the man for his unforgivable actions?

All this did not restrain the righteous from ordering the Ten Commandments to be posted. The only thing I can suggest here is censorship. Let's blank out "You shall not commit adultery." Maybe in today's crazy world nobody will notice! Maybe the lawyers could come up with an explanation why adultery does not really mean adultery. The problem is that we probably could not stop at that commandment alone. There are all these annoying little problems with stealing and lying and cheating that would not hold up too well under serious scrutiny. The "false testimony" problem is under control, because the original text specifies "against your neighbor". The lawyers will be able to find a really narrow interpretation for this, excluding 99.99999% of humanity. But there certainly would be a couple of examples for a not so nice treatment of parents. The contemporary version of that is to have them declared incompetent by a court, seize their money and tuck them away in a nursing home.

The righteous might in the end post empty sheets of paper! That might not be so bad, because it would really totally cover the core of their message.

The only result of all this is increased cynicism and nihilism, which are the *real* problems of our time! If we could do something about those by taking their *causes* away, even our schools would get better.

3. We need a basic form of health insurance for everybody. Public health is a real hot potato, and it is going to get worse. The structure of the problem is best understood by looking at Fig. 25.1.

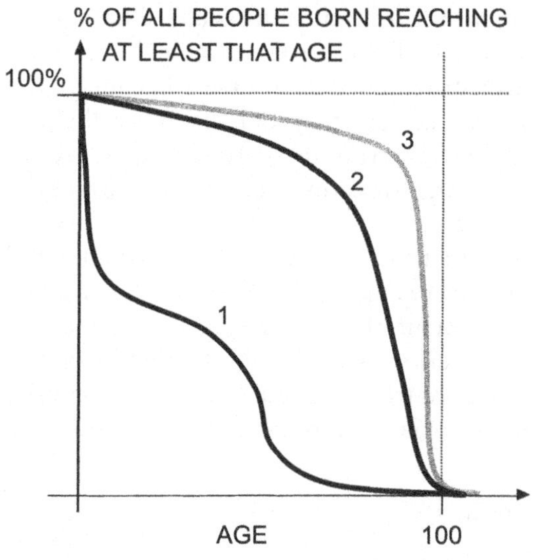

Figure 25.1

Please do not pin me down on the exact numbers. My only purpose is to make this problem understandable.

Line 1 represents the typical pattern of primitive societies. There is a high infant mortality and only a few people will get 50 years old. Some very few however can live to become 100. This is what you will see in most under-developed regions of the world. But at the beginning 19th century the pattern in the US and Europe was not much different. As horrible and insensitive as it may sound, such a longevity distribution is a very effective one. It keeps the demographic structure healthy with a relatively low average age. The number of non-productive people that have to be supported by society is low. Some get really old, which is important for the conservation of the collective tribal memory, but not so many that they would become an economic burden. Further, also easy to see, in such a society evolution just works faster.

Modern society in industrialized countries follows the curve 2. You immediately notice the consequences. An aging population will put a lot of strain on social security. The debate about these problems is raging throughout the whole "first world". Modern medicine was certainly not the only contributing factor to this development, but probably the most important one. This came with a very hefty price tag. The problem is recursive again, because the older people that now constitute a growing percentage of the population are also bigger consumers of the medical system. It is easily visible that modern medicine does indeed create its own market! This is an important example to show that things like "creating your own market" are not always the work of con-artists. In the case of medicine it happened with overwhelmingly noble intentions, but it happened nevertheless. The debate about the affordability of the medical system is also in full swing throughout the industrialized nations.

But how would the distribution be if all diseases were curable? That is what curve 3 represents. Now the devilish structure of the problem becomes clear. We are again dealing with one of these asymptotic problems. It is rather safe to say that we cannot reach the green curve. It is also certain that we are still able to make some more progress into that direction. It is equally certain that the latter would come at a terrible cost.

The prize question in situations like this is "how good is good enough?" That is never an easy thing but here we are talking about our life! So on a personal level we will have a tendency to claim that "nothing is good enough to extend *my* life." But on the level of society we simply *know* that we cannot afford that. This will be one of the big controversial questions of the coming years. It is laden with more potential social, economic and moral explosives than anything else I ever saw!

4. We need to invest in basic research.

We also need to do this smartly. If you know that the next generation particle accelerator is not going to offer you fundamental new insights in the questions that really bother us, just don't build it! Rather wait until you find an idea that will deliver the bang for the buck. Doing such a thing without retreating from high-energy physics all together is not easy.

Biotechnology is probably the hottest topic around in these days. We simply must keep abreast of rogue nations in this respect with a safe distance of at least a decade. It becomes increasingly difficult. Recombinant DNA technology is important and controversial. Especially in Europe, there is a lot of resistance to genetically altered fruits and vegetables. Because of the very real risks, there needs to be regulation of some kind, but it must be a form of regulation that does not asphyxiate our research efforts. There are difficult moral questions surrounding this.

As missile technology and weapons of mass-destruction become more widespread, a missile defense system for the USA and possibly Europe is no longer a luxury. One needs to be really good in at least half a dozen high-tech areas to address this problem with any chance of success.

At the same time we notice a trend in society that seems to point towards *less* enthusiasm for innovation. It is as if we were growing weary of our relentless progress. One symptom is a decreasing willingness to spend money for basic research. Many people have an easy way to rationalize this. The capitalistic conventional wisdom says that one can always buy what one needs. We have by now told each other so long and so loud that essentially everything is for sale that we start to believe it. I just can hope and pray that you will not need to go shopping for a missile defense system the minute you noticed beyond reasonable doubt that you need one. That's right after the first impact! You will find to your amazement that not everything can be bought, even *if* money isn't the issue.

5. In Europe we need an organization modeled after the FBI.

I do not believe that Europeans in positions of power, be it in government, big business or organized crime (and all those are not as neatly compartmentalized as we might whish!), are essentially more corrupt than their American counterparts. They are just more likely to get away with whatever they elect to do. We definitely should increase their risk.

Wouldn't that be a terrible thing to happen?

- The left will immediately cry: "police state!"
- The right would have problems with all kinds of freedoms.
- Most political parties will voice strong objections. In at least a couple of cases we have solid proof that a part of their income was generated through bribery in connection with arms purchases.
- The regionalists would suspect a gigantic plot to enforce European bureaucracy over local autonomy.
- The trade unions will be against it. I do not yet have predictions for their excuse, but the financial dealings of some of them are so corrupt that they will have to find one.

- Big business will have serious objections. Earnest looking men will formulate their doubts on TV, with deep sorrowful grooves in their stern.
- The center will have its eternal problem: how do we explain this to the general population?

But again, all these objections are nothing but powerful arguments to go for it.

Before I continue this list longer than your patience allows, an intermediate observation. You may think: "If this is what this guy calls prudent, unobtrusive, small and slow change, we know what else we have to expect from him!" But please think again. We are not going to make fast progress in any of these issues, but if we do not clearly set our sights on them, there will be no progress at all!

Can you see our contemporary breed of politico's deal with any of these issues in a productive way? Maybe you really should take things in your own hands after all! I beg you to do this, even if you have to take a sea sickness pill before going to the meetings.

But of course society is much more than just politics. We are as much the builders of the Zeitgeist as we are its victims. We underestimate our ability to change anything, because our individual contribution is obviously very much restricted in scope and time. That makes us often forget that, while we can only do very little for the world, we are quite capable of making a real difference in our immediate surroundings. Even if you really can't bring yourself to joining or forming a political party, there is still a lot you can do.

True and honest religiosity is a way. There are immense problems with that. First of all, one can never be ultimately certain that there is a God. Although for me, a single glance at the amazing process of evolution tells me that there simply *must* be a Supreme Being, I can quite well understand – and accept – other people that do not have the same experience. But why not approach this problem the way Pascal did? Blaise Pascal was one of the most towering geniuses that walked the face of the earth. He offered groundbreaking contributions to mathematics, physics and philosophy. He invented the first truly workable calculator, the ancestor of our contemporary computers. Reading his "Pensées" [13] – the quite erroneous title publishers posthumously gave to a collection of his work intended to deliver a kind of rationalization of the Christian faith – was one of the most moving experiences of my adolescence. Pascal proposed a wager. It is true that we cannot determine whether there is a God or not with ultimate certainty. So we have to bet (Pascal also offered important contributions to probability theory). We can either assume that there is a God, or there isn't. We can of course also take the position that we will not take a position. What are the consequences? We can bet that there is no God. In that case, nothing of what we see around us makes any sense. We can refuse to take a position, in which case we just don't know. We can of course just throw our life into the – undeniably real – stream of evolution like a gambler throwing one quarter after the other into a slot machine. At the end we will find no meaning in it. If we do on the other hand bet that there is a Creator responsible for the emergence of the universe, albeit through less naïve processes than many of us believe, there suddenly is sense, beauty and hope. Pascal sugarcoated the whole thing by pretending that in the latter case, one might be "saved". I believe he only did this to make the idea more enticing to his rather primitive environment. I do not need such a reward, and I can't conceive that Pascal would have needed or wanted it. If I am allowed to see the sense, the meaning and the beauty of the universe, I *have been* saved.

I believe that this is one of the simplest and most powerful ideas ever thought. How can anybody be so stupid to bet on the losing proposition? One reason for not accepting Pascal's wager is the destructive work of all kinds of fundamentalists. They distort and degrade religion to the point where many intellectuals will rather stay agnostics than being a part of that. That is why I will fight fundamentalists of every denomination in every street and at every corner. I will fight them in their churches, their synagogues and their mosques. An apology to Sir Winston Churchill is in order here, but it was necessary to make the point.

The problem is that we cannot really conceive morality without religiosity. It has been tried, with enormous efforts, in the communist countries as well as elsewhere, and it has failed. How do we define "universal values" without transcending the obscure and temporary desires of dear old me?

But if we truly embrace religion, and whether it is the Bible or the Koran does not matter all that much, we have a way to see values. In the traditional Christian setting I would suggest to look not just at the Ten Commandments, but also at the Sermon on the Mount. The latter has always overwhelmed me as a powerful piece of wisdom. It supports the cooperator without crushing the competitor. Somehow it must be divine.

Please do not start to post these documents on every available billboard or door. A zealous missionary propaganda campaign will hurt much more than it would help. The obvious and very visible contradiction between doctrine and actions contributes more to the contemporary nihilistic groundswell than anything else. Churches of all denominations have handled this very clumsily. The emphasis was always more on "cover up and deny" than on "admit and repair". As compelling as the text can be for some of us, it is only seeing the *living* that will convince people to absorb it in their value set.

Accepting these principles as a beacon for your life is a deep and rewarding but also a terrifying decision. They are so noble that we never will be really able to measure up to them. We will fail, and we don't like to fail. Only a mindset like "nobody said that we have to be perfect, we only must do our best" will help. But "our best" really means that we cannot do any better. All the forgivingness and compassion I recommend towards other people does not include "dear old me". "Dear old me" has to *perform* to earn his place in evolution, end of line.

Now let us suppose that you cannot embrace religion as a possible part of the solution. There still are many other things you can do. Every time a human being does something really unselfish and noble, he or she pushes the wall of nihilism a little bit back. There are so many opportunities. Please do not try to *buy* yourself out of the situation with an expendable donation to some charity. That may be an option of last resort for those of us who really see no opportunity to do anything else. But the whole point really is that we need to *prove* that there are alternatives to greed and selfishness. Giving some of your time is much more important than giving some of your money. Time is a part of your life, money is, well, just money, and the people that say that "time is money" have not thought deeply enough. You may be able to convert time into money whenever you choose. But try the opposite, and you will soon see the limits.

Care for people in your neighborhood, your workplace, everywhere. By all means use money when that seems appropriate. But do not do this in a sterile "donation" fashion – with tax kickbacks – but in a personal way. It can have an enormous impact on a person's attitude in life, if he once heard: "I truly believe in your capabilities, in your character and your morality. That's why I put my money where my mouth is!"

We probably should concentrate our attention on young people. I honestly believe that my age group has chained itself so strongly to materialism and hedonism that it is way beyond repair or recovery. That is fortunately a very temporary problem, as long as it does not spill over too badly into future generations.

If we could make serious progress in society, our enterprises would in the end fix themselves. But we know that progress, if there is any at all, will be painstakingly slow. So we will have to open an additional front within the enterprise itself.

25.3 Re-Conquer the Enterprise!

Our enterprises have been taken away from us, the stakeholders. They are now controlled by a class of people with a very limited accountability and no real loyalty to any of the stakeholder communities. We need to take them back.

We can do this! Many of us are in various positions of power, and even those that are not can contribute. It's just a matter of *wanting* it. More than anything else, this is a matter of awareness and paying attention. Of course, none of us, as an individual, has a trace of a chance to make a relevant lasting difference. But it is not really necessary for any of us to make heroic sacrifices. If we would all start to pay attention to just a couple of things, we would be a formidable, albeit invisible force.

25.3.1 Values

Our first priority must be to reenter human values into our management and decision processes. We are talking about moral values like:

- honesty
- loyalty
- justice
- compassion.

Of course, nobody is in a position to just proclaim that, from now on, these are going to be the touchstones for our decisions. But we surely can enter them into the debate. Imagine, if we could just start to routinely ask in any one of our zillion meetings: "is this morally justifiable?" wouldn't that make a lot of difference, especially if a lot of us did it? It would at least mightily embarrass the opposition. They are not quite willing to admit to their profound amoral attitude! And there are those of us that do occupy positions of power. To a certain extend, we can use moral values as a benchmark for our own decisions. There should be no misunderstanding here. Negligence and indifference that let the shareholders sit on a miserable return are immoral. So is throwing a 60 year old sick woman on the street, a couple of weeks before she would have permanent health benefits. The problem is that those that will readily do the latter are also our prime suspects for the former. Fortunately the perpetrators are very seldom exceptionally brave, and a bit of resistance will go a long way. We should not fool ourselves. There will be a price to pay: a serious reduction of the likelihood that you will ever reach the very top. Whether that is an affordable price or not depends on your values, but if you are the kind of person that is concerned with these problems and wants to do something about them, you probably will not be devastated if you can't become the president.

We should by all means form and maintain alliances between people that share these values and opinions. All too often we see what I call the positive forces in an enterprise destroy each other over relatively unimportant issues. In a world of intense competition, without much restrain from relicts like decency, a true alliance is a formidable force. Alliances as such are the breeding grounds and carriers of important values, like loyalty and mutual support.

25.3.2 Employees and Leadership

We need to accept our employees as what they are: one of the stakeholder communities certainly, but first and foremost our fellow men (also if they are female). We need to know that we are either going to represent them honestly, on an equal level with all other stakeholders, or that they are going to be represented by someone else. That someone else highly likely is going to be someone we will have a lot of problems with. He will be a union official, as interested in the fate and future of our enterprise as I am in baseball, and I didn't even bother with understanding the rules. But "representing" people, means leading them.

The problem is that you can't truly lead people if you do not like them. Leadership is neither a science nor a craft. Those things you could learn. But it is indeed an art and a state of mind, which you can obviously not learn. You could of course read a couple of the zillion books on this topic and even apply some of the tips and tricks. That will hurt more than it helps. It is like being determined to become a great violinist without having the necessary talent. All you are going to do is make a couple of teachers rich and unhappy.

Unless you can make and maintain the deep biological bond with your people that has existed between leaders and their flocks for ages past, you will never become more than an administrator. Being an administrator is not all that bad, most of us are in that situation. However, if you have the stuff, please do more and become a real *leader*. It is the most thankless job on earth. It is agonizing and lonely. Your superiors will mistrust you, because they will believe you to be some kind of a communist. Your subordinates will need an eternity to determine whether or not you are for real, and in the mean time deny you the so much needed support. All the weight is on your shoulders. But it is worthwhile nevertheless. We may not be able to fix the world, but we can fix a small part of it, to a certain extend, for a certain time.

This is where those of us that are not in positions of power can contribute decisively. You can say a couple of words of encouragement and appreciation to your leader. He needs it badly. He needs to see at least somebody appreciate his efforts in order to gain the strength to continue on his path. If he is a *true* leader, he will receive your heartfelt comments very positively. If he isn't, it's time to look for another job anyway.

I am not too enthused about all that karma stuff, but there is this belief of the Salvation Army, an organization I deeply respect. It goes as follows. There is in the universe a pot of good, and a pot of evil. Every second of our life, we have a choice to which one we will contribute. And our albeit small contribution will be there forever and help to tip the balance one way or the other. I find this a powerful thought.

Today I experienced how one of my previous coworkers, a rather hard-nosed Texan, came to visit me. He had heard about my impending retirement, and wanted to say his good-byes. I had found this jewel in one of our sites, contracted him to work in headquarters, and developed him. At face value, that's what I am paid for. But then he started to tell me how this changed his life, and the life of his family. He now could afford to have his two children attend college. While he told me all this, mentioning how grateful he felt, he cried. I responded that I had just done my duty, which is of course totally factually correct, but I felt – Lord forgive me the vanity – a kind of pride about what I had done.

When I had to say good bye to the organization I had led for many years, I got a lot of e-mails. I will print three of them, exactly as they arrived, typos and all. I only replaced the company identifiers by XXX.

I have always been moved by the passion with which you speak, which is why I have continued to make every effort to attend your communications meetings. Today was no exception.

As you spoke of silos and internal wars, I was reminded of a Viet Nam era anti-war slogan, which you may want to borrow:

"What if they gave a war and nobody came."

Thanks for leading XXX out of the dark ages and into the modern age, and for being an approachable human being while doing it. Maybe you feel that you have not accomplished everything you intended, but you have certainly earned my respect.

Best wishes always,

Diane

***

I wanted to ignore the announcement from Klaus about you moving on to different things, but now that you have started the goodbye, I want to say what I feel. I know if I delay or think much, I will probably not write this note. But my emotion is too strong to let it slide by.

Your last note at the communication meeting suddenly made me realize that you will not be able to lead us directly the way you had been and that is unsettling in my heart. Mainly because I hate separations especially with good people.

I always looked at you as a ghost guide/mentor. The most touching aspect of you is that you are an original ... you are honest, open, caring, sincere, and do and say what you mean. You instill confidence and trust and therefore peace of mind. I wanted to be around because you were the leader.

Your idea about publishing the constitution was bold and brilliant. The time and effort you took to personally understand all of XXX folks was impressive. The project reviews, routing slips, project tracking, all were a BIG step in opening up communications and information. Until then, folks at the bottom had no idea what XXX was about and what we were in together for! I used to have a view of just my work because information was guarded and secretive.

You lead by example. You roll up your sleeves and are in the pit, hands on, knowing and relating to what we do, fighting for us. And I appreciated that.

You reminded us to work on the important things. You cautioned us of the potential pitfalls. You let us grow and learn and I am sure you have payed a price for that. And that is just like a father. We knew that as long as we give our 100% and are committed to XXX we will have a job. That allowed focusing more on doing the job rather than worrying about looking elsewhere.

Others may have had good, bad or mixed experiences with you, but I had only good. And I wish you well. I will miss you.

As a concerned friend ... rightly or wrongly, I believe you should watch that cigarrette ... the last thing that should come in the way of what you want to do should be your health.

Even though I don't want you to leave, you have to do what is best. Good Luck, and it was indeed a great pleasure knowing and working for you.

Chetan

***

Gerard

Your goodbyes at the end of the meeting today really moved me. I will never forget how you gave a naive and scared little girl a chance to do something she really wanted to and I will never be able to thank you enough.

I will miss you.

Erika

And then there is the one I received the first day after my retirement.

Dear Gerard:
This is the first day of a brand-new and undoubtedly exciting new chapter in your life, and Vita's also.
We have weathered many a storm together, and I appreciate the privilege bestowed upon me by the Universe, to be your faithful partner-in-crime.
I doubt that you will ever fully realize (much less acknowledge) the extent of the legacy you left behind at XXX. Thankfully, it far exceeds your contributions in the corporate area, although there is no doubt that you were always seeking to do "what is best for the company". But this is something several other effective executives could be credited with as well.

But your biggest impact was made where it counts the most:

You were willing to always ignore your self-interests for the good of the "little guy"; you were willing to make yourself (immensely) unpopular with the political ranks by standing up for WHAT was right not WHO was right.

This took courage. And it cost a lot of energy. I know.

I know, because I have watched this kind of thing suck all the energy out of you.

And you fought on ... even when you knew that it would probably be an effort in futility, and the cost would be very high.

And I am proud and pleased to know that what irked the "upper-levels" the most, was to be forced to secretly acknowledge and admire your courage, while they had none.

You may have taught some valuable computer-principles to some computer nerds.

You may have saved XXX from some disasterous decisions.

You may have developed some computer skills in talented people.

But what will remain ... always ... is the EXAMPLE you set for the people around you, especially the irrelevance of superficial glitter and "appearance".

Some will go on to become executives.

Some will develop and stagnate at the (despicable) manager-level.

Some will stay in their own little comfortable world.

No matter.

What MANY (far many more than you will EVER realize) will have internalized and will be making a part of their lives is what you showed them to be important.

Really important:

PRINCIPLES.

INTEGRITY.

ACCOUNTABILITY.

TAKING RESPONSIBILITY.

KINDNESS and FLEXIBILITY that come from a position of STRENGTH.

None of us really like to be forgotten.

But – as time goes on – undoubtedly your name and your person will become a distant memory within XXX.

However, many will carry within them the character-shaping lessons you've taught them.

And they will be better people for it.

No matter what their career pursuits.

You've encouraged those around you, to surround themselves with people WHO WILL HOLD THEM TO HIGHER STANDARDS. And that is a never-ending quest.

So ... go on ... and play with your toys and work with some more wood.

Drive some company-executives nuts, whenever you can.

And, given the opportunity ... continue to do what you do best: TEACH and BE OUR FRIEND.

HAVE FUN.

WEAR A BROWN SHOE AND A BLACK SHOE.

CUT UP ALL YOUR TIES. They've done their duty.

JOIN A COMPETITIVE SWIM TEAM.

SURPRISE VITA (and Helena) BY CUTTING OUT "THAT AWFUL HABIT".

ENJOY A SUNRISE OR A SUNSET.

REFLECT, IF YOU MUST...AND KNOW THAT YOU'VE DONE THE BEST YOU COULD ... AND IT WAS VERY VERY GOOD.

Your devoted-as-ever

- Helena

I did not print these in order to appear as a good guy. After all, why should I care? It would not help too much if you thought well of me: I know myself. I am, like you, a weak human being. I have made more stupid moves than I can recall, also involving people, hurting them! But even if my previous coworkers were pushed by their emotions or otherwise mistaken, they felt that they had found true leadership and it had enriched their life. Just suppose I ever would have had the choice to either become president and CEO of XXX or receive those e-mails. What do you think that I would have picked?

THIS IS WORTH IT. It is worth every hardship, every disappointment, and every nerve wrecking battle. Chetan and Helena were right. I had to pay a price. But all things considered, it was a very reasonable price for what I was allowed to do and I would pay it again without a second thought!

25.3.3 Compensation

Compensation needs to be result oriented. The question is what we mean by result.

Would Earnings after Taxes be the right thing to measure? That may be a suitable yardstick to measure the CEO, but Joe at the assembly line has only very limited influence over it, so for him it's probably not the right thing. For him the percentage of faulty pieces, rejected by quality assurance might be a more accurate gauge. It is however also necessary to let him participate in the over all financial success of the company. He does undeniably contribute to that, and he needs to feel to be connected to it.

The above indicates that we need a rather complex and compounded system. I will not try to design one here, but I will rather limit myself to listing a couple of guiding principles.

- The underlying philosophy is equitable sharing of the created value among the stakeholders.
- The result dependant part of total compensation should be substantial for *everybody*, and not just for top management.
- There should be a clear and established relationship between the funds that will be used for the variable compensation and the dividends we offer our shareholders.
- There needs to be a mix of short term and long term components in the determination of the variable income. The higher up in the hierarchy, the more dominant the long-term component should become.
- No stock options!

We also must stop the widespread transfer price fraud. I described how this works in Chapter 16, "The Almighty Bonus". There are indeed creative ways to cure this. Here comes one example. Suppose we have a value chain as represented in Fig. 25.2.

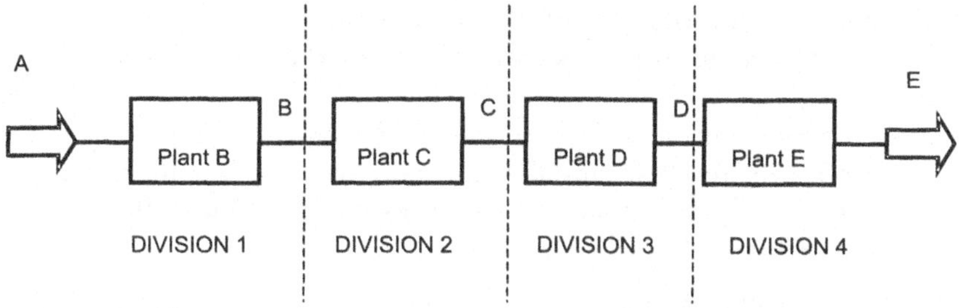

Figure 25.2

We buy product A, convert that to B, the latter to C and then D which finally is processed to yield E, which we sell. There are four plants involved, operated by four different divisions. Such a construct is not at all uncommon in the chemical industry. As each division has its own profitability goals, transfer prices need to be determined for B, C and D. This is normally done by "negotiations", which have a tendency to deteriorate into a kind of "cloak and dagger" story, because bonuses are linked to your division's profitability, and it is much easier to take advantage of you colleagues than of the competition. The short story is: the shrewdest, the most ruthlessly inwardly focused win! That is obviously rather counter-productive. For the enterprise, the outcome of this whole thing does not matter a bit, but think of the energy that goes into this! Divisions hide their information often more jealously for each other than for the competition or the IRS (Internal Revenue Service)! It does not have to be that way. Let's take the enterprise view as shown in Fig. 25.3.

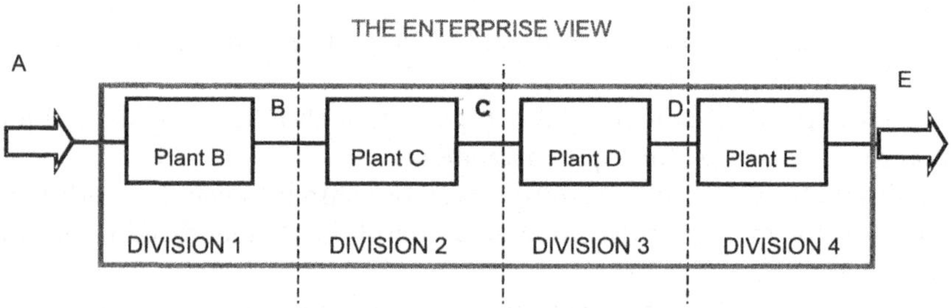

Figure 25.3

All that matters: what happens within the big rectangle?

- How well do we buy A?
- How well do we sell E?
- What cost do we incur on the road from A to E?

Once we have that information, we can do a number of things:

- We can look at the profitability of the whole chain.
- We can rationally determine as a corporation whether we really want to do this or not.
- We can *calculate* transfer prices, so that every involved division gets the same return for its invested capital. We can do this for much more complicated and meshed systems than our simple example, and it really does not take more than high school algebra!

Now the skeptics will say: what if the calculated transfer price for C considerably exceeds the known market price? The question here is what you mean by "known market price". But if it is real and proven, the solution is quite simple. Obviously plant C is not up to snuff. That can have a number of reasons, but we are not going to bother with those. We will simply assume that the technology is obsolete, and thus the value of the plant is lower than the book value. We will hit division 2 with a depreciation that will bring the transfer price of C in line with the market price. That will have a number of wholesome effects:

- The participation of division 2 in the profitability of the whole chain will be reduced. That will hurt their own profitability that is used to determine their bonus.
- The fact that they are hit with an extraordinary write off will compound their problem.
- If division 2 corrects the problem and the calculated transfer price for C drops, we can *appreciate* the value of their plant. Internally, we are able to do such things.
- If it really was the technology, division 2 has the opportunity to invest, in which case their share of the profit goes up too.

You may think: "What's the point? We are still negotiating. Very true, but the negotiations do no longer take place between divisions, but between a division and the neutral instance that is responsible for setting the transfer prices. That unit has no own stake in the outcome. Their bonus is totally linked to the bottom line profitability of the *enterprise.* It is important to stipulate that in the end, if an amicable agreement cannot be achieved, said unit will decide without the possibility of appeal.

I was blessed with the opportunity to implement such a system once in my career. It worked like a charm and gained us over the years several $ 100 million!

The bonus should have components reflecting

- individual performance,
- performance of the unit lead by the individual,
- performance of the individual's peer group.

Although a team can never be a substitute for leadership, team*work* is still an important success factor and should as such be rewarded.

We must keep a lot of leeway for the supervisor's discretion in the process. This may look like introducing an opportunity for injustice, and it is. But going the other way, trying to mechanize the whole process, means absolving our leadership from their duty to judge. That will not just erode their leadership role, it will also create even greater injustice.

We must penalize myopic behavior. We must have a component that rewards thinking for the enterprise.

As long as I was an executive, I had as an objective for all my direct reports:

To be known as a good team player, sensitive to the problems of my peers and subordinates, and being known to contribute to their resolution.

I happen to believe that this is quite important! The evaluation of performance against this goal will be an eternal bone of contention. It requires courage and a deep-rooted sense of justice on the part of the leader. But on the other hand, if he has problems with those, why is he a leader?

If we want to employ entrepreneurs, and we clearly do, we must subject them to the unpredictability of the markets, just as we do with our shareholders. Adverse external circumstances will hit them just as unfairly as those will hurt our shareholders. But even if our employees were no part of the problem, they can contribute to the solution. This principle should be clearly anchored into the compensation system.

Last but not least: audit the process. Find and punish the con artists that sandbag or cheat in other ways.

A bonus system developed along these lines would support our company culture and decision making instead of impeding those.

25.3.4 Decisions

There is a lot of room for improvement here. Our modern dinosaur enterprises have the fatal habit to dilute responsibility and accountability to a degree where even our most sensitive instruments will no longer detect a trace of them. A very popular way to achieve this is "shared" responsibility. Another very effective way to deflect responsibility, are computerized systems. But didn't I read somewhere that a camel was originally intended to become a horse? It's just that a committee (or team) designed it with the help of a computer! Please do not believe that the now so fashionable "team" concept is essentially a new invention to that end. Before the teams we had committees, and they served the same purpose. After the teams, we will have something else. The rationalization is that 10 people will know more than one. That is not always true!

- Ten ignorants do *not* know more than one expert. They can just make a lot more noise.
- But ten experts, if they really cooperate, can work marvels.

At any rate accountability and responsibility cannot be shared, but only distributed.

Accountability is necessarily an attribute of a *person*. But of course, if a person is expected to assume accountability, that person must be given the corresponding authority. Authority is not fashionable. We do not like to subject ourselves to authority. We rather prefer to pretend that we can do without it. Hence, all the BS about self managed teams. But please ask yourself the following question: "Would I board an airplane if I knew that the decisions in the cockpit are not going to be made by the captain, but by a self managed team?" I suspect the answer from a large majority of people will be a resounding "NO!" But if it isn't OK for your airplane, why is it then acceptable in a chemical plant or at an assembly line? Is it really only the physical presence or absence of "dear old me" that defines my judgement in such issues?

What a real team can do is to give good and sound advice. But at the end of the process there has to be a *person* that states: "I had 500 teams advising me on this issue, but it was *my* responsibility to accept their recommendation." Teams cannot be accountable, individual people can. The idea behind all this is not to find somebody guilty to behead in case of the occasional mishap. We should not punish or reward success or failure. We should judge the quality of the decision.

If a carefully calculated risk goes sour nevertheless, protect the poor victim.

If a foolish risk succeeds against all odds, punish the fool in spite of his apparent success.

This will be difficult, because it violates the supreme law that success excuses everything. That is one more law born out of the complacency and laziness of the leading class. It is so much more comfortable and secure to judge success than to bother with the quality of the decision process. But if we really want to improve our decision making, we will have to do the latter. Otherwise we will keep spending much more time and effort on avoiding mistakes than on doing the right thing.

The culture of blame that has developed in many of our enterprises has lead to risk adversity. Do not condone that attitude. Point out, with Frederic the Great of Prussia, that the worst of all choices one can make is making none at all.

25.3.5 Beware of Culture

Culture is one of these words with an enormous content and an even bigger context. Let's look at the dictionary.

The totality of *socially transmitted* behavior patterns, arts, beliefs, institutions, and all other products of human work and thought.

These patterns, traits, and products considered as the expression of a particular period, class, community, or population: *Edwardian culture; Japanese culture; the culture of poverty.*

These patterns, traits, and products considered with respect to a particular category, such as a field, subject, or mode of expression: *religious culture in the Middle Ages; musical culture; oral culture.*

This is of course a very cursory definition. I strongly feel that culture has much to do with the socially accepted value system. It is obvious that if a subentity deviates in its value system from the general population this will create stress. Therefore, one cannot deviate too much, but there always is a difference. It is that Δ that we have to watch. Are we more honest than the general population, or less? Are we more committed to quality or less? That difference matters, because one way to look at culture is to see a set of pre-packed behavioral modules that let us act or react in unexpected situations without much deliberation. Culture continuously directs action, and action feeds back on culture.

The question now is: what influences define that Δ? There are fascinating and complicated group dynamics involved here. One cannot simply design and enforce a culture, but the leadership does have an above average input. We should be very careful when we speak about our culture. The leadership has the understandable tendency to overestimate its achievements, also in this field. Tolerating a huge discrepancy between "the official truth" and the "true truth" is one of the most damaging things you can do to your culture. If it happens out of dishonesty, it is bad. When it happens out of ignorance, it is in a way even worse.

Culture has a paramount influence on whatever we do and on how we do it. If our culture is not healthy, nothing else, no other measures will be able to compensate for that. While it may be possible to kick off culture changes with declarations and directives, the only way they are going to happen is by living example. This needs to be a constant concern.

25.3.6 Courage

Another worn out word! The dictionary says:

The state or quality of mind or spirit that enables one to face danger, fear, or vicissitudes with self-possession, confidence, and resolution; bravery.
[Middle English corage, *from Old French, from Vulgar Latin* *corâticum, *from Latin* cor.*]*

This is again one of these properties that one cannot acquire. You have it or you don't. The etymology suggests that it has something to de with the heart, and it has. You cannot send people to a course and at the end proclaim "from now on you will be brave".

I believe that courage is a rather complex phenomenon. The short formula for courage is: accepting risk for the sake of a higher good. The nature of that "higher good" is the key to the direction of courage. It can be fully altruistic or totally selfish. It can be extremely noble or abysmally evil. Fortunately, the distribution of the different motivations is skewed. People will be more readily prepared to expose themselves to perils for causes that they consider more important than their own "dear old me". I may not agree with their cause, but from their perspective, it is a noble one. Evil people may take occasional chances, but they are generally much more focused on self-preservation than the ones who have the mission to improve the world. Courage leads to action; it belies and transcends the laming indifference that threatens our contemporary world.

While courage cannot be truly learned, it can certainly be suppressed if present. We seem to do everything possible to that effect. We manipulate the odds by punishing failure much more intensely than rewarding success. A careful observer would, purely based on the facts, come to the conclusion that courage is counter productive. The question is only: what is the objective here?

- Is it to rise through the ranks at all cost? Will that not lead to emotional impoverishment, to a point where one stops, takes stock and suddenly discovers that one has sacrificed everything of importance for something that, in the end, proves quite worthless?
- Or is the real goal a fulfilled and meaningful life, something one can look back upon with a smile and deep satisfaction?
- Or is it, as must have been the case with Gorbatchov, to acquire the necessary power to be able to right something that one is deeply convinced of to be catastrophically wrong?

In the first case, courage is the wrong prescription.

In both other cases, considerable courage is required, albeit differently distributed over one's life span.

The obvious contempt I feel for our modern cynical nihilistic prudent managers is clearly exceeded by my compassion for them. I believe that they cheat themselves much more than their fellow men. They deprive themselves of the most precious of all commodities: a real life. The ones among them that are so perverted that this never dawns to them are blessed. The awakening, if it ever comes, must be terrible.

Some of us are born without courage. They are excused, as they can't help it. But to those of you who have the gift of gallantry I say: Please do not suppress it, the effort is not worth it. From those of you that are in positions of power, I would like to ask that you protect the brave. They will occasionally encounter misfortunes. The nature of courage, however carefully deployed, dictates that. Courage is a great value. Do not allow it to be destroyed by the petty accusations that often follow a mishap!

25.3.7 The Selection Machine

There is some serious repair work overdue here.

For those of you that are at this moment struggling within the selection machine, I have the following advice. Do not sell your soul for a career. It's bad business. The problem is that, if you decided to do the deal, you will only see and understand the full implications when it is way too late. If you do sell your soul, you ruin much more than just your own life. You contribute that little bit to the "pot of evil" that might, with some bad luck, become decisive for the final outcome. By diminishing the background of responsibility and conscience, you greatly facilitate the undetected progress of the real con artists. It is better to be sorted out standing, with an intact spine, than to be selected by performing all kinds of unnatural bends.

Those in positions of power could observe the following:

- Be constantly aware of the pitfalls of appearance. If the guy puts up a brilliant show, the more reason to dig for the substance. He might have neglected the latter for the sake of the former.
- If somebody does not take good responsible care of his subordinates, he will probably not be too committed to the enterprise either. Chances are that he is only committed to his dear little self. Do not try to fool yourself. You *cannot* deflect such an attitude to the favor of the company.
- Beware of flattery.
- Conformity is not a virtue. It just is convenient.
- Before you decide to sponsor somebody, make sure that he has the priorities right. Moral values should come first under all circumstances. People that handle this aspect indifferently are not just long-term liabilities to your company. They might prove quite destructive in the short term.
- Respect technical competence. While it will in and by itself not save the day, without it nothing goes.
- Never trust people that will let you do dumb things unopposed.

25.3.8 Change

Let's not try to glorify change. Change is like chemotherapy. You don't want it but you take it nevertheless because of the "or else". And there is a lethal overdose! Change is dangerous is many ways. It offers golden opportunities for the eager ambitious charlatans that would sell their mother for a career jump.

We should never advertise change as a value in its own right. Nevertheless change is necessary, but it needs to be carefully planned and controlled. We need to prepare our people for change, by properly informing and involving them. We need to protect them from the unavoidable adverse effects change may have on their personal lives. This can be done without waiving the enterprise's legitimate interests. It is more a matter of careful planning and solid hard work than anything else.

25.4 Conclusion

If we could create a mass movement, quietly making even modest and slow progress into the direction outlined above, we might very well change the world for the better, give it one more essentially undeserved chance. We should not expect our Creator to come to our assistance. The reason is simple and very much in line with our little naïve creation story at the beginning of this book.

God does not need to come to our rescue: He already did it!

26 Advice to a Young Entrepreneur

Dear young friend,

You are going to be the Bill Gates of the 21st century. You have it all: guts, brains, vision, endurance and on top of everything, that fire in your belly. I don't really think that you need my advice, you are going to make it no matter what. But just in case...

One should always start with the trivia. In the course of my life, I collected a number of platitudes that I called "Gerard De Beuckelaer's rules". Whether there is any wisdom in them is your call to make, but even if they are not all that useful, they might at least be somewhat amusing.

1. Never check your conscience in at the cloakroom, you might not get it back.
2. Industry is an activity by the people for the people.
3. If you can't win, don't fight.
4. If you don't truly want to win, you can't win, so don't fight.
5. An ounce of decency is worth more than 50% of Microsoft.
6. If you don't love your people, you can't lead them.
7. If you cheat or lie, blue collar workers will notice first. They will never trust you again.
8. Real leaders are willing to die for their people. Managers won't even risk a cold.
9. If you automate a mess, you get an automated mess. It will be faster and able to do more damage in the same time.
10. If you don't understand it, you can't automate it.
11. The most common reason for heroism is lack of information.
12. The poorer the understanding, the more flamboyant the enthusiasm.
13. Sometimes people just refuse to listen. Don't automatically blame that on the communication skills of the speaker.
14. Logic and enthusiasm
    - Logic without enthusiasm will allow you to understand the world, not to change it.
    - Enthusiasm without logic will allow you to change the world, not to improve it.
15. Whatever your worries, in 50 years from now it doesn't matter anymore.
16. Make sure that your engineers understand the gist of your balance sheet and profit and loss statement.

17. Make sure that your accountants understand the gist of what your engineers are doing.
18. Encourage prudently calculated risks, even if they happen to go sour.
19. Punish foolish risks, even if they happen to succeed.
20. Always look for a few good men, and if they happen to be female, that shouldn't bother you.
21. Constructive criticisms is so important that you can't leave it to outsiders. You need your own personal critics just as much as you need your doctor. Take good care of them. Ideally you should have a second in command that is at the same time your best friend and the opposition leader. This is your only insurance against really *big* mistakes.
22. There is nothing dirty about profits, as long as you truly *earn* them.
23. Stupidity is worse than bad character. A smart bad person can still be guided by convincing him of his own interests.
24. Never bother with secrecy. The only thing it will do is slow you down, so that in the end you might need secrecy.
25. Mistrust fanatics in any shape and form. Losing sight of the relativity of things is losing sight of the universe.
26. Gossip should never be mistaken for a form of communication.
27. If you have bad news: give it to them right away. Tell your people what you will do to protect them as well as what contribution you need and expect from them.
28. Trust is like your retirement plan. You cannot expect to build it in three months, but with one reckless act you can ruin the whole thing in the blink of an eye.
29. If you don't understand it, don't touch it. This rule applies to
    - complicated electronic equipment
    - financial deals
    - human relationships
    - and everything else …
30. Determination is often inversely proportional to insight, but not always!
31. The moral high ground is never cheap real estate, but usually a very good investment.
32. It is not true that 10 idiots together know more than one expert.
33. But it is true that 10 experts, if they really cooperate, will together achieve a lot more than one of them.
34. Beware of language. It is imminently imprecise. And don't believe the French when they claim that theirs is different.
35. In a collision between form and substance, form always wins round #1.
36. In a collision between form and substance, substance will always win the last round.
37. You may not live long enough to see the last round.
38. Never believe propaganda, especially not your own.

39. If you observe a discrepancy between the official truth and the true truth, one of the following things is going on:
    - There is a serious disruption in the communication system. It needs to be repaired urgently.
    - Some people are playing silly games. They need to be fired urgently.

    But no matter what: it's an urgent problem.
40. If you see that your official chain of command and the real one differ, the most promising course of action is to have a serious look at the former.
41. Paranoia is worse than cancer. The latter may terminate a life. That is a quite natural thing. Paranoia will ruin a life, and that's a terrible waste.
42. Life is when
    - the things you can do are not desirable.
    - the things you really want to do are impossible.

    But there are exceptions.
43. The physicists have it all wrong. Strong interaction is not the dominating force in the universe. It's stupidity! Stupidity is omnipresent and it explains more of what you see in the world around you than any physical law.
44. Stupidity comes in layers.

    Level 1: normal stupidity. That's just "I don't know". There is nothing catastrophic about this. It happens to all of us all the time, and after all, we can learn.

    Level 2: meta-stupidity. That goes like: "I don't know but I don't know that I don't know." This is worse, because now we don't even understand that we need to learn and there is no remedy in sight.

    Level 3: aggravated meta-stupidity. "I don't know and I don't know that I don't know. Therefore I consider myself an expert." Not only do I fail to understand that I should learn but I am prepared to teach the course!

    Aggravated meta-stupidity destroys more wealth than wars, earthquakes, hurricanes, tornadoes, volcano eruptions and landslides combined.
45. If you need a dress code, you must have hired the wrong employees.
46. If you want to operate with the world as your market, you need to learn languages. Just as a vehicle for communication, English might do fine. But languages are about much more than just communication: they are tools of thought and thus gateways to different mindsets and cultures.
47. There may be another way to say: "Your explanation is too complicated." How about "My approach is too simplistic."
48. Never underestimate the qualitative aspects of big numbers. One mosquito is no problem, but how about 7 million mosquitos? Arithmetic would suggest that zero times 7 million is still zero, but is it really?
49. Reasonable people can always find a compromise. That's why we have all those wars!
50. The most fundamental difference between a medieval baron and a modern top executive is that a jet is a lot faster than a horse.

51. Machiavelli was an idealist.
52. "How can I know what I think unless I hear what I have to say?" Well, before starting up your mouth, check if your brain is operating normally.
53. Are you sure that when you said "focused" you didn't mean "single minded"?
54. It's never the substance that kills, it's always the dose.
55. What you say is not important. What they hear doesn't matter. The all-important thing is what they *understand*. However, if you don't say it in such a way that they can hear it loud and clear, there isn't going to be much to understand!
56. Communication is complicated. It is all about me having a mental image of something, which I want to replicate into your brain. But look at all the things that can go wrong. First I need to convert "something" into language, then into the appropriate phonemes, which I send to my vocal cords. It is important to understand what we have now: vibrating air! Then the vibrating air reaches your ears, and the process has to go all the way backward. That is even more complicated, because all kinds of transmission problems must be repaired on the fly. The point I want to make is that there is no guarantee that the "something" you sent will arrive in one piece. But you can improve the odds by keeping it simple!
57. If religion and materialism should ever compete to obtain the title "Opium for the people", the latter wins hands down.

References

1 Bernstein, Peter L. (August 31, 1998). Against the Gods: The Remarkable Story of Risk
John Wiley & Sons; ISBN 0471295639.

2 Comte, Auguste. Auguste Comte and Positivism: The Essential Writings
Transaction Pub; ISBN 0765804123

3 Gide, André. The Immoralist
Vintage Books; ISBN 0679741917

4 Gorbachev, Mikhail. George Shriver (Translator). On My Country and the World
Columbia Univ. Press; ISBN 0231115148

5 De Waal, Frans and De Waal, F. B. M. Chimpanzee Politics: Power and Sex Among Apes
Johns Hopkins Univ. Press; ISBN 0801858399

6 Huxley, Aldous. Brave New World
Harper Perennial Library; ISBN 0060929871

7 Kauffman, Stuart A. The Origins of Order: Self-Organization and Selection in Evolution
Oxford Univ. Press; ISBN 0195079515

8 Kennedy, Paul M. The Rise and Fall of the Great Powers: Economic Change and Military Conflict from 1500 to 2000
Vintage Books; ISBN 0679720197

9 Machiavelli, Niccolò, Peter Bondanella (Editor), Mark Musa (Translator). The Prince
Oxford Univ. Press (Trade); ISBN 0192833979

10 Michalewicz, Zbigniew and Fogel, David B. How to Solve It: Modern Heuristics
Springer-Verlag; ISBN 3540660615

11 Minsky, Marvin L. The Society of Mind
Simon & Schuster (Paperback); ISBN 0671657135

12 Orwell, George. 1984
Buccaneer Books; ISBN 0899663680

13 Pascal, Blaise, Krailsheimer, A.J. (Translator). Pensées
Penguin USA (Paper); ISBN 0140446451

14 Peursen, Cornelis Anthonie van. The Strategy of Culture: a View of the Changes Taking Place in Our Ways of Thinking and Living Today
North-Holland/Elsevier; this title is out of print

15 Reichheld, Frederick F. and Teal, Thomas. The Loyalty Effect: The Hidden Force Behind Growth, Profits, and Lasting Value
Harvard Business School Press; ISBN 0875844480

16 Schumpeter, Joseph A. Capitalism, Socialism and Democracy
Harper Collins (Short Disc); ISBN 0061330086

17 Shakespeare, William. The Tragedy of Romeo and Juliet
Washington Square Press; ISBN 0671722859

18 Teilhard de Chardin, Pierre. Phenomenon of Man
Harper Collins (paper); ISBN 006090495X

19 Thurow, Lester C. The Future of Capitalism: How Today's Economic Forces Shape Tomorrow's World
Penguin USA (Paperback); ISBN 0140263284

The manufacturer's authorised representative in the EU is Springer Nature Customer Service Centre GmbH, Europaplatz 3, 69115 Heidelberg, Germany. If you have any concerns regarding our products, please contact ProductSafety@springernature.com

Printed and bound by CPI Group (UK) Ltd, Croydon, CR0 4YY
30/09/2026
02225573-0007